A
History
Of The
Joke

J K Dowd

For Marie

Contents

Preface

Introduction
What is a joke? - Set-up/punch-line – Ambiguity/Incongruity - Hidden meanings - Words count - Timing - Narrative jokes - Shaggy dog - Observations - Theories - Laughter and Health – Cognitive - Joke Cycles - Time

A History of the Joke

Chapter One – *Philogelos*
Sumerian - Egyptian - Greek - *Philogelos* - Socrates - Irony - Diogenes - Roman - Cicero - Jewish - Buddhist - Hindu

Two – Medieval
Lord of Misrule - *The Exeter Book - Scattered Pearls* - Middle-East - Nasreddin Hodja - Muslim - Petrarch - Boccaccio

Three – Chaucer
The Canterbury Tales

Four – Poggio Bracciolini
Facetiae

Five – Merry Tales

One Hundred Merry Tales - Tales and Quick Answers - Howleglas -
Tarlton - Armin - Puns

Six – Archee's Jests

Joque to Joke - Puritans - Irish "Bull" - Scotch Jock

Seven – *Joe Miller's Jests*

Tom Brown's Jest Book - Malapropism - *Dictionary of the Vulgar Tongue*

Eight – Hooked

Practical joke

Nine – Music Hall

Grimaldi - Music Hall - Wits - *Cambridge Jests - New London Jest Book*

Ten – Cartoon

Punch - French satire

Eleven – Why did the chicken cross the road?

Waiter, waiter - Cannibals

Nineteen – Who's There?

Dark House jokers - Jewish - American Radio - Joke writers - Knock, knock - Little Audrey

Twenty – British Stand-up

Max Miller

Twenty-One – World War Two

Italian - Nazi - Cabaret - GI's - Bennett Cerf - "Glamour" magazines

Twenty-Two – American Wit and Humour

Schmulowitz - *Encyclopaedia of Wit, Humour, and Wisdom* - *Over Sexteen*

Twenty-Three – *The Green Book*

Goons - Hancock - Death of Variety

Twenty-Four – *Rationale of the Dirty Joke*

Mort Sahl - Lenny Bruce - Gershon Legman - Dead Babies - Wind-up Doll – Moron - Gay - Feminist

Twenty-Five – Race

Elephants - Rastus - Dick Gregory - *Deep Down in Jungle* - Water Wit - Flytings - Dozens - Yo Mamma - Light Bulb

They say the seeds of what we do are all in us, but it always seemed to me that in those who make jokes in life the seeds are covered with better soil and with a higher grade of manure.

Ernest Hemingway: *A Moveable Feast.*

Preface

For as long as I can remember I have loved jokes. Some of my earliest memories are of telling and being told jokes, and throughout my school years, while I would hesitate to call myself the class clown, I was always a keen participant in the schoolyard joke cycle crazes of the sixties and seventies.

Post school I became a stand-up comedian and jokes became my business as well as my pleasure, but it was not until a few years ago when I began researching the history of stand-up comedy for what was to be my first book, that I realised what a tour de force jokes are, and how much they can reveal about people who enjoy certain types. It is not, and never has been, "just a joke".

Jokes are invented and then they evolve, the best are updated, rearranged and chosen time and again from the insurmountable mass of jokes that have been told down the centuries. The following is from the 1535 English jest book, *Tales and Quick Answers*:

A father tells his newly widowed daughter, who is weeping uncontrollably beside her husband's deathbed, that he has another, richer husband ready for her and thus she should stop mourning. The daughter is very angry that her father would suggest such a thing, her husband not yet cold, and her lamentations continue all the louder.

Two days later the husband is buried and after his soul-mass the girl, between sobs and heavy wails turns to her father and whispers in his ear, 'Father, where is the young man that ye said should be mine husband?'

Some four hundred years later:

A man at his wife's funeral becomes hysterical, attempting to leap into the grave and is restrained by a friend who tells him, 'I know you're hurting, but time will pass, a month from now, a year from now, you'll meet someone else, and everything will be alright.' And the man wiping away his tears says, 'A year from now? What about tonight?'

A Jewish version, less than a century old, incorporated sex:

Abe's wife died, and the house rang with his sorrowful cries. The next day the Rabbi called only to find him in bed with the housemaid. 'Vot are you doing?' the Rabbi cried, 'and your wife not dead twenty-four hours!' Abe stopped, looked up and said with a shrug, 'In my grief how should I know vot I'm doing?'

Some people may be offended by some of the jokes within, the cruelty, blatant racism and sexism, and the choice of language, but readers should remember that this is a history book, the jokes reflect the times they lived in.

Joke cycles most especially, those joke fads that seemingly come from nowhere and are briefly fashionable and disappear almost as quickly as they arrived. They reflect a section of the population's sense of humour at a given time.

"Dead baby" and "wind-up doll" jokes are just two examples of the many "sick" joke cycles popular in the 1960's. They were gross, deliberately so, but we should note that it was society that produced the jokes and omitting them would not be a true reflection of what some people found funny then, or indeed, reveal why such jokes were created in the first place.

And so, as the Actress said to the Bishop: 'Let's get on with it.'

J. K. Dowd, 2018.

Introduction

The English word 'joke' was initially a slang word, a derivative of the Latin *jocus* meaning 'wordplay', introduced to the English language in the seventeenth century as *joque* or *joc*, prior to which a funny story was a 'jest', from the Old French word *geste* and the Latin *gesta* meaning, 'action, exploits' from *gerere*, 'do'. The original sense was 'heroic deed', hence a narrative of such a deed, but later it denoted an idle tale, hence a joke.

The Anglo-Saxon word, 'gag' meant 'interpolation' and described the process of improvising, adding something or introducing something new to conceal either memory loss or an unforeseen circumstance. The medieval *jape* held two meanings; 'jest' and 'sexual intercourse'.

A joke is a funny story, some information that ends with a line that hopefully elicits laughter from its audience. That's it, simple. Well, not always that simple, as we shall see. Some jokes are more complicated than others:

Take my wife... please!

The above is the American comic Henny Youngman's classic. A simple statement, 'take my wife' which implies that he is about to make a statement about his wife, but when Youngman turns it on its head with the punch-line, 'please', meaning, 'take her away', it sends our thought process in a completely different direction. An old Vaudeville double-act joke goes:

I've just spent two weeks in bed with acute hepatitis.

You lucky stiff, which one? They're both cute those Hepatitis girls.

1

The humour comes from the sudden recognition of the connection between the two dissimilar items. It's something jokers have been doing for thousands of years. The Roman orator and philosopher Cicero (106-43 BCE) observed: 'The most common kind of joke is that which we expect one thing, and another is said.'

A man walked into the living room to find his wife breastfeeding their son. 'How long do you have to do that for?' he said. 'When is he too old for it?'
'Well, it's a physical bond between mother and child isn't it? It's only society that deems it to be unacceptable beyond a certain age.'
'Shut up, Dennis,' said the father, 'I'm talking to your mother.'

A man and his wife were out shopping for an anniversary present for one another and became separated in the crowd. After frantically searching for ten minutes the wife rang her husband's mobile phone, 'Where are you?' she asked
'Well, love,' replied the husband, 'you know the jewellers where we saw that engagement ring all those years ago, the one you adored but sadly I couldn't afford?'
'Yes,' said his wife, giggling.
'Well,' said the husband, 'I'm in the pub next door.'

Other joke types include humour that arises from an unconscious statement, an observation, or a practical joke, the latter being a mischievous trick played with the intention of embarrassing or causing some form of discomfort to its victim. It is "practical" because it is someone doing something physical as opposed to a verbal or written joke.
The oldest practical joke on record involves the young Roman Emperor, Heliogabalus (CE 204-22) who played an elaborate version of the deflating seat cushion on his unsuspecting dinner guests.
Shortly afterwards the young Emperor was murdered, but one suspects that it was for his dissipated lifestyle and neglect of state affairs rather than someone overreacting to a fart cushion.

2

Observational jokes are used by comedians who point out the funny in real life:

Britain's fattest man weighs nine hundred pounds; ironically the only pants he can get to fit him are jogging bottoms.

In America's deep south citizens have been told not to fly the Confederate flag because it reminds people of its racist past. Stores have been told not to sell Confederate flags which means that the only place you can buy a Confederate Flag is on the Black Market.

The "Black Market" joke is observational satire. Comedians create satirical jokes by employing exaggeration, sarcasm, and irony. Satire takes a moral stance and its purpose is to highlight injustice through punch-lines:

The British government's *White Paper* on immigration proposes that immigrants to this country should swear allegiance to the Queen and learn to speak the Queen's English. Ironic considering that the last part would have ruled out most of her ancestors.

An unconscious statement can create a punch-line, sometimes without the protagonist being aware of it:

I'm an atheist, thank God.

Many folklorists believe that "punch-line" comes from Punchinello, the grotesque clown and bully of the Commedia dell'arte (comedy of art), a colourful theatrical form of improvised comic drama that originated in the streets and market places of Italy during the early Italian Renaissance and was extremely popular throughout Europe during the fifteenth and sixteenth centuries.
Later Punchinello was appropriated for Punch and Judy puppet shows in which the slaps metered out by Punch's slap-stick drew the biggest laughs in the same way the last line of a verbal joke does,

and subsequently the reveal of a joke became known as the punch-line.

A punch-line works because the listener's mind is subconsciously racing ahead, predicting an outcome:

Two old ladies who had been friends for decades wanted a photograph together, so they visited a photographer. He sat them on a sofa and asked them to move closer to each other.

'What did he say?' asked Edith, who was more than a little deaf.

'He wants us to sit closer,' Ethel explained, 'on the sofa, closer…'

'Now, stay perfectly still while I focus,' said the photographer.

'What did he say?' Edith asked, and Ethel said, 'He's going to focus.'

And Edith said, 'What, both of us?'

Old Hymie Rosenthal was suffering from a rare disease and could only drink human milk. 'But where should I get such milk?' Hymie asked his doctor.

'Well,' said the doctor, 'Miriam Goldblum has recently given birth and she is breast feeding, maybe she can help you.'

So, Hymie goes to see Miriam and she agrees to help him.

After two weeks of Hymie feeding at her breast Miriam one night becomes aroused and says to Hymie, 'Tell me Mr Rosenthal, do you like it?'

'Oh, very much,' says Hymie.

'And,' Miriam purrs, 'Is there anything else you might like?'

'Oh, yes,' Hymie smiles, 'perhaps a biscuit.'

A joke relies on what the listener subconsciously expects from the set-up, so it can play with hidden meaning to reveal an unexpected ending:

I said to my wife, 'From the first time I saw you I wanted to make love to you so badly', and she said, 'Well, you succeeded'.

I sat on a train opposite this stunning looking Thai woman and I kept thinking, please don't get an erection, please don't get an erection. But she did.

There are jokes that appear to have no set-up at all, when in fact the set-up exists in our prior knowledge of the subject matter:

I annoy my Israeli neighbour, any post I get addressed to 'The Occupier', I give to him...

Central to most jokes is ambiguity (open to more than one interpretation), in its simplest form using homophones (words that are pronounced the same but have different meanings) and homonyms (words that have the same spelling but different meanings):

Three tall, elderly brothers, Harry, Bert and Dick were watching the bowlers on the green when Dick decided to treat them all to an ice cream. Whilst he was gone two spinsters came walking by and one, noticing their size remarked, 'My, you're a couple of big lads, how tall are you?'
'Six-foot six,' replied Harry.
'And I'm six-seven,' said Bert.
'And look at the size of your feet,' said the other spinster, 'what size shoes do you take?'
'I take a fifteen and Bert takes a sixteen,' said Harry, 'but if you think our feet are big, wait until you see our Dicks'.'

Incongruity (incompatibility) usually plays some part too:

A man asked W. C. Fields, 'Do you believe in clubs for small children?'
And Fields replied, 'Only when kindness fails.'

Shakespeare wrote, 'Brevity is the soul of wit', and the bard was never more correct. Jokes are like poems in that they must convey the information and feeling in the fewest words possible.

Over-elaborating lessens the punch of the punch-line:

Pretentious? Moi?

Whether it is one line or one hundred, the key to a good set-up is using the minimum amount of words:

An Englishman living in Scotland went to the doctors with a large carrot wedged up his bum. 'Oh,' said the doctor, 'been exploring latent homosexual desires, have we?'
'Certainly not,' said the Englishman, 'today was my first day working in Glasgow as a door-to-door vegetable salesman.'

Anything said after the punch-line is superfluous. The following is an example from *The Encyclopaedia of Wit, Humor, and Wisdom*, 1949:

'A large percentage of accidents happen in the kitchen,' said the wife, reading from the insurance pamphlet. 'Yeah,' said her husband, 'and we men have to eat them, and pretend we like them.'

'...and we men have to eat them', is the punch-line, 'and pretend we like them', lessens its punch. A second punch-line, or "topper", is another matter entirely:

A ninety-year-old man dies while making love to his eighty-year old wife and the press, ever eager for a story turn up at the funeral. 'Madam,' said one reporter to the widow, 'I'm very sorry for your loss, but it's incredible that your husband was still sexually active at the age of ninety.'
'Oh yes,' she said, 'he was sexually active alright, but not like when he was younger. If truth be told he could only manage once a week. Every Sunday... and he wasn't as physical as he once was either, if truth be told what he used to do was just keep time with the church bells... If truth be told he'd still be alive today if that ice cream van hadn't gone past!'

6

'Nevertheless,' said the reporter, 'it must have come as a terrible shock.'

'Not really,' she said, 'I was asleep at the time.'

Two ex-military chaps were talking at their club and one said to the other, 'You know, I told my grandson that his great, great grandfather fought at the Battle of Waterloo and do you know what he said? Which platform?'

'Unbelievable,' said the other, 'as if it matters which platform it was on'.

Choice of words is equally as important as the amount. When Alan Reiss, professor of psychiatry at Stanford University used a MRI scanner to monitor brain responses to cartoons for his studies in cataplexy he was amazed at how much the wording of a joke mattered.

Reiss made subtle changes to some punch-lines and discovered that changing just one word in the caption made the difference between a hilarious cartoon and a totally unfunny one.

A group of Lancashire sewerage workers were taking their annual work's outing in the Lake District, and one of the workers was so overcome by all the fresh air that he fainted. It took seven buckets of shit to bring him 'round.

Replace 'shit' with any other word and the joke does not work as well.

Timing!

What is the secret to telling a joke?

There are various people who claim to hold records for telling the most jokes in a minute, two minutes, an hour, whatever, when in fact all they did was recite some jokes quickly. They were not *telling* jokes. Telling a joke is a mini-theatrical event, it needs a performance, and gabbling one line after another without thought to pace or timing is not telling jokes.

Ken Dodd, Steven Wright, Tim Vine are prime examples of quick fire joke tellers, comedians who tell an extraordinary amount of jokes during their shows but who perform every single one. They stay true to the beat, the beat they know gives the joke its best chance of succeeding. That is timing.

A one-line joke is obviously easier to tell.

One Buddhist said to another, 'How's life?' and the other replied, 'I've had better.'

Bringing all the performance elements together for a successful joke becomes more difficult the longer it is. The longer set-up for a "narrative" joke also heightens the expectations of the listener, and for that reason the best narrative jokes contain several smaller jokes within the set-up. These comic asides or, "jab" lines are not necessarily chasing laughs but are important because they establish a connection with the listener:

A Church of England Reverend while out on a stroll bumped into one of his parishioners. 'Reverend' said the parishioner, 'I heard a joke recently, a limerick, very good, bit saucy though…'

'Oh, don't mind me' said the Reverend 'I'm not such a prude, you know'.

'Right then,' said the fella, 'now, let me get this right:
There was a young man named Skinner
Who had a young lady to dinner.
They sat down to dine
At a quarter to nine,
And by 9.45 it was in 'er!'

'What was in 'er?' asked the Reverend, 'the dinner?'

'No,' said the fella 'Skinner, Skinner was in 'er.'

'Oh, yes,' said the Reverend, 'oh yes, I see, very amusing I must say.'

A few weeks later the Reverend is visited by his Bishop and he said to him, 'You know, Bishop, one of my flock told me a joke the other week, highly amusing, a bit ribald...'

'Oh, never mind that,' said the Bishop, 'I love a good joke, pray do tell.'

So, the Reverend said, 'Jolly good, now how does it go... ah yes:
There was once a young man named Tupper
Who had a young lady to supper,
First, they had tea
At a quarter to three,
And by 3.45 he was up 'er.

'Up 'er?' the Bishop asked, 'What was up 'er? The supper?'

'No, no, Bishop,' said the Reverend, 'some fellow named Skinner.'

A narrative joke is altogether different from a "shaggy dog" story, which is a kind of joke about jokes, a long, drawn out and often complex set-up which usually ends with a painful punch-line, making the person who was duped into listening the butt of the whole thing.

The original shaggy dog story according to Eric Partridge's 1953, *The Shaggy Dog Story, Its Origin, Development, and Nature* was told at the beginning of the twentieth century, and goes:

A grand householder in Park Lane, London, had the great misfortune to lose a very valuable and rather shaggy dog. He advertised repeatedly in *The Times* but without any luck, and finally he gave up hope. But an American in New York saw the advertisement, was touched by the man's devotion and went to great lengths to seek out a dog that matched the specification in the advertisement and which he could bring over to London on his next business trip.

[The teller should elaborate at great length on said great lengths].

He presented himself in due course at the owner's impressive house, where he was received in the owner's absence by an even more impressive butler, who glanced at the dog, bowed, winced

9

almost imperceptibly and exclaimed, in a horror-stricken voice, 'It was indeed a shaggy dog, sir, but not so shaggy as that!'

Many great minds have tried to define humour, and yet they have barely scratched the surface when it comes to revealing its vast complexities. Indeed, close examination of humour seems only to enhance its illusiveness, and paradoxically the findings usually turn out to be anything but funny. As the *New Yorker*'s E. B. White once famously observed: 'Humour can be dissected, as a frog can, but the thing dies in the process and the innards are discouraging to any but the pure scientific mind.'

Nevertheless, with the help of a few eminent scholars and some good jokes, we shall attempt to reveal how and why funny is funny, and what benefits, if any, funny brings to our lives.

Two schnorrers [Jewish hobo-beggars] are discussing Einstein's, Theory of Relativity and one explains to the other that, 'All it means is that everything is relative. It's like this, but it's also like that. It's entirely different but it's the same thing. You understand?'

'No,' says the other schnorrer, 'can you give me an example?'

So, the first schnorrer says, 'Of course, let's say that I fuck you in the ass. I have a prick in the ass, and you have a prick in the ass. It's entirely different but it's the same thing. Now do you understand?'

'Ah-hah!' says the other, 'but I got von question. This is how Einstein makes a living?'

[The original Yiddish version is told with, '*a noz in hinten*' - *a nose in the behinder*'.]

Jokes are too diverse to have a single common denominator, but there are three major contesting hypotheses on how they work and why we tell them, those being the Superiority, the Relief, and the Incongruity theories.

The Superiority Theory, endorsed by the likes of Plato, Aristotle, Bergson, and Hobbs proposes that all humour is mockery and derision, a contemptuous snarl, whereby the humour stems from the perceived lower position of others.

10

The founder of psycho analysis Sigmund Freud believed jokes to be phenomena that does not admit too, and yet indulges our cruel streak. 'Only joking' we say, yet still we make the joke.

A husband stepped on scales that tell your character and weight. He popped in his coin and after a couple of minutes out came the small white card. 'Listen to this,' he said to his wife, 'it says that I'm witty, intelligent, resourceful, and a great person.'
'Yes,' said his wife, 'it got your weight wrong too.'

Superiority theory encompasses jokes about the diseased, deformed, and disabled:

For the first couple of years after a man is diagnosed with leprosy he can have sex numerous times a week, but then it drops off.

A midget with a speech impediment goes to buy a horse from a farmer. The farmer brings the horse to him and the midget says, 'Can I thee her mouf?' So, the farmer lifts him up to look in the horse's mouth. Then the midget says, Can I thee her eerths?' Again, the farmer lifts him up to look in the horse's ears. 'Can I thee her nothtwils?' the midget asks, and the farmer, getting pretty fed up by now lifts the midget up to see the horse's nostrils. 'Can I thee her twot?' the midget says, and by now the farmer is sick and tired of him so he picks the midget up and shoves his head into the mare's vagina. After a few seconds he puts him down. The midget quietly cleans his face with a handkerchief and then says, 'Pewhaps I should wephrase the wequest… can I thee her walk about a bit?'

A woman is walking along the beach and comes across a feller with no arms and legs, lying in the sand, crying. He tells her he's upset because it's his birthday and at fifty years of age he's never been kissed, so the woman bends down and gives him a long lustful kiss. The feller is still crying. 'What's wrong now?' she asks, and he tells her that he's never had oral sex. Feeling sorry for him the

11

woman obliges, but afterwards as she begins to walk away the feller again bursts into tears. 'What now?' says the woman, and the feller sobs, 'I've never been screwed!' And the woman looks to the sea and sighs, 'Well, you will be soon, the tides coming in.'

It also includes mother-in-law jokes:

I was thrown out of my mother-in-law's funeral. When the music started playing I was the only one dancing.

The age-old, battle of the sexes:

Two Homo Sapiens in their cave talking by the fire and one said to the other, 'I think I'll teach the wife to speak.' And the other said, 'Why not? I can't see what harm it can do…'

Lying in bed a husband asked his wife if she had any fantasies, and the wife said, 'There is one. I fantasise that we're complete strangers, we've never met…'
'And what,' he said, 'and then you pick me up in some bar?'
'No,' she said, 'that's it, just the first part.'

Old versus young:

Two young Oxbridge chaps were checking out newly acquired premises for their antique shop. There being nothing on the shelves, one turned to the other and said, 'I'll bet you while we're here some local yokel will come by, see the empty shop and ask what we're selling.'
Sure enough, an old feller came to the window, peeked in and said, 'What are you selling?'
One smiled and said condescendingly, 'Arseholes!'
And the old feller said, 'Well, you're doing well, only two left.'

Drunks, drug addicts, bankers, and lawyers:

This feller fresh out of rehab was alone in a hotel room and trying desperately not to think about booze he picked up the bible to read and miraculously out fell a leaflet: 'Alcoholic? Need help? Ring 01246 743 682'. He rang the number... it was the local Off-License.

Two junkies got married and one of the wedding presents they received was a twenty-four-piece silverware; all spoons.

The Devil said to a banker, 'I can make you rich beyond your wildest dreams, every investment you make will be successful, you will be famous amongst your peers, until you outstrip them to become the greatest banker of all time and knighted for your services to the nation's finance.'

'What do I have to do in return?' asked the banker.

'Give me your soul,' said the Devil, 'and not just your soul but the soul of your wife, the souls of your children and the souls of your children's children, in fact the souls of all your descendants throughout eternity.'

'Yeah, right,' said the banker, 'what's the catch?'

They are replacing rats in animal experiments with Accident Lawyers for three reasons, one; they are plentiful, two; lab assistants don't get attached to them, and three; they will do things that you just can't get rats to do.

Superiority theory encompasses laughing at other people's misfortunes:

There's a new book out about a young girl who takes drugs and meets some strange creatures. It ends with her getting pregnant and becoming a single parent living on a council estate and surviving on government hand-outs. The book's called, Alice in Sunderland!

The same joke type can apply upwards to someone better off, who has a better job, a bigger house, one who needs bringing down a peg or two, and what better way than making that person the butt of a joke?

Seeing the new Lord of the Manor step from his Land Rover and bend to drink from a stream a West Country farmer shouted: 'You don't wanna be drinkin' that thar wa'er from that thar creek oi tell 'ee, it be full of 'orse piss and cow shit and oo knows wha...'

And the lord shouted back: 'What on earth was that? Was that even a language? What you said was totally incoherent, could you perhaps repeat yourself in something akin to English.'

And the farmer said, 'I said, if you use two hands you'll be able to drink quicker.'

Most contentious of superiority theory types are ethnic and sexist jokes:

Whenever I see a woman driving a bus I am reminded how far we have come with equality, then I wait for the next bus.

An ethnic joke is one that refers to a perceived subculture or to a representative of that subculture. A description I realise hardly encompass the gamut of ethnic humour and throws up more questions than answers, but that would be another book entirely. For now, it is enough to recognise that ethnic jokes can be an effective way of confirming power and reaffirming superiority over someone or some group of people.

Ethnic jokes rely on stereotypes, perceptions that are sharpened and exaggerated, stereotypes that may have influenced our thinking for decades, and which sometimes can be so embedded in our thoughts and rooted in our collective folklore that they are difficult to dislodge. Irish jokes are a case in point:

An Irishman phoned a vet and said, 'I've just found a suitcase in the woods with a cat and four kittens inside.'

'Oh dear,' said the vet, 'are they moving?'

14

'I'm not sure,' said Pat, 'but that would explain the suitcase.'

Ethnic jokes purport certain characteristics to a people, and by using a stereotype that everyone is familiar with can put the listener into, "laughter readiness" mode. Rightly or wrongly, 'An illogical thinker phoned a vet...' does not set-up as well as, 'an Irishmen phoned a vet...'.

Jokes depicting a group or a race as stupid, inept, and ignorant are the most common and the most durable ethnic types, they have been around for thousands of years, and have been adapted for numberless groups of people.

English jokes about the stupidity of the Irish overlap with American jokes about the Polish, Canadian jokes about Newfoundlanders, French about Belgians, Brazilian about Portuguese, Russian about Estonians, Estonians about Finns, Australians about Tasmanians, etc., etc:

A young Pollack was talking to his Dad the day after his wedding.
'So, how did last night go, son?' said his Dad.
'Great,' said the son, 'You know, the way she was acting, I think I could've fucked her.'

Ethnic jokes are condescending and cruel, that is the point of them, though in his excellent 1997 book, *Seriously Funny* the author and humourist Howard Jacobson proposes: 'When we listen to a joke we are in a theatre of cruelty, but it is cruelty not hate, and it is a theatre not actuality... Of all the unquestioned assumptions on the politically correct agenda, this is the most indurate: jokes with ethnic content promote the rhetoric of racism... We know when we listen to a joke that we are entering, of our own violation, a world of dramatic make-believe and that we are lending ourselves to a fiction...'

Jacobson believes that we can indulge in racist jokes without being racist if (and it is a huge if), we are willing to accept that they are, 'just jokes'.

It is all about intent. The feelings and sentiments behind a joke cannot be inferred by an analysis of its content, it is a question of tone and context. From content alone, all we can deduce is that the teller of the joke knows what is perceived about the people who are the butt of the joke, because without that knowledge such a joke could neither be invented nor appreciated.

Asians drive so badly I'm starting to think that Pearl Harbour was an accident.

Jokes are the result, not the cause of a social situation. We should remember that the reason a race joke works is because there is some truth in it, not necessarily about the people, but about how they are thought of. The traits and characteristics may be exaggerated, wrong even, but the knowledge of how they are perceived makes the joke work.

Jewish men watch porn movies backwards because the best part for them is watching the prostitute giving the money back.

In his *Jokes: Philosophical Thoughts on Joking Matters* (2001) Ted Cohen offers his thoughts on Jewish jokes: 'More than once someone has demanded of me that I explain exactly why anti-Semitic jokes are not funny. I have come to realise that if there is a problem with such jokes, the problem is compounded exactly by the fact that they *are* funny. Face that fact. And then let us talk about it.'
Cohen believes that those who refuse to laugh at a race joke just because it upsets them is an indication of denial that solves nothing, and does not change the principal problem, which is why and how people hold negative opinions about certain social groups.

Jews were always discriminated against and persecuted and they found the best way to survive was to become a doctor, because no one is going to persecute a doctor. Who's going to walk into a doctor's office and say, 'My foot hurts, you Jew bastard!' (Jackie Mason).

Generalisations about cultures or nationalities can be harmful, history is littered with examples of unfavourable stereotypes that

16

contributed to prejudice, discrimination, persecution, and even genocide. But just how accurate are those generalisations?

An international study on cultural stereotypes published its findings in the July 2017 edition of the journal, *Science*.

The researchers tested the likelihood of cultural stereotypes being based, at least partly, on real experiences from people interacting with each other. If it were true, then the stereotypes would reflect the average personality of members of that culture. Robert McCrae and his colleagues at the *National Institution on Ageing* studied real and perceived personalities in fifty different countries and found it was not the case.

'These are in fact unfounded stereotypes. They don't come from looking around you and doing your own averaging of people's personality traits…' said McCrae, and added, 'National and cultural stereotypes do play an important role in how people perceive themselves and others and being aware that these are not trustworthy is a useful thing.'

The Relief Theory was first proposed by British philosopher Herbert Spencer (1820-1903) and endorsed later by Sigmund Freud (1856-1939).

Psychoanalyst Freud was an avid joke collector who thought that by treating our forbidden impulses lightly, that is with humour, not only allows us to relieve inner tensions but permits us to express ourselves in otherwise forbidden ways.

He also believed that the best jokes were the most provocative ones, and that jokes which fail to make us at least a little uneasy never succeed as well as those that do. The type of jokes we laugh at instinctively before our brain has time to analyse the content, that outwit our inner censor, leaving us free from our instincts of wrong and right, bad and good:

Two Paedophiles were walking through a park and as they passed a sixteen-year-old girl, one nudged the other and said, 'I bet she was a looker in her day.'

17

Relief Theory is characterised by the notion that laughter is a way of relieving pent-up emotion, letting off steam, while liberating ourselves from the inhibitions of forbidden thoughts. It includes smutty, cruel, and blasphemous jokes:

After his wife's funeral Tom was standing at her graveside when her attractive younger cousin came up to him. She lightly touched his arm whispered in his ear, 'Irene's gone, but you know Tom... there's no need for you to be lonely.'
'I don't think I'm quite ready yet,' said Tom, 'I need a bit more time.'
'I'm sorry,' she said, 'how insensitive of me, too soon, please forgive me.'
'Yeah,' said Tom, 'your sister just sucked me off in the vestry so give me ten minutes.'

This old feller drove to a local supermarket where they have special parking for pensioners, unfortunately he found that he had forgotten proof of his age but had a brainwave and opened his shirt and revealed all his grey chest hair to the attendant who then let him park. When the feller relayed the story to his wife she said: 'You should have dropped your trousers, they would have let you park in a disabled bay.'

And Jesus happened upon a crowd about to stone a woman accused of being a harlot. And Jesus spoke to the crowd saying, 'Let any virgin here cast the first stone...' and a big rock came from the crowd and hit the woman smack in the face. And Jesus said, 'You know, sometimes mother, you can be a right pain in the arse.'

Freud also proposed that innocent jokes were not entirely innocent and were, 'equated with exhibitionism in the sexual field,' and believed such jokes are closely linked to aggression and sex. He claimed that those who laugh hardest at malicious jokes are the ones who are more likely to hide their aggressive tendencies, while those who laugh loudest at lewd jokes are the most likely to be sexually repressed.

However, recent studies by British psychologist Hans Eysenck found the very opposite to be true and concluded that those who laughed most at aggressive and sexual jokes were in fact the least repressed and the least inhibited in displaying their true feelings.

Finally, there is the Incongruity Theory, the theory most agreed upon by modern academics, one which proposes that humour arises when the decent and logical become the low and ridiculous, or as the seventeenth century French philosopher Blaise Pascal wrote when he conceived the concept: 'Nothing produces laughter more than a surprising disproportion between that which one expects and that which one gets.'

After my son was born I said to the midwife, 'how long before we can have sex?' she said, 'I'm off duty in ten minutes, I'll meet you in the car park.'

Jokes are incongruities that conversely depend upon a certain amount of congruity which itself sounds incongruous but is nevertheless true. What makes a joke funny rather than nonsense is that the punch-line is not entirely unexpected, because in the light of the punch-line we can see that there were subtle clues in the set-up.

The crucial thing is believability, the listener must at least accept a certain amount of plausibility in the narrative. The surprise ending should make sense with what has gone before, unless of course the whole point of the joke is for it not too, which is another joke type entirely:

A joke is a natural set-up leading in one direction, followed by a sudden turn in another direction to the punch- line. So, here goes: Walk forward, turn left, pasteurisation!

John Morreall's 2009 book, *Comic Relief* linked the cultivation of a sense of humour to our well-being. 'Through humour,' he wrote, 'we can learn to enjoy life, and take pleasures in its absurdities rather than let them bring us down. Through humour we can learn to step back when necessary, and take a more objective perspective of life…'

He explores specifically the benefit of "gallows" humour, citing jokes told by Jews while imprisoned in ghettos and war camps during World War Two, many of whom said that telling jokes helped them cope:

Two Jews met in the Warsaw Ghetto and one was eating scented soap, the other asked him, 'Why are you eating scented soap?'

'Well,' said the first Jew, 'if I'm going to be turned into soap I might as well smell nice.'

Two Jewish brothers in a Berlin ghetto discussing their plight and one said, 'Terrible persecutions, no rations, discrimination, death threats, sometimes I think it would be better if we had never been born.'

'You're right,' said the other, 'but who has that much luck, maybe one in fifty thousand?'

Gallows humour is often created from real tragedies which makes it inevitable that the jokes will receive mixed reactions. What people consider tragic is pretty much universal, what people consider funny is anything but:

Why did the American cross the road? To escape the buildings falling on his head.

A few weeks after the New York terrorist attacks on September 11, 2001, the New York, Friars Club hosted a "Roast" for *Playboy* founder Hugh Heffner. The guest comedian, Gilbert Gottfried began his set with a couple of innocuous Viagra jokes before announcing that his new Muslim name was, 'Hasn't Been Laid', to which the audience laughed and applauded.

Then Gottfried said, 'I have to leave early tonight, I have to fly to L. A. I couldn't get a direct flight, I have to make a stop at the Empire State Building.'

The audience booed, and the sound of, 'too soon' rang out around the room. But how soon is too soon?

A feller on the Titanic went to the bar and said to the barman, 'Pint, please.' And the barman said, 'Are you mad? The ships at forty degrees, we're sinking, and you want a pint?'

'Look,' said the feller, 'it's women and children first, and then the old and infirm, I'm not getting off this ship, I'll be going down with a lot of others.'

'Well sir,' said the barman, 'perhaps you're right, a pint it is...'

He got his pint and asked, 'How much do I owe you?' and the barman said, 'A penny.'

'A penny?' said the feller, 'that's cheap.'

'Yes,' said the barman, 'it's Happy Hour.'

In 1912 the *Titanic* ocean liner ploughed into an iceberg off the coast of Newfoundland and fifteen hundred and seventeen men, women, and children either drowned or froze to death. Yet Titanic jokes abound.

We each have different and complex emotional reactions to tragedy and adversity. In his *Great Humour* study, Danish philosopher Harald Hoffding theorises that great humour reflects an appreciation of life not just from the perspective of happiness or sadness but from a more complex synthesis of these emotions.

Hoffding believes that the best jokes do not just make you feel one way or the other, they do much more, and that is why we can laugh at "sick" jokes and still have sympathy for their targets.

It is well documented that doctors, murder detectives, firemen, and various other professionals whose jobs expose them to some tragic situations often use humour to help them cope. The following American anecdote, which also happens to be true, is about a group of doctors who were working late one night in ER and decided to order pizza:

21

It was early hours of the morning and their pizza still hadn't arrived when suddenly a nurse burst in to tell them a patient had been brought in suffering a cardiac arrest.

The doctors rushed to surgery and immediately recognised the patient as the pizza delivery boy who must have had a heart attack whilst delivering their pizza. They worked for an hour trying to save his life but to no avail, he died.

Tired and depressed they all sat solemnly in the hospital canteen until one of the doctors piped up, 'Wonder what happened to the pizza.'

They rushed to the window and sure enough there was the box lying in the car park. One doctor rushed out and retrieved the pizza and set it out on the table in front of his colleagues. And as they munched away one doctor said, 'How much do you think we should tip him?'

Was the doctor being cruel? Maybe it was it just his way of handling the death of a patient. Maybe he was reminding his colleagues that we are all going to die while trivial matters like tipping will live on. Maybe he was saying that life is special, and we should not waste it, just like pizza. Maybe he just needed to laugh.

Because of my gambling addiction, I no longer see my wife and kids... I won a fortune and moved to Spain.

Last week I surprised my wife during sex, I came home early.

A feller murdered his wife and chopped her into pieces and placed the body parts into several bin bags and left them out for the bin men.

Two hours later there was a knock on the door, it was one of the bin men, he said, 'Excuse me, have you got another bin bag? The arse has fallen out of this one!'

If you dig deep enough there is tragedy or at least some unpleasantness in almost every joke. A gambling addiction can lead to a broken home and divorce, which is not funny, nor is adultery, or murder. Yet still we make the jokes.

Still, the question remains. When is it okay to joke about a tragedy, and when is it not? No one can say. It comes down to the individual every time, you and your own moral sensibility. What people consider inappropriate is purely relative and to a degree meaningless, and jokes considered such are judged subjectively on a person's life experiences and anxieties. People who profess to not liking "sick" jokes are not morally any better than those who do, they just have a different sense of humour.

Similarly, when it comes to "dirty" or "vulgar" jokes, terms some might use when referring to jokes about sex, or those containing expletive language.

In Britain, explicit sex jokes, until relatively recently, were for male ears only, the British in mixed company usually reverting to allusion and innuendo. In his introduction to the 1975 Penguin Edition of D H Lawrence's 1928 classic, *Lady Chatterley's Lover*, Richard Hoggart wrote:

Most of us know "four letter words" from an early age. We know them as swear words or parts of dirty jokes. But if we wish to speak simply and naturally about sex we are baffled. We tend to take roundabout ways, most of which are ashamed escape-routes. There is an old war-time story which illustrates both these characteristics. A soldier on leave from abroad was charged with assaulting another man. He explained why he had done it: 'I came home after three fucking years in fucking Africa, and what do I fucking-well find? My fucking wife in bed, engaged in illicit cohabitation with a male.'

We may be shocked when we hear expletives in a joke, it disturbs our superficial social values, yet most of us laugh anyway because we are not really shocked, it is earthy humour, and correctly used, can turn an average joke into a gut punching one. Comedian Dave Allen was discussed in the House of Commons after telling the following joke:

23

You get up to the clock, you go to work to the clock, eat to the clock, go home to the clock, sleep to the clock, wake to the clock, and go back to work to the clock. And after fifty years of work you retire and what do they give you? A fucking clock!

When asked why he felt the need to use the expletive Allen explained; 'I'm a believer in language, and there's only certain ways of saying things… It's not a damn clock, it's not a silly clock, it's not a doo-doo clock, it's a fucking clock! I'm Irish, we use swearing as stress marks. Language is there to be used. If you sanitise it, you take everything out of it.'

He who laughs, lasts.

The development of a sense of humour is a cognitive one, and beneficial not only to our social skills, but also to our health.
When we enjoy a joke, chemicals flood the brain, mostly dopamine, which results in laughter, and laughing is good for us. (Food and sex also stimulate the brain and increase dopamine levels, as does cocaine, which is why it is so addictive. Chocolate does the same, though it has a milder "kick" than cocaine and more calories.)
Research has proven that people who laugh more, while experiencing no less stress in their lives, tend to get over stressful times quicker than those who laugh least. In other words, people with a good sense of humour do not have easier lives than anyone else, they just feel like they do.

A feller said to his wife, 'What turns you on the most, my handsome face or my sexy body?' And she said, 'Your sense of humour.'

Humour in general has a direct impact on our relationships and having a good sense of humour improves the quality of our social relationships, even our romantic ones. Numerous surveys have asked women what they most desire in a partner and a sense of humour is always close to the top of the list.

24

Developing a sense of humour is part of the process of acquiring knowledge and understanding, and learning to deal with situations, people, and the world about us.

Laughter develops in infants long before language, usually between ten and twenty weeks of age, not that babies are discovering humour as adults understand it, they are responding to certain pleasurable stimulants such as tummy kissing or peek-a-boo.

Children begin to see things as funny during their second year, when they recognise that certain objects have meaning and can be rearranged in a funny way, such as using a soup bowl as a hat, or a banana as a telephone.

In their third year they begin to use their developing language skills to make jokes, usually by deliberately misusing or misapprehending words and names. Changing names, especially if they can match it to gender swapping is comedy gold to three-year-olds. Saying, 'You're Melanie' to Michael is funny, and cruel, and a child knows it, the joke is meant to hurt.

Around the same time children also learn that taboo words are funny, and are aware of the shock value of words like, 'pooh' and 'bum':

Why did Tigger look down the toilet?
To find Pooh.

At about four years old children begin to understand simple riddle jokes, ones easy to remember and tell, surreal but with a certain amount of logic:

What time is it when an elephant sits on your fence?
Time to get a new fence!

The humour of older children is defined by an increased portion of logical elements and higher levels of intellectual and language sophistication, while taboo words are likely to be ever more expletive:

25

What's yellow and smells of bananas?
Monkey shit.

By their mid-teens young people "get" and enjoy jokes with more adult themes, especially sex:

My maths teacher asked me what comes after sixty-nine? Apparently, 'I do' is not the correct answer.

Young people laugh a lot more than older people, studies show that five-year-olds laugh on average seven times an hour, whereas the average adult laughs just eighteen times a day, a figure that decreases with age.

At last we come to the history of the joke, but before we do I would ask you to cut the old jokes some slack, to keep in mind that most were jokes of their time and never aspired to be anything else. Most jokes have a relatively short shelf life, a few on the other hand live on for centuries, like the following, first recorded in Ancient Rome during the reign of the Emperor Augustus (63BCE-14CE):

The Emperor Augustus who, observing a slave passing the palace, and surprised to see how he looked remarkably like himself shouted to him: 'Ho there, slave, did your mother ever pass this way?' And the slave shouted back: 'No, sir, but my father did.'

The joke is known in numerous other countries and has been told at different times with different heads of state as the butt, including four British monarchs.

The fact that jokes rely on so many variables, not least changing tastes and changing cultures, it is remarkable how many do survive, even topical ones.

History often repeats itself and with a little imagination topical jokes can be redressed for new occasions. When it was discovered that American president Bill Clinton *did* have sexual relations with a

White House intern in the late nineties a Clinton cycle of jokes began that included:

The president is walking across the Whitehouse lawn one winter day and comes across the words, 'I Hate Bonking Bill' written in urine in the snow. He tells the Secret Service to investigate, and a week later they come back with their findings: 'Well, Mr President, we've analysed the urine and it turns out its Al Gore's. We've also analysed the handwriting, its Hillary's.'

It is an updated joke from the Nixon presidency with Henry Kissinger and Pat Nixon the protagonists, and an Asian version featuring Salman Khan, Vivek Oberoi and Aishwarya Rai Bachchan. The same joke was passed down orally by the Ozark people of the Arkansas-Missouri hills. Folklorist Vance Randolph recounts the joke the Ozarks claim was told to their ancestors in 1885, in honour of which he titled his 1954 book, *Pissing in the Snow*:

One time there were two farmers that lived out on the road to Carrico. They were always good friends, and Bill's oldest boy had been a-sparking Sam's daughter. Everything was going fine until the morning they met down by the creek, and Sam was pretty goddam mad, 'Bill,' said he, 'from now on I don't want that boy of yours to set foot on my place.'
'Why, what's he done?' asked the boy's daddy.
'He pissed in the snow, that's what he's done' said Sam, 'right in front of my house.'
'But surely, there ain't no harm in that,' Bill said.
'No harm,' hollered Sam, 'Hell's fire, he pissed so it spelled Lucy's name right there in the snow.'
'The boy shouldn't have done that,' said Bill, 'but I don't see nothing so terrible bad about it.'
'Well, by God, I do!' yelled Sam. 'There were two sets of tracks! And besides, don't you think I know my own daughter's handwriting?'

Time is not always so kind. A seventeenth century Japanese joke:

27

The chief of the monkeys orders his one thousand monkey followers to bring him the moon that is reflected in the water. All try and fail except for one monkey who gets the moon in the water and brings it to his chief. 'Here is what you asked for,' said the monkey.

Delighted the chief said, 'What an exploit, you have truly distinguished yourself.'

Then the monkey asked, 'By the way, master, what are you going to do with the moon from the water?'

And the chief replied, 'Ah, well, I didn't think of that.'

And to think only a few hundred years ago it brought the house down.

Chapter One

Philogelos

The oldest joke on record is a Sumerian Proverb dated around 1900 BCE:

Something which has never occurred since time immemorial – a young woman did not fart in her husband's lap.

The Sumerians were the indigenous non-Semitic people of ancient Babylonia in southern Mesopotamia (modern day Iraq), and the first historically attested civilization. Aside from inventing an advanced system of mathematics, and the socio-political institution of the city state, the Sumerians also created the oldest known written language.

Inscribed on a recently discovered Mesopotamian tablet dated around 1500 BCE are joke riddles:

In your mouth and in your urine. Constantly stared at you. The measuring vessel of your lord - What is it?
Answer: Beer.

He gouged out the eye. It is not the fate of a dead man. He cut the throat. A dead man - Who is it?
Answer: A governor. [We assume that a governor was also an executioner.]

The deflowered girl did not become pregnant. The un-deflowered girl became pregnant - What is it?
Answer: Auxiliary forces. [This even confused the experts!]

The Sumerians were not the only ancient civilisation to record their jokes. The Egyptian, *Westcar Papyrus Texts* written sometime between the eighteenth and sixteenth centuries BCE include several jokes. An abridged version of one goes:

How do you entertain a bored Pharaoh?
You sail a boat full of young women dressed only in fishing nets down the Nile and urge the Pharaoh to go and catch a fish.

Egyptologist Peter Clayton believes that the jokes told today by Egyptians about the stupidity of the Nubians are based on a stereotype that is thousands of years old and, states Clayton, 'probably go back to the dawn of time.' Nubians lived on the southern periphery of ancient Egyptian civilization:

An Egyptian said to a Nubian, 'I walked past your house last night and passing your bedroom window I heard you and your wife in copulation.'
And the Nubian said, 'Well, the joke is on you, because I was not home last night.'

In the beginning there was a laugh and that, according to an Egyptian alchemical papyrus dating from around the third century BCE, is how God created the world. With a laugh! How cool is that? (Okay, at Karnak in Upper Egypt, God Amun supposedly gave life to the world by masturbating over it, but a laugh better suits this book).
God surveyed the chaos and laughed, and there was light. Another laugh and the waters were created, and every time he laughed something else sprang up, and he kept on laughing until the Ancient World was complete.
So, when Ancient Egyptians laughed (or masturbated) it was their way of clearing the air, literally a joyful way of creating the world anew.

The first recorded laugh in Western literature occurs in Homer's *Iliad* (eighth century BCE) when Hephaestus, the Greek God of fire and crafts, having made a beautiful set of cups and forged a serving tray, filled each cup with wine which he intended to serve to the other Gods. But Hephaestus was lame, and his ungainly gait caused him to spill the wine over himself, upon which the Gods broke out in, 'unquenchable laughter.'

In Ancient Greece lameness referred to any infirmity, but especially to weak-wittedness. It was also used to describe bad meter in poetry. Hence today when we say a joke is, "lame" we refer to its lack of wit and timing.

The Greeks established comedy as an art form, "comedy" coming from the Greek word *Komos* a complex word which translates as: "a noisy, happy, drunken procession", add the suffix *ody* (song) and you have "happy drunks singing", *Komody*!

Comedy's official birth date is 486 BCE when for the first time a comic play was allocated a slot in the dramatic competitions at the Athens' festivals.

The dramatists took advantage of their newly created status by dethroning Gods, mocking heads of state and philosophers, parodying and satirising authorised customs and religious rites, and generally shaking things up.

At the beginning of his play, *Frogs* the playwright and poet Aristophanes (448-380 BCE) has the God Dionysus boasting to Heracles (Hercules):

Dionysus: We sank twelve or thirteen enemy ships.

Heracles: Just the two of you?

Dionysus: Yes, by Apollo.

Xanthias: And then we woke up.

Sex was also a prominent feature. Aristophanes' politically disenchanted *Birds* use bawdy word play for comic effect, the Greek word for 'wing' being a euphemism for 'phallus'. The character Tereus explains how they, 'feed in gardens on white sesame, myrtle berries, poppies and bergamot', plant names that all allude to female genitalia. There are few such allusions in *The Knights*:

31

Sausage Seller: Here is a camp-stool to sit on, for your comfort, and to carry it, an incredibly well-hung young slave. And if you fancy it, just turn him over and use him as a camp-stool.

Demos: Oh my, am I back in the good old days?

The first stage comedians were created at the Ancient Greek, Komos Festival of Music and Dance where the most popular entertainers were the "Komoidos", comic poets.

The stage Jester meanwhile, though well-liked by the people, was despised by Greek philosophers who often found themselves the butt of his jokes. One of the Seven Wise Men, Cleobolis (sixth century BCE) advised, 'Do not laugh at the jester, for you will be hated by those who are ridiculed.'

Nevertheless, many rich Greeks owned their own jester, slaves referred to as *Bomolochos* (parasites), described in one Greek drama as, 'smooth tongued witty varlets whose aim is to make themselves agreeable and who are ready to submit to any humiliation so that they may live at other people's expense.'

Noble Roman households also kept jesters, and it was a precarious existence, there always being a fine line between funny and disrespectful, and a jester was wise to know where that line was.

An Athenian jester called Philoxenus in the service of Dionysius of Sicily (around 400 BCE) noticed at dinner one evening that his patron's fish was much larger than his. The jester put the fish to his ear and when his master asked why he did so Philoxenus answered that he was intending to write a poem and wanted to hear news from the kingdom of Nereus, but unfortunately the fish knew nothing having been caught so young. 'No doubt that the fish set before Dionysius would know everything,' he added.

His master laughed and duly sent the larger fish to the jester, however, shortly afterwards a similar joke backfired which resulted in Philoxenus being sentenced to hard labour in the stone quarries.

Like Ancient Greeks the Romans enjoyed comic dramas which began to flourish in Rome around 300 BCE with Fabula Raciniata companies whose performances incorporated tumblers, jugglers, fire eaters, sword swallowers, singers, stilt walkers, character comedians, and a Scurra (from *scurrilous*), a solo jester who was given license to satirise and mock the ruling elite.

Ancient Romans also created the Lord of Misrule, a comic lord who reigned during the winter festival of Saturnalia. Throughout his reign he and his entourage played practical jokes and issued ridiculous commands and proclamations that usually involved up-ending normal customs, such as slaves being waited upon by their masters.

All good fun you might think, but there was a catch. At the end of his reign the Lord of Misrule had to die. We know this occurred at least until 303 CE because records show that in that year a garrison of Roman soldiers at Durostorum (Bulgaria) chose a soldier named Dasius to be their Saturnalia Lord. He reigned for thirty days during which time he and his friends indulged in all kinds of earthly pleasures and drunken mayhem. However, when it came time for Dasius to kill himself he refused. His friends beheaded him.

Ancient orators were largely responsible for developing the joke beyond a one-dimensional riddle, they were also the first public speakers to use humour to win over the crowds and deride their opponents.

The Greek philosopher, Socrates (470-399 BCE) was said to be, 'in both praise and blame sarcastic' (from the Greek *sarkazein*, 'to tear flesh'):

My advice for you is to get married; if you find a good wife you'll be happy, if not you'll become a philosopher.

The witticism is believed to be a truth told in jest as Socrates was married to Xanthippe, who by all accounts was a nagging hag of a wife who he allegedly married to practise his patience. The following is a joke that has appeared in numerous jest books down the ages:

Socrates had a cursed scolding wife called Xanthippe, the which on a day after she had altogether chided him, poured a piss pot on his head. He, then talking all patiently, said, 'Did I not tell you that when I heard Xanthippe thunder so fast that it would rain soon after?'

Socrates' wit was likely influenced, and one hopes encouraged by one of his teachers, the philosopher Archelaus who himself possessed a wry sense of humour:

My barber asked me how I would like my haircut. I told him, in silence...

Plato (428-348 BCE) termed Socrates' oratory as, 'a pretended self-deprecation or affected ignorance' and in calling him '*eiron*' effectively introduced *irony* to the world.

Not that Plato was a fan of jokes, he believed that a joke could be permitted only if, 'innocent in its purpose and free from anger', while other types he felt, 'lacked dignity'.

Somewhat begrudgingly he did concede that humour could be an effective aid in the education of ordinary citizens. Mild harmless jokes Plato concluded, could be helpful in making a serious point more acceptable, a concept he introduced as his own ('speaking truth under cover of a jest'), even though the Cynics and the Stoics had earlier come up with the idea.

Like Plato they too strove to correct the excesses of others, but unlike Plato the Cynics and Stoics believed that excess grew out of people taking themselves too seriously.

Not all Greek philosophers agreed with Plato and several took pleasure in jokes. One such was Democritus (460-370 BCE) who when asked, 'what wine do you prefer to drink?' famously replied, 'Another man's'.

The greatest theologian of the age, Hippolytus (170-235 CE) wrote how Democritus laughed and joked so much that his contemporaries called upon the physician Hippocrates (460-377 BCE) to heal him. But Hippocrates declared that Democritus was laughing at the folly of mankind and thought him a wise and sincere philosopher who joked to make serious issues more palatable to ordinary citizens.

Then there was Diogenes (400-325 BCE), the father of cynicism who other philosophers referred to as, 'Socrates gone mad' and called him, *kuon* (the dog).

When asked: 'When should a man marry?' Diogenes replied: 'A young man not yet and an old man not at all.' His greatest joke goes:

Life is good and bad. Mostly and.

Diogenes believed that happiness could only be attained by satisfying one's own natural needs, and what was natural was not indecent and therefore could be done in public. And Diogenes did everything in public!

He made a virtue of poverty and lived in a large ceramic jar in the market place in Athens where he often wandered half-naked in the daytime carrying a lighted lamp, searching, he said, 'for an honest man'.

His legacy is the medical term, "Diogenes Syndrome" for people diagnosed with a personality disorder, who live in domestic squalor, are self-neglectful, compulsive hoarders, socially isolated, apathetic, and have a complete lack of shame.

Democritus and Diogenes were the exception rather than the rule, most Greek philosophers believed that wit defined breeding while jokes were for uneducated commoners, of whom Aristotle (384-322 BCE) said were, 'forever doomed to lives of boorishness and crude jesting'.

In *Rhetoric* Aristotle wrote: 'Irony better benefits a gentleman than buffoonery; the ironical man jokes to amuse himself, the buffoon to amuse other people.'

Aristotle and his kind favoured the Greek *apophthegm* and its Roman successor *apothegm* over the joke, an apothegm being a humorous expression, maxim, observation, a brief narrative of a topical event, or an anecdote that carried a moral lesson, and though often humorous that was not its primary purpose. Its purpose was to teach.

Nevertheless, the Greeks were the first civilisation to create joke books. It is reputed that Philip of Macedonia (382-336 BCE) paid handsomely to have the Greek "Court of Humour" jokes recorded but the volume, if it ever existed, has never surfaced, though the second century Greek writer Lucian of Samosata recalled a joke allegedly from one of the court gatherings:

While a man is riding his horse, the horse is stung by a wasp and bolts. Someone he knows shouts at the rider: 'Where are you going?' And the rider shouts back, 'don't ask me – ask the horse!'

The Court of Humour was held at Heracleum in the Temple of Heracles near Athens and organised by the famous "Group of Sixty" (a group of elite Greeks) who met each month to eat, drink, and swap jokes.

In the second century the Greek writer Diogenes Laertius, author of *Lives of the Philosophers* produced a collection of jokes in the form of attributed anecdotes, many of which appear in numerous medieval jest books:

Diogenes the Cynic observing a bastard throwing rocks into a crowded street warned him; 'Be careful lad, the man you hit might be your father.'

The oldest existing joke book is the Greek *Philogelos*, 'Laughter-Lover', dated between the fourth and fifth century.
It contains two hundred and sixty-four jokes, some of which appear twice in slightly different form, suggesting that *Philogelos* may even be two joke books combined, which would account for its two authors, the Greek scholars, Hierocles and Philagrius.
The collection has a gallery of stock comic characters including fools, drunkards, braggarts, sex starved women, men with bad breath, misers, scholasticus (scholars lacking common sense), and pedants (pedantic types):

Did you hear about the scholasticus who asked his father how much a five-litre flask holds?
(The joke is also a double entendre, the ancient Greek word for flask being, *lekythos* which was slang for penis.)

A scholasticus was on a sea voyage when a big storm blew up causing his slaves to weep in terror. 'Don't cry,' said the scholasticus trying to console them, 'I have freed you all in my will.'

Wishing to teach his donkey not to eat, a pedant did not offer him any food. When the donkey died of hunger, he said, 'I've had a great loss. Just when he had learned not to eat, he died.'

Philogelos contains Monty Python's famous "Dead Parrot" sketch in joke form:

A pedant bought a slave who soon afterwards died and when he complained, the slave seller said, 'Well he did not do that when I owned him.'

Numerous others have survived the ages, including:

Someone needled a jokester, 'I had your wife'. And the jokester replied, 'It's my duty as a husband to couple with her, but what made you do it?'

The following *Philogelos* joke is possibly the longest recorded joke lineage:

Said a young man to his randy wife, 'Wife, what shall we do, eat or make love?'
And she in reply said, 'Whichever you like, there's no food.'

The same joke appears in the 1470, Latin, *Facetiae* and in the sixteenth century French poem, *Mais le Souper ne'st pas Encore*

Cuit (but the supper is not yet cooked), and again in the late eighteenth century Scottish rhyme, *The Supper Is Na Ready*:

> Roseberry to his lady says,
> 'My hinnie and my succour.
> O shall we do the thing ye ken,
> Or shall we take oor supper?'
>
> Wi modest face, sae full o' grace,
> Replied the bonny lady;
> 'My noble lord, do as ye please,
> But the supper is na ready.'

Philogelos produced the first documented, "Doctor, doctor" joke:

'Doctor,' said the patient, 'whenever I awaken after a sleep I feel dizzy for a while and then I'm alright.'
'Well,' said the doctor, 'wait a while before you get up.'

We learn from *Philogelos* that Ancient Greek ethnic jokes were aimed at Boeotians, the citizens of Abdera in Thrace, and the people of Cyme in modern day Turkey, all of whom were regarded as dim witted. Today the Greek word *boeotian* means dullard, while *abderite* and *abderitic* define a simpleton.

The father of a man of Cyme died and his son dutifully took him to the embalmers. When he returned to collect the body, there were a number of bodies in the same place, so he was asked if his father had any peculiarity by which his body might be recognised. And the son replied, 'He had a cough.'

A mere century younger than the *Philogelos* is *The Golden Words of Pythagoras* by Hierocles of Alexandria (active around 430 CE, no connection to Hierocles of *Philogelos*). Attached to the manuscript is a collection of twenty-one jokes, including:

A pedant, seeing a deep well in a field asked his hired man if the water was good to drink. 'Oh, yes' was the reply, 'your ancestors drank from that well.'

The pedant said: 'What long necks they must have had to drink from such depths.'

A pedant who almost drowned in a river vowed never to enter into water again until he had learned how to swim.

Romans too created joke books, the playwright Platus (255-184 BCE) refers to jest books in several of his plays, while the historian Suetonius noted that Gaius Maecenus Melissus the early first century Roman writer compiled as many as a hundred and fifty joke anthologies.

Roman scholars were however, much of the same opinion as Greek philosophers when it came to jokes and joking, and dubbed the famed orator, philosopher, and joke lover, Cicero (106-43 BCE) 'scurra consularis', consular buffoon.

Buffoon he was not, Cicero understood the power of jokes and wrote, 'The orator jokes with an object, not to appear jester, but to obtain some advantage.'

Cicero added jokes to his speeches not only to gain favour with the crowds but also with Rome's elite. Emperor Augustus (63 BCE-CE 43) collected many of Cicero's jokes, no doubt including his most famous:

A Sicilian lamented to a friend that his wife had hanged herself from a fig tree. 'I beseech you,' the friend said, 'give me some shoots from that tree that I may plant them.'

In *De Oratore* Cicero discussed the two prominent and distinct kinds of wit used by speech makers, that being irony and raillery, but also encouraged *hilaritas* (general jesting) and *iocus* (jocularity/joking), he wrote: 'The highest art of the rhetorician is the sheer delight in telling funny stories.'

Cicero made jokes an acceptable and important part of rhetoric, but that is not all. He wrote extensively on the fusing of the comic with fiction which established fiction as a new context for humour.

It was a monumental contribution to the history of western literature, not to mention the history of the joke, fusing the comic with fiction, '*iocare in re*:' a story about the truth of a person, but fabricating the details.

Prior to Cicero's idea, a joke was forged from truth, or at least exaggerated truth, or social commentary, but he encouraged original creation, a lie, a fabrication, a tall tale told purely for fun. In effect Cicero invented the narrative joke.

Unfortunately, it did not end well for our hero who in 43 BCE made jokes at the expense of Mark Antony and the Roman general, short of a comeback, had him executed.

Like most Greek and Roman philosophers, ancient Jewish elders did not look kindly on jokes and went so far as to condemn joyous laughter as something unnatural and pagan. *The Bible* makes numerous negative references to humour and laughter. *Ecclesiastes* 7: 3-4:

Sorrow is better than laughter: for by the sadness of the countenance the heart is made better. The heart of the wise is in the house of mourning; but the heart of fools is in the house of mirth.

The only laugh in the Old Testament, apart from the derisive laughter of God, is when Abraham and Sarai are told that they will have a son. Abraham was a hundred years old while Sarai was in her nineties and had been infertile her entire life. When they both laugh God gets angry and when Sarai denies laughing God has a quick comeback, saying, 'You did laugh.' (Gen 18:15)

After Sarai gives birth to her son (Isaac), God changes her name to Sarah (princess) and names her son by his Hebrew name, Yitzchak, which means, 'He laughs'. Did God make a joke?

The fourth century rabbi, Chanina Bar Papa advised: 'When you have an impulse toward frivolity, resist it with the words of the Talmud.' (The Talmud is a collection of Jewish lore and law written in the sixth century BCE which was refined and added too over the following thousand years.)

Despite the advice of their dour ancient religious leaders, Jews developed a unique sense of humour through irony, subverted meanings and understatement, and a gentle mocking themselves and their customs. Jewish jokes tend to deal in incomprehensibility, surrealism, and illogical logic:

During a service in a wealthy synagogue the Rabbi got carried away and fell to his knees and put his forehead to the wooden floor and cried, 'Oh, God, before thee I am nothing.'

The Cantor not to be outdone also fell to his knees and forehead to wood also cried, 'Oh God, before thee I am nothing.'

Seeing this, Levy, a poor tailor in the fourth row, jumped from his seat, fell to his knees, and forehead to wood cried, 'Oh God, before thee I am nothing.'

And the Cantor nudged the Rabbi and sniffed, 'Huh, look who thinks he's nothing.'

Many modern Hindu reformists and other uptight religious apologists wish to impose a prohibitive seriousness on their scriptures and ancient literature, believing that laughter somehow makes their religion less respectable. But Indian Gods are magic and illusion and are playful, and religious texts and ancient folklore contain an abundance of jokes and humorous tales.

The Hindu sacred texts, the *Rig-Veda*, dated around one thousand years BCE, is a collection of hymns addressed by the seers to the Gods. The texts highlight the human side of the Gods and tell of marriages, adulteress affairs, and flaunting their sexual prowess. Thunder-God Indra's wife, Shachi brags: 'There is no woman more fair-assed than I, nor better lubricated, nor any more counterthrusting, nor better thigh spreader...'   *Rig-Veda* 10:86:6.

41

In the *Itihasa-Purana* literature of the first century BCE Indra seduces a priest's wife and is punished by having his body covered with a hundred vaginas. Magical curses cannot be revoked so Indra asks Brahma, the Creator God of Hinduism for help and Brahma comes up with the rather fetching solution of filling each vagina opening with an eye. A satirical twist on the imagery of a hundred-eyed (all-seeing) God.

Indra, hundred eyed vaginas, God was not as popular as Indra, Thunder-God who disappeared from the Hindu pantheon, although the Gods Shiva and Ganesh are heirs to his symbolism.

Son of Shiva, Ganesh is called, 'Laughing God' and is invoked at the beginning of religious rituals to remove mental obstacles and leave worshippers worry free. He is portrayed as red, with an elephant-head, one tooth, pot-belly, and riding on the back of a rat.

Since ancient times Hindu jokers have made Brahmins (priests) and Pandits (scholars) the butt of their jokes. Generally perceived as a being a bit too clever for their own good and ridiculed for always insisting that their word is the only truth:

A neighbour came to Brahmin and asked to borrow his cow. 'It's out on loan,' the Brahmin said. Just then the cow snorted loudly in the stable. 'But I can hear it snort,' said the neighbour. And the Brahmin said, 'Who are you going to believe, me or a cow?'

Pandit Vajpeyi was crossing the river in a ferryboat and he said to the ferryman, 'Hey boatman, have you studied grammar?' And the ferryman sheepishly said, 'No.'

'Then a quarter of your life has been wasted,' said Vajpeyi.

After a short silence the Pandit then asked, 'Have you studied philosophy?' and again the ferryman said 'No.' And Vajpeyi said, 'then half your life has been wasted.'

After another short silence the ferryman said, 'Hey Pandit-ji, have you studied swimming?' And the Pandit said, 'No.'

'Well,' said the ferryman, 'then all your life has been wasted, the boat is leaking, we're sinking.'

Initially Buddhist leaders considered laughter an evil and in Ancient India it was an offence for a Buddhist monk to laugh out loud.

The *Vinaya*, a code of conduct for monks and nuns stipulated that all laughter is bad, and by the fourth century BCE Buddhist scholars had a kind of league table of the six types of laughter ranging from *sita*, a faint, almost imperceptible smile all the way down to *atihasita*, boisterous, uproarious laughter.

Buddhists could only indulge in *sita*, though one of lesser attainment could occasionally indulge themselves with a *hasita*, a smile that does not expose the teeth.

We need to fast forward a thousand years to China and Ch'an (Zen) Buddhism where the slim, aristocratic figure of the Indian Buddha and his faint smile is replaced in art by Pu-Tai, a jolly, fat, laughing Buddha, and where laughter is not only permitted but encouraged.

Zen uses humour as a learning tool, particularly through koans, paradoxical anecdotes or riddles without a solution which are meant to demonstrate the inadequacy of logical reasoning and thus provoke enlightenment. The most famous of which is: What is the sound of one hand clapping? Nowadays; what is the sound of one hand texting?

Other joke koans include:

If there is no self, then whose aching bones are these?

Wherever you go, there you are.
Your luggage is a different story.

Breathe in, breathe out... forget this and Enlightenment will be the least of your problems.

Chapter Two

Medieval

Jamie Kreiner in her 2014, *The Social Life of Hagiography in the Merovingian Kingdom* explores early medieval jokes from the Kingdom of Gaul where the "French" were making jokes in what were supposed to be serious works of literature.

The most popular Gaul literature at the time was hagiography, of which Kreiner said in her article for *Fifteen Eighty-Four; Academic Perspectives from Cambridge University Press*: 'In medieval and modern library catalogues these writings are shelved away as "saints' lives". That's not all they were... sometimes they were funny.' She cites a few examples, including:

There was a man who left his job as a Deacon and started working for the royal treasury. He was so corrupt he even illegally confiscated some sheep owned by the church of St. Julian: he was essentially stealing from a dead saint ('What, does Julian eat sheep?' he cackled to the shepherds.) But one day he had a bad fall in front of Julian's tomb and could not get up again. When the servants found him lying there they said, 'Why have you been down on the ground all this time? You don't usually take so long to pray.'

Hagiography was not however, exclusive to Gaul literature and extends throughout much of medieval Europe. In 1926 Dr Robin Flower, compiler of the *Catalogue of Irish Manuscripts in the British Museum*, dated the Irish hagiographic *Triar Manach* (three monks) early medieval. *Three Monks* is a joke, and a rather good one at that:

Three monks turned their back on the world. They go into the wilderness to repent their sins before God. They did not speak to one another for the space of a year. Then one said to another at the end of the year, 'We are well.'

Thus, it was for another year.

'It is well indeed,' said the second monk.

They were there after that for another year.

'I swear by my habit,' said the third monk, 'if you do not allow me some quiet I will abandon the wilderness entirely to you.'

There have since been numerous versions, peopled by Christian, Buddhist, and Hindu monks. The tale is also listed in *The Types of International Folktales* by Hans-Jorg Uther (Helsinki 2004) in which Uther recites centuries old versions of the joke from across Northern Europe.

Early medieval times in Britain were the Dark Ages for jokes, or at least for recording them, the highly religious intent on suppressing any kind of frivolity.

In his *Homo Ludens: A Study of the Play Element in Culture* author Johan Huizinga characterized Medieval culture in England as one, 'whose play-spirit was extraordinary' and described the Middle-Ages society as, 'one desperate to put its playfulness into practice, but one held back by rules and regulations.'

Throughout the Middle-Ages the church in England grew increasingly angered at their religious festivals being hijacked by ordinary folk for the sole purpose of making merry.

The annual Feast of Fools for example, hosted by the Lord of Misrule, a jester also known as the Abbot of Gaiety, the Cardinal of Bad Measure, Bishop Flat-Purse, and Duke Kickass, was one such festival the church felt had gotten out of hand.

For the peasantry it was a few days of liberation and disorder with the Lord of Misrule instigating the two great levellers, mockery and derision, while flipping the order of power.

The Lord as "Motley Fool", dressed in multi-coloured suit and cap with floppy ears and bells, symbolized mankind in general and great men in particular, while his fooling revealed the folly and vice that are basic to all human instincts.

He proved so popular a character that a comic "Lord" was appointed for other festivals and wakes (festivals of the Saint to whom the parish church is dedicated and so called because the previous night, or vigil, the people kept watch, or "wake" in the church until the morning came). A wake was initially one day where the inhabitants of the parish kept open house and entertained friends and relatives who visited from other parishes. Meanwhile booths and tents were set up near the church for all to feast, pray and say thanksgivings. But by degrees the prayers and thanksgivings were forgotten as eating and drinking became the order of the day (and night), and by the middle-ages wakes as religious festivals had given way entirely to summer fairs which went on for days, sometimes a week, and attracted people from far and wide.

The church meanwhile, laid out strict guidelines for its monks regarding laughter. The sixth century *Regula magistri* described it as a despicable vice that wounds the soul, while the *Regula Pauli et Stephani* warned how laughter tempts the devil.

With religious leaders in Britain so set against laughter, and they at the time being the learned and literate, it is no surprise that few jokes exist on record until the Middle Ages. There are however, several texts of Medieval humorous rhymes, such as the anonymous:

Say me, wight in the brom.
Teche me how I shal don
They min housebonde
Me lovien wolde.

'Holde thine tongue still
And have al thine wille.'

It is a woman asking a man (Wight), how she can get her husband to love her, with him delivering the punch line: 'Hold your tongue, and you'll get what you want.'

46

Not until the eleventh century *Exeter Book* do we have recorded examples of popular joke types in Medieval Britain.

The book was written between 960-990 and bequeathed by Leofric, the Bishop of Exeter to his cathedral after his death in 1072. It contains devout poems, legends of saints, meditations, and ninety-nine joke riddles which are surprisingly quite ribald:

A curiosity hangs by the thigh of a man, under its master's cloak. It is pierced through in the front; it is stiff and hard, and it has a good standing place. When the man pulls up his own robe above his knee, he means to poke with his head of his hanging thing that familiar hole of matching length which he has often filled before.
Answer: Key.

I am a wondrous creature for women in expectation, a service for neighbours. I harm none of the citizens except my slayer alone. My stem is erect; I stand up in bed, hairy somewhere down below. A very comely peasant's daughter dares sometimes, proud maiden that she grips at me, attacks me in my redness, plunders my head, confines me in a stronghold, feels my encounter directly, and woman with braided hair who squeezes me. What be I?
Answer: An onion.

I have heard of a something-or-other, growing in its nook, swelling and rising, pushing up its covering. Upon the boneless thing a cocky-minded young woman took a grip with her hands, and with her apron a lord's daughter covered the tumescent thing.
Answer: Dough.

Written around the same time as the *Exeter Book* was the Middle Eastern *Nathr al-durr* (*Scattered Pearls*), a seven-volume encyclopaedia of jokes, anecdotes, and humorous tales compiled by Iranian author al-Abi (died 1030).

Scattered Pearls began seriously with the pillars of Islam and the early caliphs, but gradually moved on to jokes about uninvited guests, greedy people, lunatics, transvestites, homosexuals, dishonest professionals (dyers, weavers, and lowest of all, canal-cleaners), robbers and their victims, sectarians and fanatics, and farts and farting (silently and noisily):

Ahmed Al-Mohammed was in the bazaar when he was overcome with terrible stomach cramps and unable to control himself let out a long and loud fart. Everyone around stared at him and Ahmed felt his face redden with embarrassment as he fled from the bazaar. Feeling totally shamed he packed his belongings and journeyed to the far side of the world vowing never to return.

Over the years he longed for his home, and at eighty-three years old, his face aged and unrecognisable from his younger self, and confident that after sixty years the incident was long forgotten, he finally returned home.

The following morning Ahmed strolled through the bazaar feeling happier than he had for over half a century. Passing one stall he smiled at the owner and asked, 'My friend, I have not been here for some time, tell me, when were these paving stones re-laid so neatly?'

And the owner of the shop said, 'Ah by the grace of Allah, it was forty-four years, three months and two days after Ahmed Al-Mohammed farted in the bazaar.'

From the Middle-East and dated early twelfth century is *Disciplina Clericalis* by Petrus Alphonsus (born Moses Sephardi in 1062), a collection of Jewish and Arabic jokes, the sole purpose of which Alphonsus said was for religious leaders to keep their congregations from sleeping during their services.

Around the same time Muslim preacher Ibn al-Jawdi compiled a triad of books containing jokes and comic anecdotes. In his introduction al-Jawdi advised followers, 'Enjoy recreation, since the soul tires at times from continuous sobriety and longs for permitted pastimes.'

(The Koran does not set any specific rules regarding laughter, though surah 53, verse 43, states that God is the one who makes men laugh and makes men weep. There is no mention of God laughing joyously in the Koran, however various *Hadiths* [official reports of

48

the life and teachings of the Prophet] speak of Mohammad laughing on numerous occasions and sometimes so intensely that his molar teeth were visible. Religious author, the learned Muhammad Ibn Sirin (died 728) when asked if the Prophet's early companions used to jest, said: 'They were just like everybody else.')

The most famous comic character in Middle Eastern folklore is the trickster Nasreddin Hodga, a Seljuc Sufi who ridicules state and religious affairs.

There are many contrasting accounts of Hodga's life including that from the 1483, *Sultakname* which contains folk tales, anecdotes, and jests of Hodga's alleged exploits. The book claims that Hodja was born in the Hortu village of Sivrihisar, in the Eskihir province in Turkey, whose natives were renowned for their strange behaviour and innocent ways.

Sultakname also states that Hodja died in 1284 at Aksehir, a province of Konya. However, Hodja jokes are on record long before he was supposedly born and continued long after his death, and he is not exclusive to Turkey but shows up throughout the Middle East, Far East, Eastern Europe, Russia, southern Siberia, and North Africa. The jokes are the same, only the places differ:

One of the neighbours found Hodja Nasreddin scattering bread crumbs all around his house.
'Why are you doing that?' he asked.
'To keep the tigers away,' replied Hodja.
'But there aren't any tigers around here,' said the neighbour.
'That's right,' said Hodja, 'see how well it works?'

In 1344 the Italian poet and Humanist Francesco Petrarch (1304-74) presented his *Rerum Memorandaum Libri* (*Book of Memorable Things*), a collection of a hundred and forty-four jests mostly adapted from Cicero, Macrobius' *Saturnalia,* and Suetonius' *Lives*. His *Dante and the Boring Speaker* was originally a Macrobius joke:

The poet Dante Alighieri was at the table with some noble guests and the lord of the feast, merry with wine and food, was sweating freely and talking all sorts of frivolous, false and pointless things. Dante listened in silence for a long time. Finally, the lord grabbed hold of Dante with clammy hands and shouted, 'What? Don't you agree that he who speaks the truth doesn't have to work at it?' And Dante replied, 'Yes, I was just wondering why you were sweating so much.'

Petrarch's close friend and fellow Humanist, writer and poet Giovani Boccaccio (1313-1375) was author of many notable works including the classic masterpiece, *The Decameron* (1353), a book of one hundred tales told by a group of seven young women and three young men whilst sheltering from the Black Death in a secluded Florence villa.

The plots of the tales have various origins including Spain, India, Persia, and ancient Middle-Eastern civilizations which Boccaccio adapted to mock the greed and lust of the Italian clergy, tensions between the new wealthy commercial class and old families of nobility, the exploits of travelling merchants, and strained marital relationships.

Unlike Dante and Petrarch before him, Boccaccio created strong female characters and rather than portray them as seductive, corruptive creatures, accepted woman's sexual urges. In Dioneo's tale of *Ricciardo and Paganino*, a wife takes her husband to task over his unwillingness to perform his husbandly duties:

'And I can tell you this, that if you had given as many holidays to the workers on your estates as you gave to the one whose job it was to tend my little field, you would never have harvested a single ear of corn.'

It is a typical example of Boccaccio's wit and clever euphemism, playing on the idea of husband and husbandry, and sex in terms of farming and earthy fertility.

What also separated Boccaccio from most other Medieval writers is that he used the Italian vernacular, the language of the ordinary people, *Decameron* is particularly noted for its realistic dialogue, while the use of common issues made it accessible to more people.

Though *Decameron* is not a collection of jests it was a major influence on arguably the most important joke book in history, *Liber Facetiarium* written by another Florentine, the Italian papal secretary, Poggio Bracciolini.

However, prior to Bracciolini's joke book another writer greatly influenced by Boccaccio, the English poet Geoffrey Chaucer released his seminal work, *The Canterbury Tales* (c1387-1400) and was duly dubbed by the eminent poet Thomas Hoccieve as, *'the firste fynder of our fair language'*.

He was some joke writer too.

Chapter Three

Chaucer

Geoffrey Chaucer (1342-1400) was the first great English poet, and one who legitimised the literary use of English at a time when the dominant literary languages in England were French and Latin. He also knew a thing or two about writing jokes.

In creating fully rounded characters, recognisable characters with all their faults, foibles and sensibilities, and putting them into situations that were funny and yet plausible, Chaucer constructed perfect humorous narratives.

His *Canterbury Tales* is a cycle of stories told by a group of travelling pilgrims, a collection of comic tales brimming with jab-lines and punch-lines.

The cycle begins with *The Knight's tale*, a chivalric romance that a fellow traveller, the Miller, finds boring and endeavours to liven up proceedings by launching into a rollicking, bawdy account of infidelity and deceit.

The Miller's Tale is a direct antithesis of *The Knight's Tale* and a real gem, one in which Chaucer took the physicality of a practical joke and converted it into a verbal one.

The Miller and a co-traveller, the Reeve, are enemies (so it is a tale within a tale), and the Miller makes it clear that the Reeve is his character John, an old carpenter who has taken for his wife the young and beautiful Alison (the Reeve himself has a young wife).

John is past his prime and unable to satisfy Alison and suspects she is cheating on him with Nicholas, a poor student who is renting a room in his house. He has good reason to suspect, when Nicholas and Alison are alone:

...privily he caughte hire by the queynte,

And said, 'Indeed, unless I have my will,
For secret love of thee, sweetheart, I die.'

Afraid of alerting her husband, Alison insists they wait for the right opportunity. Enter Absolon, another young man in love with Alison and one who every day sits at her window and serenades her. Meanwhile Nicholas convinces the old carpenter that God is sending a flood and so John decides to sleep in a bathtub suspended by chords from the ceiling, which leaves Nicholas and Alison free to spend the night together.

Shortly before daybreak the following morning, Absolon shows up outside Alison's window and begs for a kiss, to which Alison eventually agrees, but as Absolon closes his eyes and puckers up she instead thrusts her bare bum out of the window:

And at the window out she put her hole,
And Absolon, to him it happened no better nor no worse,
But with his mouth he kissed her naked ass
With great relish, before he was aware of this.
Back he jumped, and thought it was amiss,
For well he knew a woman has no beard.
He felt a thing all rough and long haired,
And said, 'Fie! Alas! What have I done?'

When Absolon kisses her bare bum, which Chaucer describes as, 'ful savourly' it evokes from Alison the first laugh recorded in English: 'Teehee,' quod she, 'and clapte the window too.'

Humiliated, Absolon runs off only to return with a red-hot poker and tells Alison he will give her a ring in return for another kiss, at which point Nicholas decides to get in on the joke:

This Nicholas was risen to piss,
And thought he would make the joke even better;
He should kiss his ass before he escapes.
And he opened up the window hastily,
And puts out his ass stealthily

53

Over the buttock to the thigh;
And then spoke this clerk, this Absolon,
'Speak, sweet bird, I know not where thou art'.

This Nicholas immediately let fly a fart
As great as if it had been a thunder-bolt,
So that with the stroke he was almost blinded;
And he was ready with his hot iron,
And he smote Nicholas in the middle of the ass.

Off goes the skin a hands breadth about,
The hot plough blade so burned his rump
And for the pain he thought he would die.
As if he were crazy, for woe he began to cry,
'Help! Water! Water! Help, for God's heart!'

The carpenter woke suddenly out of his slumber,
And heard someone cry 'water!' as if he were crazy,
And thought, 'Alas, now comes Nowell's flood!'
He sits up without more words,
And with his axe he smote the chord in two,
And down goes all; he found nothing to sell [wasted no time],
Neither bread nor ale, until he came to the pavement
Upon the floor, and there he lay in a swoon.

The Miller's Tale demonstrated how people (in this case the Miller and the Reeve) can play out their hostilities and humble their adversaries through jokes, and how their adversaries have little choice but to accept it with a grin or risk being perceived as one without a sense of humour, unable even to take a little joke.

Chaucer's genius broke new ground for English literature and for humorous prose especially, which conversely was not good for the joke as it was already suffering from a lack of identity, indistinct amongst the numerous types of humorous tales and jolly anecdotes.

Medieval Latin collections such as *Gesta Romanorum*, the *Alphabetum Narrationum*, and the *Speculum Exemplorum* are compilations of humorous tales rather than jokes, although admittedly the spirit of the joke is apparent.

Medieval French *fabliaux* (literally, fabulous) and *nouvelles* (short story) found in collections like *Les Cents Nouvelles*, and *Le Vilain Mire* said to have been composed by jongleurs and troubadours in the twelfth and thirteen centuries, were much closer in style and content to the joke. The following is from *Les Cents Nouvelles*:

A woman entertaining a lord in her bed is interrupted by another nobleman lover. The lord hides in the canopy over the bed. But then the husband returns and interrupts the second lover who hides under the bed. As the husband is about to ejaculate into his wife, she tries to draw aside and objects, 'But husband, how can we afford another baby?' And the husband says, 'The lord above will provide, the Lord will provide.' And a voice from the canopy above shouts, 'Oh the lord above will provide, will he? And what about that bugger of a Baron under the bed?'

As Europe entered the Renaissance period that saw a revival of art and literature, the joke was in dire need of a separate identity from various other forms of humorous literature, and it found an unlikely champion in the Italian papal scholar and Vatican secretary, Poggio Bracciolini.

Chapter Four

Poggio

Gian Francesco Poggio Bracciolini (1380-1459) was an Italian humanist, scholar, writer, and secretary to seven different Popes.

His great passion was books, he travelled extensively throughout Europe where he rescued numerous precious manuscripts from monasteries before laboriously deciphering and copying them for posterity. It is thanks to him that we have Lucretius's *De Rerum de Natura*; Quintilian's *Institutio Oratoria*; many of the speeches of Cicero; the architectural writings of Vitruvius; and Apicius's transcriptions on cooking.

He was also a keen joke collector and his *Liber Facetiarium* (Book of Trifling Jests) published in 1470 and known simply as, *Facetiae* (Jests) established the joke as unique folklore, something quite separate from a humorous tale or anecdote. By calling the collection 'facetiae', Poggio gave the title to this genre of fiction.

Facetiae is a volume of jokes which had been shared by scholastic monks, priests, and papal scribes for decades, possibly centuries. A collection of two hundred and seventy-three jokes, quips, and puns which Poggio gathered from his travels in Europe, but mostly from his nights at the "Bugiale" (Bugiale meaning literally, "lie"), a kind of humour club in the Vatican where papal scholars gathered to drink wine and swap jokes.

Poggio described the Bugiale as: 'a kind of fib factory, founded by the secretaries to give us a laugh. Since the time of Pope Martin, we had the habit of choosing a quiet place in which we could tell one another news, and speak of various matters, either serious or frivolous, to distract our minds. Here nobody was spared, and we spoke ill of whatever or whomsoever displeased us. Often the Pope himself provided material for our criticisms, and this was the reason why many attended our gatherings, for fear of being ridiculed in their absence.'

The collection was written in Latin, chiefly because Poggio wanted to demonstrate how every kind of subject could be treated in the ancient language, even the coarseness of common life.

In the introduction he wrote: 'I myself wished to make a trial to see if many things which were reputed as being unable to be said or written in Latin could nevertheless be so written without falling into baseness. So, I did not seek either elegance, or an ample style, but I contented myself and am now content that my tales do not seem badly told. And in any case, let all those who are over-rigid censors and too bitter critics spare themselves the reading of these conversations - for it is so I would call them - and, as once Lucilius said, I like my readers to be of serene and happy mind. If, on the other hand, they are too little cultured, I do not deny them the right to think as they will, provided they do not grow angry with the author, who has written only to exercise his talent and refresh the spirit.'

Perhaps because the collection was in Latin, which only the learned could read and thus left the masses free from its corruptions, it was never officially condemned by the Vatican, surprising in that no previous jest book had anything like the level of irreverence or crudeness found in *Facetiae*.

Poggio's English biographer, the Reverend William Shepherd had no such reservations and roundly condemned the book saying how disgraceful it was that, 'an apostolic secretary who enjoyed the friendship of the pontiff, should have published a number of stories which outrage the laws of decency and put modesty to the blush.'

Prior to Poggio's work facetiae were not so licentious, more akin to classic Greek and Roman apophthegm which was reverent and adulatory toward royalty, the aristocracy, and religious leaders. *Facetiae* was irreverent and disrespectful, *especially* toward religious leaders:

The worst men in the world live in Rome, and worse than the others are the priests, and the worst of the priests they make cardinals, and the worst of all the cardinals is made Pope.

One day, during the war waged by the Spanish cardinal against the enemies of the Pontiff, the two armies found themselves face to face at Agro Piceno, forced to fight a decisive battle. With many prayers, the cardinal exhorted his soldiers to fight, assuring them that those who died would dine with God and the angels, and in order that the combatants should kill each other with greater good will, he promised his men the remission of all their sins. Then, having made this exhortation, he withdrew to a great distance from the battle. Then, said one of his soldiers: 'Why then, Eminence, are you not coming with us to this dinner?'

The cardinal replied: 'I am not in the habit of dining at this hour. I haven't an appetite yet.'

Facetiae's priests and friars are either debauched or fools, and more often both:

A countryman of Pergola wanted to marry the daughter of a young neighbour, but, when he saw her, she seemed to him much too young and childish.

The father of the young girl, in answer to remarks of the peasant said, 'She is much older and more mature than you think. She has already had three children by our Parish priest.'

A friar who was not at all circumspect was preaching to the people of Tivoli, and denounced at great length, and with much fury, the sin of adultery. Among other things, he said that he himself would rather have ten virgins than one married woman. Many of those present were of the same opinion.

The oldest recording of a "Welsh" joke is in *Facetiae* and portrays Welshmen as braggarts with a great fondness for cheese:

58

There was in Heaven a great company of Welshmen which with their crackling [bragging] and babbling troubled all the others. Wherefore God said to Saint Peter that He was very weary of them and that He would fain have them sent from Heaven. To whom Saint Peter said, 'Good Lord, I warrant you that it shall be done.' Wherefore Saint Peter went out of Heaven gates and cried with a loud voice, 'Caws Pob!' that is to say, 'roasted cheese' which the Welshmen hearing ran out of Heaven at great pace, and when Saint Peter saw them all out he suddenly went into Heaven and locked the door, and so locked all the Welshmen out.

Such was *Facetiae's* popularity that there were twenty editions of the book in the fifteenth century alone, including the earliest known translation, a 1473 edition printed in Poland. Unfortunately, translators took it upon themselves to exclude the bawdiest jokes and not until 1878 was the first unexpurgated translation published, in French, although the crudest jokes were not translated and remained in Latin, including:

In Florence a young woman, somewhat a simpleton, was on the point of delivering a baby. She had long been enduring acute pain, and the midwife, candle in hand, inspected her secret area in order to ascertain if the child was coming. 'Look also on the other side,' said the poor creature, 'my husband has sometimes taken that road.'

Poggio also patterned the technique of connecting jokes to real people, known celebrities such as Razello of Bologna, Cencio Romano, and Mateo Franco:

Messer Mateo Franco, walking with Lorenzo de Medici, and coming to an Inn where some bad wine was served to them, which, however, the host declared to be very old, said, 'It seems to me in its second childhood.'

That the collection was the best of its kind to date is without question, and it is because of *Facetiae* that jokes got shorter and punchier, but it is also evident that the joke still had a way to go before it manifested into the modern type we know today. Take the following:

The Abbot of Septimo, an extremely corpulent man, was travelling towards Florence one evening. On the road he asked a peasant, 'Do you think I'll be able to make it through the city gate?' He was talking about whether he would be able to make it to the city before the gates were closed for the night. The peasant, jesting on the Abbot's fatness said, 'Why if a cart of hay can make it through, you can too!'

Pre-empting the punch-line to explain the Abbot's meaning almost ruins the joke. Many jokes also carry a superfluous post punch-line moral:

A woman who, owing to some disease, had shaved all the hair off her head, was one day called out of doors by her neighbour for a certain matter, and rushed out, forgetting to put anything on her head. When the other woman saw her in that fashion, she reproved her for having come out without any covering and looking so ugly. Whereat, the woman in order to cover her head, lifted up her skirt, and in doing so displayed her arse. And all who saw this laughed.
So now they say, 'to cover your head,' of one who, to hide a small misdeed, commits a greater crime.

Despite such shortcomings *Facetiae* is an incredible body of work, and one that is recognised by folklorists as *the* jest book that set the joke apart from other humorous folklore and literature.
In effect, Poggio Bracciolini re-introduced the art of the joke to Western culture.

Chapter Five

Merry Tales

The invention of the mass marketing printing press in the middle of the fifteenth century made literature more accessible and affordable to a greater number of Europeans.

It was invented in Germany by Johann Guttenberg in 1455, or by Dutchman Laurens Koster a few years earlier depending on whether you believe allegations of stolen printing blocks etc. etc.

Guttenberg's new printing process attracted the attention of William Caxton (1422-91), a rich expatriate Englishman living in Belgium who promptly established his own publishing house and in 1474 produced the first printed book in English, his translation of the French romantic novel, *Recuyell of the Historyes of Troye* by Raoul Lefevre.

Two years later Caxton set up a printing works at Westminster in London where he produced the first printed book in English in England, Chaucer's, *Canterbury Tales*.

In 1484 he translated a translation of *Aesop's Fables* (Aesop was an Ancient Greek storyteller active around the sixth century BCE), which is generally considered the first English joke book.

The German physician and author Heinrich Steinhowell was the first to publish Latin and German translations of *Aesop's Fables* in 1477 which he padded out with jokes from Alphonsus and Bracciolini.

Six years later Steinhowell's German version was translated into French by the Lyon monk, Jules de Machault, and the following year Caxton translated Machault into English. Caxton's *Aesop and the Fables of Avian, Alfonce and Poge* is therefore credited as being the first English joke book.

There are many things that Caxton deserves great credit for, not least being the first English retailer of printed books through which he helped standardise the English language, but the creator of the first English joke book? Is *Aesop's Fables* with a few *Facetiae* jokes really an English joke book?

In my opinion, for what it is worth, Sir Thomas More (1478-1535), English scholar, writer, and Lord Chancellor produced the first English joke book in 1526; *A Hundred Merry Tales*.

The collection was published anonymously but More, and a few like-minded friends were almost certainly the compilers. It was More who transmuted the Old French word *geste*, "story" into the English *jest*, meaning "funny story", a word used frequently in *Merry Tales*.

A close friend of More's, Erasmus had two years earlier published a much smaller "joke" book, *Convivium Fabulosum* which is an account of a night of drunken gaiety with friends who each swapped humorous tales. But as the title suggests, it is a collection more in the style of French fabliaux than jokes.

A Hundred Merry Tales became known as, "Shakespeare's Joke Book" due to the bards' habit of dipping into it for comic inspiration. In *Much Ado About Nothing* the acid-tongued Beatrice admits: 'I had my good wit out of the Hundred Merry Tales…'.

It is the first distinctly English joke book, tales without foreign influences, and just as Poggio Bracciolini wrote his *Facetiae* in a colloquial Latin style, *A Hundred Merry Tales* was written in a colloquial English style:

A man asked his neighbour who was but late married to a widow how he agreed with his wife – for he said that her first husband and she could never agree. 'By God,' quod the other, 'we agree marvellously well.'

'I pray thee how so?' said the man.

'Marry,' quod the other, 'I shall tell thee: When I am merry, she is merry, and when I am sad, she is sad. For when I go out of my doors I am merry to go from her, and so is she. And when I come in again, I am sad, and so is she.'

Some jokes are obviously intended to introduce the unlearned to the mysteries of the Paternoster, the Creed, Ave Maria, and the Seven Deadly Sins, but the majority are purely for pleasure:

In a certain parish a friar preached, and in his sermon, he rebuked them that rode on Sunday – ever looking upon one man that was booted and spurred, ready to ride. This man, perceiving that all the people noted him, suddenly half in anger answered the friar thus: 'Why preach thee so much against them that ride on Sunday, for Christ himself did ride on Palm Sunday – as thou knowest well it is written in Holy Scripture.' To whom the friar suddenly answered and said thus: 'But, I pray thee, what came thereof? Was he not hanged on the Friday after?'
Which hearing, all the people in the church fell on laughing.

A certain scholar there was, intending to make priest, which had neither great wit nor learning came to the bishop to take orders, whose foolishness the bishop perceiving – because he was a rich man's son – would not very strongly oppose him but asked him this small question: 'Noah had three sons – Sem, Cham, and Japhet. Now, tell me who was Japhet's father and thou shalt have orders.'
Then said the scholar: 'By my troth, my lord, I pray you pardon me, for I never learned but little of the bible.' Then quod the bishop: 'Go home and come again and solve this question, and thou shalt have orders.'
The scholar so departed and came home to his father and showed him the cause of the hindrance of his orders. His father, being angry at his foolishness, thought to teach him the solution of this question by a familiar example and called his spaniels before him, and said thus: 'Thou knowest well Coll my dog hath these three whelps – Ryg, Tryg, and Tryboll. Must not Coll my dog needs be sire to Tryboll?'
Then quod the scholar: 'By God, father, ye say the truth. Let me alone now. Ye shall see me do well enough the next time.'
Whereupon the morrow he went to the bishop again and said he could solve the question.

63

Then said the bishop: 'Noah had three sons – Sem, Cham, and Japhet. Now tell me who was Japhet's father?'

'Marry, sir,' quod the scholar, 'if it please your lordship – Coll, my father's dog!'

A Hundred Merry Tales remained in print until the beginning of the seventeenth century despite the popularity of the 1535, *Tales and Quick Answers* which discarded the limits and the pattern of its predecessor and gave the joke another nudge toward the modern type of today.

As an example, number eight of *A Hundred Merry Tales* is, 'Of the Woman that followed her fourth husband's bier [moveable frame upon which the deceased is displayed] and wept.':

The widow made great moan and waxed very sorry in so much that her neighbours thought she would swoon and die for sorrow, wherefore one of her gossips [female relative] came to her and spoke to her in her ear and bade her for God's sake comfort herself and refrain that lamentation.

'I was good gossip I have great cause to mourn, if ye knew all, for I have buried three husbands besides this man, but, now I am sure of no other husband and therefore ye may be sure I have great cause to be sad and heavy…'

The joke goes on to describe at length how the widow had previously lined up her next husband, until finally arriving at the punch-line, '…before the corpse came out of my house.'

The *Tales and Quick Answers* jests are noticeably leaner:

A young man of Bruges that was betrothed to a fair maiden came on a time when her mother was out of the way and had to do with her. When her mother was come in, anon she perceived by her daughter's countenance what she had done. Wherefore she was sore displeased that she sued a divorce and would in no wise suffer that the young man should marry her daughter.

Not long after, the same young man was married to another maiden of the same parish, and as he and his wife sat talking on a time of the foresaid damsel, to whom he was betrothed, he fell in a foolish laughing. 'Whereat laugh ye?' asked his wife.

'It chanced on a time,' quod he, 'that she and I did such a thing together and she told it to her mother.'

'Therein,' quod his wife, 'she played the fool. A servant of my fathers played that game with me a hundred times, and yet I never told my mother.'

The first edition of *Tales and Quick Answers* was printed by the royal printer, Thomas Berthelet and contained one hundred and thirteen jokes. The second edition, printed in 1567 by Henry Wykes added twenty-six more, all of which were updated versions of Erasmus and Bracciolini jokes:

A certain curate, preaching on a time to his parishioners, said that our Lord with five loaves fed five hundred people. The clerk, hearing his error said softly in his ear: 'Sir, ye err. The gospel is five thousand.'

'Hold thy peace, fool,' said the curate, 'they will scantly believe that they were five hundred.'

Two years prior to *Quick Answers'* second edition Andrew Borde published *The Merry Tales of the Mad Men of Gotham*. The villagers of Gotham in Nottinghamshire having been the butt of dim witted jokes for at least a century:

The men of Gotham were once greatly scared by a report that enemies were about to invade their country. They were anxious to save as much as they could from falling into the hands of the invaders, and first they decided to save the church bell, which they prized above all else. After a great deal of trouble, they managed to hoist it down from the church steeple.

'Where shall we hide it so that the enemy cannot find it?' asked one of another. Someone said, 'Let us sink it into the deepest part of our pond.'

'Agreed!' said his fellows, and they dragged the bell down to the shore of the pond and got it aboard a boat. They then rowed out to

65

the middle of the pond and hoisted the bell overboard. After it had disappeared the worthy citizens of Gotham began to think that they had been too hasty.

'The bell is now truly safe from the enemy,' said they, 'but how are we to find it when the enemy has left us?'

One of them, who was wiser than the rest, sprang up and cried, 'That's easy enough. All we have to do is to cut a mark where we dropped it in.' He snatched his pocket knife and cut a deep notch into the side of the boat where the bell had been thrown overboard. 'It was right here where we heaved the bell out,' said he.

Then the men of Gotham rowed back to the shore, fully assured that they would be able to find their bell by the mark on the side of the boat.

The book went through several reprints, unchanged but for the title, which saw *Mad Men* replaced by the ironic, *Wise Men*. Nigh on a century later it was one of the first English joke books to have notable success in America where many wits took to referring to New York as, "Gotham City".

While *Merry Tales* and *Quick Answers* were both enjoying success in Britain, in Italy the largest collection of jokes to date was published by the distinguished poet and orator, Ludovico Domenichi (1515-64).

Italian jest books like those by Giovanni Pontano (1429-1503), secretary to King Ferdinand, plundered most of their jokes from Poggio's collection. Domenichi's joke book was no different, first published in Florence in 1548 and compiled largely of updated *Facetiae* jests, but over the following years he added a great many German jests, notably from the 1508 *Margarita Facetiarum* by Johan Mulich, and from the poet laureate of the Emperor Maximilian, Heinrich Bebel (1472-1516).

The 1571 edition of Domenichi's *Fecetie, motti, et burle, di diuersi signori et persone private* (Jokes, witticisms, and gags, by various Nobles and private persons) contained nine hundred and eight jests, more literary in style than Poggio's, and less bawdy:

A Doctor of Law, well known for a learned and eloquent man in his time, coming to the court of the Emperor, where he had been a long time, found a friend of his recently returned from Nuremberg who said to him that his wife was alive and well. And he replied, 'If my wife is alive, then I am dead.'

Messer Bartolomeo Gottfriedi, a person of great wit and spirit, being asked one day what the safest kind of ship was, replied: 'The one which arrives in port.'

In England meanwhile, the 1565 *Merry Tales* set the precedent for connecting jokes with known figures, a technique adopted from *Facetiae*.

Merry Tales features the English poet John Skelton (1460-1529), court poet to Henry VIII, famed for his short irregular rhymes based on colloquial speech. It is a collection of fifteen amusing tales, some long enough to be considered a short story:

How Skelton handled the friar that would needs lie with him in his inn:

As Skelton rid into the country there was a friar that happened in at an alehouse where Skelton was lodged, and there the friar did desire to have lodging. The alewife said, 'Sir, I have but one bed whereas Master Skelton doth lie.'
'Sir,' said the friar, 'I pray you that I may lie with you.' Skelton said: 'Master friar, I do use to have no man to lie with me.'
'Sir,' said the friar, 'I have lain with as good men as you, and for my money I do look to have lodging as well as you.'
'Well,' said Skelton, 'I do see then that you will lie with me.'
'Yea, sir,' said the friar.
Skelton did fill all the cups in the house and plied with drink the friar that, at last the friar was at peace with the world. Then said Skelton: 'Master friar, get ye to bed and I will come to bed within a while.'

67

The friar went and did lie upright and snorted like a sow. Skelton went into the chamber and did see that the friar did lie so, said to the wife: 'Give me the washing stick.' Skelton then cast down the clothes and the friar did lie stark naked. Then Skelton did shite upon the friar's naval and belly, and then he did take the washing stick and did strike a hard stroke upon the naval and belly of the friar and did put the candle out and went out of the chamber.

The friar smelt his belly and smelt a foul savour had thought he had been gored and cried out and said: 'Help! Help! Help! I am killed!' They of the house with Skelton went into the chamber and asked what the friar did ail. The friar said: 'I am killed. One hath thrust me in the belly.'

'Fo,' said Skelton, 'thou drunken soul, thou dost lie. Thou hast beshitten thyself. Fo, let us go out of the chamber, for the knave doth stink.'

The friar was shamed and cried for water. 'Out with the whoreson,' said Skelton, 'and wrap the sheets together and put the friar in the hog sty or in the barn.'

The friar said: 'Give me some water into the barn –' and there the friar did wash himself and did lie all-night long. The chamber and bed were dressed, and the sheets shifted, and then Skelton went to bed.

The public took the tales at face value, believing them to be anecdotes of real events and so Skelton the poet gained added celebrity as Skelton the trickster.

Authors and publishers quickly latched on to the marketing ploy of attaching jokes to a celebrity and the likes of *Scroggan's Jests* featuring John Scoggan, jester to King Edward IV, *The Merry Conceited Jests of George Peale,* and *Tarlton's Jests* were common titles. They also used fictitious characters like Gargantua, Mother Bunch, Robin Goodfellow, Old Hobson, and Howleglas.

Howleglas is the English version of Till Eulenspiegel, a trickster of German folklore whose joke answers and comic exploits were "borrowed" from Marcolf, the ancient and mythical Middle Eastern jester of King Solomon's court.

He first appeared in the 1520 German *An Amusing book about Till Eulenspiegel*, a random collection of antics and foolery with Eulenspiegel taking on a variety of roles including fool, peasant, rogue, country bumpkin, and apprentice to various professions.

Some forty years later Robert Copland translated the German book into English with the title *Howleglas* (from a drawing of Eulenspiegel with an owl perched on his arm and a looking glass in his hand), though Copland did more than translate *Till Eulenspiegel*, he cleverly edited the jests and added jab lines to the texts which resulted in a far superior book:

On a time Howleglas served a tailor:

And the tailor asked him if he could sew woollen cloth that no man might see the seam. And then Howleglas said yes. And then went Howleglas and sewed under a barrel. Then said his master: 'What dost thou now? This is marvellous [terrible] sewing!' Then answered Howleglas: 'I sew so close [pun on secretly] that no man can see, as you bade me. Nor I myself see not.' Then answered his master: 'Good servant, I meant not so. I bade thee sew that every man might see.'

And then the third night, the master had laboured so sore that he must needs sleep. Then cast he to Howleglas a husbandman's gown and he bade him take a wolf and make it up. And then said Howleglas: 'I shall do it.' Then went he to bed. Then cut Howleglas the husbandman's gown and made thereof a wolf with the head and feet. And when that he had sewed it together, then he set it upon the table with staves.

Then in the morning arose his master and came down, and when he saw the wolf standing upon the table, he was afraid and asked him what he had done. And he said: 'Master, I have made a wolf as you bade me.' Then said the master: 'I meant that you should have made up the russet gown – for a husbandman's gown is called a wolf.'

Then answered Howleglas: 'If that I had known that before I would have done so. For I had lever [rather] have made a gown than a wolf.'

And, at last the master was content.

69

And then within four days after, watched [stayed awake] the master so much that he must needs go to sleep. And there was a coat ready-made, but it lacked the sleeves. Then the master took the coat and the sleeves and gave them to Howleglas. And he bade him that he should cast on the sleeves, and he said he would. Then went his master to bed.

And then took Howleglas the coat and hanged it on a balk [beam on the ceiling] and set on every side a candle, and stood up, and cast the sleeves at the coat all the night long. And then arose the tailor and that spied Howleglas, and he cast the sleeves faster than he ever did before, at the coat.

And that espied well the tailor, and said: 'What foolish touches be those that you do there?' And then answered Howleglas very angrily: 'This is no foolish touch, for I have stood all the night casting the sleeves at the coat, and they will not abide thereon.'

The popularity of joke books was such that *Howleglas*, like most other books of humorous stories was marketed as a jest book, collectors and publishers alike deliberately blurring the line between comic prose and jokes.

Thomas Deloney's 1583 translation of Bonaventure des Perier's French, *Mirrour of Mirth* is another example. Des Perier had earlier published a genuine jest book, his excellent 1558, *Nouvelles Recreations*. The following is a translation from *Nouvelles*:

A young fellow arrives at his work the day after his wedding looking extremely worried. He explains to his friends that having consummated the marriage he forgot himself and left two gold coins on the dressing table. 'Don't worry,' his friends tell him, 'your wife will just think it's for household expenses.' 'That's not what bothers me,' says the young fellow, when I sneaked back I found my bride biting shrewdly, with a distressing air of experience, at one of the coins.'

Deloney's adaption of *Mirrour of Mirth* employs techniques of dramatic realism and characterisations in the same way a narrative joke does.

However, its artistic form makes it more of a collection of humorous stories:

Of a monk that answered altogether by syllables:

A certain monk travelling the country arrived at an inn at suppertime. The host willed him to sit down among others that had already begun supper. The monk, to overtake them, began to lay on a load with his teeth, and with such an appetite as though he had eaten no meat for three or four days before. The old lad had put himself in his doublet, the better to fill his paunch – the which being perceived by one that sat at the table, he began to ask the monk questions that were not greatly to his mind for he was busy filling his belly. Because he would not lose much time, he answered the party that spake to him altogether in syllables. And I think he was practised with this language long before, for he was very expert in it. The questions and the answers were thus:

'What garment do ye wear?'
'Strong.'
'What wine do ye drink?'
'Red.'
'What flesh do ye eat?'
'Beef.'
'How many monks are ye?'
'Nine.'
'How like ye this wine?'
'Good.'
'You drink no such at home?'
'No.'
'What eat ye on Fridays?'
'Eggs.'
'How many have each of you?'
'Two.'

And this while, he lost not one mouthful of meat, for his teeth were still going, and yet answered well and readily to all his demands. If he said his matins so short, out of doubt he was a notable pillar of the Church.

71

It is testament to the popularity of joke books that some authors attempted to pass off their humorous tales as jokes, but *Mirrour of Mirth* marks the point where the two begin to separate for good. By the end of the sixteenth century the two forms of comic literature separated, helped greatly by the fact that publishers of humorous tales could market their books as such, thanks in no small way to Ben Jonson's comic drama, *Every Man in His Humour and Every Man out of His Humour*.

Prior to Jonson's play, humour was not associated with comedy. The word originated from the Latin *umor*, meaning fluid or moisture, and it was believed that the fluids in the human body were blood, phlegm, and yellow and black bile, all of which needed to be in balance for a healthy body.

Too much blood made people over-excited and overly cheerful, too much phlegm made them phlegmatic and inert, too much yellow bile gave them colic, and too much black bile caused melancholy, irritability and depression. Trying to make people feel better was known as "humouring" them, trying to get their fluids balanced, into good humour, i.e. into good health.

However, when the English playwright and satirist Jonson presented his *Every Man in His Humour and Every Man out of His Humour* in 1598, the characters on stage were portrayed in such an exaggerated fashion that they were perceived as comical, and in a relatively short time humour was associated with non-aggressive amusement (as opposed to joking which is usually aggressive).

Humorous tales were therefore considered less provocative, less cruel, and less likely to cause offence than jokes, while being of good humour was considered a virtue, and a "sense of humour" was something worth cultivating.

During the sixteenth century contests in verbal wit became ever more common in Britain, so much so that playwrights began incorporating them into their plays.

Since medieval times "flytings" as the contests were known (from the Anglo-Saxon *flitan*, to strive, to contend or quarrel) were usually contested in verse which meant that the participants not only had to be quick witted but adept rhymesters. They were called, 'skalds', from the Middle-English word, 'scold' which specifically referred to ribald speech.

The earliest literary example of a flyting contest is Sir Thomas Maitland's, *Satyr upon Sir Neil Laing*, between a priest and one of the Pope's Knights which took place around the middle of the sixteenth century:

Canker'd, Cursed Creature, Crabbed Corbid Kittle,
Buntin-arsed, Buegle-backed, Bodied like a Beetle;
Sarie Shitten, Shell-padock, ill-shapen Shit,
Kid-bearded Gennet, all alike Great:
Fiddle-douped, Flindrikin, Fart of a Man.
Wa worth thee, Wanwordie, Wanshapen Wran.

The above is taken from John Watson's 1706, *A Choice Collection of Comic and Serious Scots Poems* which also includes *The Great Flyting betwixt Polwart and Montgomery*.

The contest is dated at 1580 and was staged purely for entertainment, neither of the assailants being angry at each other, nor did they harbour any grudge afterwards. It took place in the presence of King James and the contestants were Captain Alexander Montgomery, poet-laureate to the Scottish court, and Sir Patrick Hume of Polwart who we assume emerged victorious as Hume's final outburst receives no reply.

Montgomery begins the contest with, 'kiss my arse' to which Hume answers, 'upon thy knee and kiss my foul foundation', before Montgomery counters:

Yet wanshapen Shit thou shupe such a Sunzie,
As proud as you Prunzie your Pens shall be plucked,
Come kiss where I cukied and change me that Cunzie,
Your Gryzes Grunzie is graceless and gowked.

They go back and forth for some thirty pages until a great flourish from Hume ends the contest:

73

Lean Limmer, steal Grimmer, I shall skimmer I thy mouth.
Fly'd Fool, made Mule, die with Dool, on an Aik'
Knave Kend, Christ send, ill end, on thee now,
Pudden Wright, out of sight, thou's be dight, like a Draik.
Jock-blunt, thrawn Frunt, kiss the cunt of a cow.
Purs-peiler, Hen-stealer, Cat-killer, now I quell thee,
Rubiator, Fornicator by Nature, foul befall thee.
Tyke-sticker, poisoned Vicar, Pot-licker, I mon pay thee,
Jock blunt, dead Runt, I shall punt while I slay thee …

Evidence of similar verbal conflicts in jest have been recorded by numerous cultures, the gentlest of which was surely contested by Zen monks who played out battles of wit, attempting to outdo each other in a series of puns, witticisms and low-brow quips aimed at themselves rather than their opponent. The following took place in the ninth century between Chao-chou and his disciple Wen-yuan:

Chau-chou: I am an ass

Wen-yuan: I am the ass's buttocks

Chau-chou: I am the ass's faeces

Wen-yuan: I am a worm in the faeces

Chau-chou: What are you doing here?

Wen-yuan: I'm on my summer vacation.

Chapter Six

Archee's Jests

In 1605 two successful hack writers, George Wilkins and T. D. (most likely Thomas Dekker) published *Jests to Make You Merry*, sixty jokes they claimed were drawn from contemporary life, and which to date were the closest in style to the modern joke.

The method by which the writers set the scene, introduced the characters and let the action unfold through the dialogue captured the rhythms and diction of real speech, a dramatic technique taken from the writers' experience as playwrights:

A Justice of the Peace found his man laying his mistress on the lips, at which the Justice in a rage and rapping out a great oath, called him 'Rascal' and asked him what he did.

'Why,' says the fellow and swore as deep as he, 'I was kissing your wife.'

The Justice told him that if he saw him kissing there again, he would make him kiss in another place.

'Truth, sir,' says the serving man, 'had you not come in I would had kissed in another place indeed.'

One called a Captain a coward and said he had no heart. 'It's no matter,' quoth the Captain, 'I have legs.'

Perhaps the book was ahead of its time, or without a celebrity attached did not catch the public's fancy, but for whatever reason it had modicum success and quickly went out of print. In contrast the 1607 *The Merrie Conceited Jests of George Peale* was extremely popular:

How George served a gentlewoman as she put out her arm to take the capon:

George sitting next to her, jerks out a huge fart, which made all the company in the maze, one looking upon the other, yet they knew it came that way. 'Peace,' quoth George and jogs her on the elbow, 'I will say it is I.'
At which the company fell into a huge laughter, and she into a fretting fury...

The collection was released in the same year as *Tarlton's Jests*, a jest book purporting the antics and jokes of Richard Tarlton (d 1588), the supreme jester of his day who supposedly served as Queen Elizabeth's personal Fool.
The supposition is supported only by biographical details in the joke book which cannot be relied on as absolute fact. However, that Tarlton was the greatest comedian of his era is without question, John Stow in his 1598 *Survey of London* described him as: 'A man of wondrous plentiful pleasant extemporal wit... the wonder of his time.'

By the seventeenth century circumstances had changed dramatically for court jesters in Europe, where they had risen from the lowest servant only a couple of centuries earlier to that of trusted confidant to their master who also gave them license to speak the truth cloaked in jest.
Queen Elizabeth once reprimanded her Fool, Clod for not criticizing her enough and always relished her meeting with her Jester, John Pace: 'Come Pace,' she would demand, 'now we shall hear of our faults'.
The English historian Thomas Fuller wrote that Pace told the Queen, 'more of her faults than most of her Chaplains and cured her melancholy more than all of her physicians.'

It is probable that Richard Tarlton served as jester to Queen Elizabeth, we know that he was the comedian in an elite drama company known as the "Queen's Men", a select group of twelve actors brought together at royal command by the *Lord Chamberlain* and the *Master of Revels* (two powerful governing bodies whose duties included protecting the monarchy and church from mockery, and censoring anything in the public domain they considered distasteful).

At the time the title "Comedian" was given to any actor who specialised in light dramatic parts, as opposed to a "Tragedian" who played heavier, more serious roles, while the Low German *clown*, described an unsophisticated peasant, a rustic, a bumpkin, a role Tarlton played to its fullest.

Dressed in red russet suit with a buttoned cap, a great bag by his side, and wielding a large slap-stick, he was either country simpleton at odds with town folk's ways, or a drunken oaf in the presence of royalty.

It was not an original character but what made Tarlton unique was his ability to ad lib, go off script, step out of character and break down the fourth wall between audience and performer. One such event was recorded in *Tarlton's Jests*:

At the Bull at Bishopsgate was a play of Henry the Fifth wherein the judge was to take a box on the ear. And because he was absent that should take the blow, Tarlton himself (ever forward to please) took upon him to play the same judge, besides his own part of the Clown. And Knell, then playing Henry the Fifth, hit Tarlton a sound box indeed, which made the people laugh the more because it was he. But anon the judge goes in, and immediately Tarlton, in his Clown's clothes, comes out and asks the actors what news. 'O,' saith one, 'hadst thou been here thou shouldst have seen Prince Henry hit the judge a terrible box on the ear.'

'What man!' said Tarlton. 'Strike a judge?'

'It is true, I faith,' said the other.

'No other like,' said Tarlton, 'and it could not be but terrible to the judge, when the report so terrifies me that methinks the blow remains still on my cheek that it burns again.'

The people laughed at this mightily, and to this day I have heard it commended for rare but no marvel, for he had many of these. But I would see our clowns in these days do the like. No, I warrant ye, and yet they think well of themselves, too.

Unlike other comic thespians Tarlton performed solo after the play had ended and in much the same way a modern stand-up comedian might, he took subjects from the audience and engaged them in a battle of wits. Once when asked what he thought of soldiers in time of peace he quipped back: 'Why, they are like chimneys in summer!' The very height of humour in Elizabethan times.

Tarlton's Jests was published anonymously by someone obviously determined to preserve the legacy of Tarlton as the supreme jester of the age. Published in 1607 it contained seventy-three jests featuring Tarlton on stage, at court, in town, and in the countryside:

Tarlton, going toward Hogsdon, met a country maid coming to market. Her mare stumbling, down she fell over and over, showing all that God had sent her. And then rising up again, she turned her round about unto Master Tarlton, and said, 'God's body, sir, did you ever see the like before?'
'No, in good sooth,' quoth Tarlton, 'never but once in London.'

Renowned travel writer, poet, and humourist John Taylor produced *Wit and Mirth* in 1632, one hundred and twelve jokes the author said were drawn from, 'relation and hearsay':

A countryman brought his wife's water to a physician, saying, 'Good morrow to your worship, Master Confusion.'
'Physician thou wouldst say,' said the other.
'Truly,' said the fellow, 'I am no scholar but altogether unrude and very ingrum and I have here my wife's water in a pittle pot, beseeching your mastership to cast [analyse] it.
The physician took the water, which having put into a urinal and viewed it, he said, 'My friend, thy wife is very weak.'

78

'Truly,' quoth he, 'I think she be in a presumption.'

'Consumption thou wouldst say,' said the physician.

'I told you before,' the fellow replied, 'I do not understand your allagant speech.'

'Well,' quoth the doctor, 'doth thy wife keep her bed?'

'No, truly sir,' said he, 'she sold her bed a fortnight since.'

'Verily,' quoth the doctor, 'she is very costive.'

'Costive' said the man, 'your worship says true for I have spent all that I have upon her almost.'

Said the doctor, 'I do not say costly, but costive! And I pray thee tell me, is she loose or bound?'

'Indeed sir,' said the fellow, 'she is bound to me during her life, and I am bound to her.'

'Yea, but I pray thee,' said the doctor, 'tell me in plain terms how she goes to stool.'

Truly,' said the fellow, 'in plain terms, she goes to stool very strangely. For in the morning, it is so hard that your worship can scarce bite it with your teeth, and at night it is so thin that you might eat it with a spoon.'

Seven years later Robert Chamberlain published the first English joke book dedicated entirely to puns.

Chamberlain was a lowly lawyer's clerk who impressed his employers enough that they paid for him to study at Oxford University. While a degree eluded him, he did establish himself as a witty poet, playwright and joke writer, and was almost certainly the author of the 1637 anonymous, *New Book of Mistakes*. Two years later he did put his name to the book of puns, *Conceits, Clinches, Flashes, and Whimsies*:

A Dyer who was an idle drunken fellow was complaining to a scholar that he had very ill fortune in his business, and that commonly those things that he undertook to dye were spoiled. The scholar told him that the only way to have this amended was to reform himself, for he that lived ill could never dye well.

One persuaded another to marry a whore because she was rich, telling him that perhaps she might turn. 'Turn?' said the other, 'she hath been so much worn that she is past turning.'

The most popular and successful joke book of the seventeenth century was *A Banquet of Jests*, commonly known as, "Archee's Jests", a collection of jokes allegedly told by Archie Armstrong, jester to King James I.

Armstrong is portrayed in the book as a jolly and decent fellow, although he was neither, his jesting reportedly made up of vitriolic raillery and acerbic insult, and by all factual accounts he was a devious politician and a thoroughly unpleasant man.

First published in 1633, *A Banquet of Jests* claimed to contain many of, 'Archee's jests never published in his lifetime', despite Armstrong being alive and prospering in Cumberland. The book, plus its 1660 update, *A Choice Banquet of Jests* remained popular throughout the century:

A captain at the siege of Bergen that had a wooden leg booted over had it shattered to pieces by a cannonball. His soldiers crying out, 'A surgeon! A surgeon for the captain!'

'No, no,' said he, 'a carpenter! A carpenter will suffice.'

A silly country gentlewoman, being begot with child by one that was much her inferior, accused the man of rape, whereupon the matter was had in question before a neighbour Justice of the Peace, who, somewhat perceiving the matter, after he had heard her complaint how deeply she had been injured, as pitying her said, 'Alas, poor gentlewoman, I warrant this was not the first time the rogue ravished you.'

She, to aggravate his crime, replied, 'No, I'll be sworn he ravished me above twenty times' – which procured much laughter and the fellow's freedom.

On one occasion the habit of associating jokes with a living person led to tragic consequences when the Puritan preacher Hugh Peters became the principle character of the 1660, *Tales and Jests of Hugh Peters*.

In the book he is depicted as jocular preacher and buffoon who will go to any lengths for a laugh. The Puritans forbade jocularity amongst their clerics and brought Peters to trial where the preacher swore on oath that he had never told a joke, either inside or outside of church. He was found guilty and executed.

The rise to power of the hard-line Protestant moralists, the English Puritans, during the seventeenth century brought about an expurgation of joke books and a crack-down on jokers.

The Puritans began by forbidding their ministers from telling jokes or adding humour to their sermons and closed their churchyards to pipers, rush-bearers, Morris-dancers, and comedians.

Jokes about God, the Eucharist and the clergy were already prohibited in Britain, but as Puritan influence grew government also banned traditional "Miracle" and "Mystery" plays, which were humorous dramas of Biblical tales performed by local parishioners.

Puritans objected to jokes in general but were particularly angered at ones mocking religion, jokes about sex, and those containing profanities. They were determined not only to "cleanse" the English but their language also.

A 1623 Act of Parliament had already made it illegal to swear, fines were handed out for the mildest of oaths, but that did not satisfy the Puritans and in 1648 the punishments were extended to fines and short imprisonments while swearing at one's parents became punishable by death.

In 1651 following a long and bloody civil war Charles I of England was overthrown and the Puritan Lord Protector, Oliver Cromwell became head of state. One of his first orders was to ban all forms of live entertainment, festivals (including Christmas), carnivals, and dancing round the May-Pole, the latter according to Cromwell being a symbol of, 'a heathenish vanity, generally abused to superstition and wickedness.'

Cromwell committed some of the most heinous crimes in British history, but his persecution of Irish Catholics was particularly brutal. The English Civil War at one point turned into a battle for Irish independence and by the end of Cromwell's invasion in 1653 half of the population of Ireland had been slaughtered, so it was perhaps justice that he contracted malaria in Ireland and died in 1658.

Two years later the monarchy returned to the throne and after a decade of puritanical pish, things slowly returned to normality and despite heavy state censorship of stage productions, live performances were again permitted, along with festivals, fairs, wakes, dancing round the Maypole, and swearing at one's parents.

Jocus was a word frequently used by Latin scholars when referring to a funny story or a jest, the French derivative was *joque* which in 1699 officially became the English, *joke* when famed lexicographer Abel Boyer compiled the standard *French-English Dictionary* and his translation of the French *joque* was, joke.

A year later Boyer published *The Wise and Ingenious Companion*, a collection of translated French jokes including, from the 1642 edition of Beroalde de Verville's, *Le Moyen de Parvenir*:

A man is given money from his unsatisfied wife to buy a better penis. After trying out the new one she asked, 'What did you do with the old one?'

'I threw it away,' he replied.

'Oh, you should not have done so,' she said, 'it would have been just right for mother.'

In 1670 the word *joke* was admitted into *The Oxford English Dictionary* where it was defined as: 'Something said or done to excite laughter or amusement.'

The following year William Hicks published *Oxford Jests*, a collection of almost six hundred jests which he referred to as, 'jokes':

The Italian proverb is, 'Three women make a market with their chatting.'

'Zounds!' says a fellow, 'if my wife had been there, it would have been a fair.'

One affirmed that he had seen a cabbage so big that five hundred men on horseback might stand under its shade.

'And I for my part,' says another, 'have seen a cauldron so wide that three hundred men wrought therein, each distant from the other twenty yards.'

Then the cabbage-liar asked him, 'For what use was that cauldron?'

Says he; 'To boil your cabbage in.'

Toward the end of the seventeenth century there was heavy migration of unskilled labour from Ireland to mainland Britain. It was a workforce that struggled with city life which gave rise to the "Stupid Irishman" joke cycle.

Irish jokes were initially created in Ireland, by the Irish, first with the Irishman as a trickster, then later as a fool.

Since 1541 when the Irish parliament recognised the English King Henry VIII as King of Ireland the official policy of "plantation" had seen the arrival of thousands of English settlers in Ireland. Those who received estates quickly became the butt of Irish trickster jokes:

An auld Dublin feller is sitting on the side of the street casting a fishing line into the road when an English lord walking by slips him a few coins and shaking his head says, 'There you go Paddy, get yourself a bite to eat.'

And as he's walking away he laughs at the old man and asks condescendingly, 'Have you caught many?' and the auld feller tips his cap and says, 'Yes sor, you're the fourth today…'

An Irish priest was so openly hostile toward the English that he would tell his congregation: 'If you do not lead a better life, you will all end up in hell with the English.'

The news of his rants reached the English Bishop's ears who told him that he would be transferred to some desolate corner of the world if he continued with his remarks.

The priest agreed to adopt a more diplomatic tone and at his next sermon he was preaching on the betrayal of Jesus, and he said: 'And Jesus looked at all of the Apostles in turn and as he held their gaze he said, "Tonight, one of you will betray me," and Peter said, "to be sure, it is not me Lord"; then he looked at James, and James said, "Ah now, it is not me Lord"; and then Jesus looked at Judas, and Judas said, "Cor blimey, guvnor, ya don't fink it's me do ya?"'

The "stupid" Irish joke began with the expansion of Dublin in the sixteenth century and Dubliners making jokes at the expense of the people of Kerry, a county in the South West of Ireland inhabited, if the jokes are to be believed, by dim-witted country folk:

How do you confuse a Kerryman?
Give him two shovels and ask him to take his pick.

The first "Irish" joke book was published in England in the 1680s with the title, *Teagueland Jests or Bogg Witticisms* (Teague is Irish for Timothy which was also a nickname for an Irishman) and by 1750 it was on its sixth edition, albeit as *The Irish Miscellany*:

An Irish servant was asked by his master to bring him a pint of claret and a pint of sack (sherry). The servant poured both into one pot and said, 'I prithee master, drink off the top first for the sack is all in the bottom.'

A great number of *Irish Miscellany* jokes are forged from "Irish bull" which *Miscellany* defines as a, 'self-contradictory proposition, or an expression containing a manifest contradiction in terms, or involving a ludicrous inconsistency unperceived by the speaker.'

84

An Irish lawyer of the Temple, having occasion to go to dinner, left these directions written, and put in the key-hole of his Chamber Door, 'I am gone to the Elephant and Castle, where you shall find me; and if you can't read this note, carry it to the stationer's and he will read it for you.'

An Irishman was trying to sell some iron window sashes, and in recommending them said, 'Sure, these sashes will last you forever, and afterwards, you can sell them for old iron.'

An Irish lawyer had a client of his own country who was a sailor. During his absence at sea his wife had married again, and he was resolved to prosecute her. Coming to advise with his counsellor he was told that he must have witnesses to prove that he was alive when his wife married again. 'Ah, now by my soul that would be impossible,' said the Irish client, 'for my shipmates are all gone to sea again upon a long voyage and will not return for twelve months.'
'Oh then,' said the Irish lawyer, 'there can be nothing done in it; and what a pity it is that such a brave cause be lost now, only because you cannot prove yourself to be alive.'

Talking bull (different to the American, "bull shit") became a common phrase in Britain and the butt of the jokes were not always the Irish, there were similar Welsh jokes about rural dwellers whose command of the English language was limited, while jokes about Gaelic Highlanders talking bull were told by Scottish, English speaking lowlanders.

Miserly "Scotch" jokes also became part of the joker's lexicon at the end of the seventeenth century, beginning in the south of England as jokes about mean northern folk, specifically the people of Yorkshire. 'He's too far north for me' was an expression meaning, 'He's too canny, too cunning, too tight fisted'. The joke type quickly spread further north into Scotland:

Two Scots were talking in a Western saloon and one said to the other: 'Did you hear about poor Jock? Scalped by Indians.'

And the other replied, 'Aye, and just two days after he'd paid ten cents for a haircut.'

Meanwhile the humorous ballad entitled, *The Unfortunate Welshman, or the Untimely Death of Scotch Jock* did much to establish the nickname, "Jock" for a Scotsman:

Jock woke one morning to find his wife dead in bed next to him. He leaped out of bed and ran horror-stricken to the top of the stairs and cried out to his maid-servant.

'Mary, Mary!' he shouted, 'come to the foot of the stairs, hurry, hurry!'

'Yes, yes,' she called, 'What is it?'

And Jock said, 'Breakfast! Just cook the one egg.'

Chapter Seven

Joe Miller's Jests

The 1729, *Comedian's Tales'* jokes involved no celebrities:

A young widow has a wooden statue of her late husband which she calls Old Simon and takes it to bed with her every night. One night a young man bribes the widow's maid to put him in bed instead of the statue. In the morning the maid called at her mistress's chamber door as always, 'Madam what will you please to have for dinner?' The widow replied, 'Roast the turkey that was brought in yesterday, boil a leg of mutton and Colley-flowers, and get a good dish of fruit.'

'Madam,' says the maid, 'we have not wood enough to dress so much meat.'

Replied she, 'Burn Old Simon.'

Poor sales forced the publisher to re-issue the book the following year under the title, *Spiller's Jests*, same jokes but with a jester called, Spiller on the cover. The book remained in print for a nigh on a decade.

The most successful joke book of the century and of any century in fact, was *Joe Miller's Jests*, published in 1739.

Joe Miller was a well-known and recently deceased London actor who was famous for being notoriously gloomy, so the idea of naming a joke book after someone who was as solemn as an unlettered gravestone was obviously a joke itself.

The book proved so popular that it went through eleven editions in as many years and was in the public domain for so long that a, "Joe Miller" came to mean a stale joke.

More than a century after its initial release Charles Dickens referred to it in *A Christmas Carol* (1843) when Scrooge remarked; 'Joe Miller never made such a joke as the sending [of the turkey] to Bob's will be'.

Eighty years later in the James Joyce classic *Ulysses* (1922), Lenehen recites a limerick to Stephen Dedalus and afterwards asks, 'I can't see the Joe Miller, can you?'.

The book contains two hundred and forty-nine jokes, transcribed by John Motley (1692-1750) who published under the pseudonym of Elijah Jenkins. Subject matter includes the illogic thinking of men, bad breath, sex, loose women, and all too often a double entendre on the word, cock. (When a woman objects to the sign of the, 'Cock and Leather-Breeches' at her lodgings, she tells the landlord: 'I'll tell you how you may satisfy both me and my daughter; take down your Breeches and let the Cock stand.')

Most of the jokes in *Joe Miller's Jests* were new, or at least re-worked to appear so, and the economy of words made it the most modern joke book to date:

A lady being asked how she liked a Gentleman's singing, one who had a very stinking breath, 'The words are good', she said, 'but the air is intolerable.'

A gentleman said of a young wench who constantly plied about the Temple, that if she had as much Law in her head, as she had in her tail, she would be one of the ablest counsels in England.

The following Motley claimed was a true anecdote concerning the famously candid Doctor John Radcliffe (died 1714):

The same physician, who was not the humblest man in the world, being sent for by Sir Edward Seymour [Speaker of the House of Commons] who was said to be the proudest; the Knight received him while he was dressing his feet and picking his toes, being at the time troubled with a Diabetes, and upon the doctor entering the room, accosted him in this manner: 'So Quack,' said he, 'I'm a dead man, for I piss sweet.'

'Do ye,' replied the doctor, 'then prithee piss upon your toes, for they stink damnably.' And turning around on his heel left the room.

The above was one of many removed from later editions by order of the Lord Chamberlain.

The final edition of *Joe Miller's Jests*, printed in 1836 informed the reader that it contained forty-nine fewer jokes than the original due to the, 'greater delicacy observed in modern society and conversation.'

Joke book compilers had to keep one step ahead of the Lord Chamberlain. C. Henderson's, *Tom Brown's Complete Jester, or The Wit's Merry Companion* made a bold statement in advertising the book as, 'free from those insipid threadbare jests, which are in many other compositions of this kind; most of these being entirely new, and never yet appeared.'

One of the Canons of St. Paul being in company with some ladies, let fall his handkerchief, and in stooping to pick it up again he happened to break wind. 'Bless me,' cried out one of the ladies, 'I believe 'tis his Majesty's birthday, for I think I hear one of the cannons at St. James's.'

'No, Madam,' answered another lady, 'I am sure 'tis not far off as St. James's for I can smell the gunpowder.'

A man asked by his neighbour how his sick wife did, made this answer: 'Indeed neighbour, the case is pitiful, my wife fears she shall die, and I fear she will not die, which makes a most disconsolate house.'

Further editions of the book were entitled *Tom Brown's Jest Book: or, Companion to the Cloister* and as quickly as the Lord Chamberlain demanded the removal of offending jokes Henderson added new ones:

A gentleman asked his daughter, what is the fastest growing thing in the world and she replied, 'The pommel of a saddle.'

'The pommel of a saddle,' her father said, 'why that's ludicrous, what on earth gave you that idea?'

'Well,' said the daughter innocently, 'when I rode behind our boy servant Bill, the pommel, when I first took hold, was no bigger than my finger, and in less than a minute it was thicker than my wrist.'

A person going through Cock-Court, Ludgate Hill, asked a young woman the name of it. 'Upon my word sir,' says she, 'it is such a nasty name that I am ashamed to speak it.'

"But pray do," says he.

'Why then,' says Miss Innocence, 'it is called by that nasty thing that you men piss with.'

Included in *Tom Brown's Jest Book* are examples of "Water Wit", flyting style insults contested by those sailing rivers and canals:

Tom Brown was travelling up the Thames in the company of an Indian friend:

No sooner had my Indian and I took to the water at Black Friars, and got into the middle of the stream, but our two watermen began to attack a couple of fine ladies with a footman, as follows: 'How now, you two confederate brimstones, where are you swimming with your fine top knots? I'll warrant your poor cuckolds are hovering about Change, to hear what news from Flanders, while you, like a couple of hollow-bellied whores, are sailing up to Vauxhall to cram one end with roasted fowls, and the other with raw sausages.'

One of the ladies taking courage, made the following return: 'Get you home you old cuckold, look under your wife's bed, and see who has been planting a son of a whore in your parsley bed. Oh, how fond the old fool will be of the fruits of another man's labour when the midwife vouches the bastard to be the true picture of his daddy.'

After mocking Brown's boat, she turns on his Indian companion:

90

... why he looks as if he had painted his face with a child's surreverence [faeces], to make his countenance shine. Out you, nasty turd-coloured dog, born upon a dunghill without a head, that your mother was forced to supply the defect with a yellow pumpkin!

The alliterative battle of words usually had such a high level of abuse that most jest books and anthologies of invective refused to print water wit. Henderson had no such reservations:

When once the master of a Thames tug, remonstrated with for fouling a pleasure boat and breaking an oar, leant over the rails and replied hoarsely: 'Oh, I did, did I, Charley? An' talking of oars, how's your sister?'

The joke type created from misapplied or distorted language gained a formal title in 1775 when R. B. Sheridan (1751-1816), Irish dramatist, politician, and celebrated orator introduced in his play *The Rivals*, the character of Mrs Malaprop.

Mrs Malaprop did not want her daughter to be a, 'progeny of learning' but rather have, 'supercilious knowledge', and not be as 'headstrong as an allegory'.

Mrs Malaprop was not the first to misappropriate words, Shakespeare's Mistress Quickly and his Officer Dogberry both preceded her, the latter when confirming that they had apprehended two suspicious persons saying, 'we have comprehended two auspicious persons'. Until Sheridan's character came along "dogsberryism" was the term for misapplying words.

In his 1785, *A Classical Dictionary of the Vulgar Tongue* Francis Grose employed jokes to demonstrate how one might apply slang words in regular conversation.

Several slang dictionaries had been published previously in Britain, the first by Magistrate Thomas Harman in 1567 who ordered beggars be dragged before him and under threat of a whipping divulge their supposedly secret language.

Over the following couple of centuries, the words and phrases Harman recorded were appertained to be the secret language of London criminals, Highwaymen, and Gypsies.

According to the British Library, Francis Grose was, 'The first lexicographer to collect slang words from all corners of society, and not just from the professional underworld of pickpockets and bandits.'

Slang is as old as speech, spoken by people of all classes, rich and poor, honest and dishonest. It has always been indulged from a desire to appear street-wise and familiar with current joke types.

Grose gathered his words and phrases from eavesdropping in drinking dens of London slums, and from conversations with soldiers, seamen, and dock workers. He believed his dictionary to be a celebration of British democracy. In the introduction he wrote: 'The freedom of thought and speech arising from, and privileged by, our constitution, gives a force and poignancy to the expressions of our common people, not to be found under arbitrary governments, where the ebullitions of vulgar wit are checked by the fear of the bastinado, or of lodging during the pleasure in some gaol or castle.'

Where Samuel Johnson's 1755, *Dictionary of the English Language* exemplified words and phrases with examples from poets and bards, Grose's sources were the working classes and criminal underworld:

Cauliflower: A large white wig, such as commonly worn by the dignified clerk, and was formerly by physicians. Also, the private parts of a woman; the reason for which appellation is given in the following story: A woman, who was giving evidence in a cause wherein it was necessary to express those parts, made use of the term cauliflower; for which the judge on the bench, a peevish old fellow, reproved her, saying she might as well call it artichoke. 'Not so, my Lord,' said she, 'for an artichoke has a bottom, but a **** and a cauliflower have none.'

Lord: A crooked or hump backed man. These unhappy people afford great scope for vulgar raillery; such as, 'Did you come straight from home? If so you have got confoundedly bent on the way.' 'Don't abuse the gentleman,' adds a by-stander, 'he has been grossly insulted already; don't you see his back's up?' Or someone will ask him if the show is behind, 'because I see the drum at your back.' Another piece of vulgar wit is let loose on a deformed person if met by a party of soldiers on their march, one of them observes that that gentleman is on his march too, 'for he has his knapsack on his back.'

Grose also describes a popular joke type at the time called a "Bargain", played out by middle-class young women, whereby the punch-line, 'my arse' is delivered:

Bargain: As a specimen, take the following instance: A lady would come into the room full of company, apparently in fright, crying out, 'It is white, and it follows me!' And on any of the company asking, 'What?' she sold them the bargain by saying, 'Mine arse!'

Chapter Eight

Hooked

In 1809 the most elaborate and notorious practical joke in history was played by the writer and humourist, Theadore Hook.

Hook was strolling through London one day with his friend the architect Samuel Beazley when he pointed to a house and wagered a guinea that within a week he could make the quiet little dwelling the most famous in London.

That quiet little dwelling was 54 Berners Street which belonged to an unassuming widow by the name of Mrs Tottenham. According to some Hook had been involved in a dispute with the widow and the practical joke was played as means of revenge, while other accounts state that the pair had no connection whatsoever and all that mattered was that she lived in the right part of the city, upmarket Westminster, and that there were rooms to rent opposite.

One week later, on November 27 at five am a chimney sweep turned up at Mrs Tottenham's door. Not unusual for a Westminster dwelling, except that Mrs Tottenham had not hired a sweep for that day, nor had she hired the further twenty sweeps that arrived over the next half an hour. Nor the pastry chefs that followed carrying fresh raspberry tarts, or the enormous custom-made wedding cakes, or the hats, wigs, dresses, men's suits, and dozens of pairs of shoes that were also delivered.

As the morning wore on the street continued to fill with disgruntled merchants, tradesmen, delivery men, all demanding payment, and all being turned away by a totally bemused Mrs Tottenham.

As a crowd of spectators gathered bulkier wares began to arrive; butchers carrying legs of mutton, upholsterers carrying carpets, tailors pushing carts of new linen, followed by carts of coal, fresh fish, furniture, and expensive glassware.

Twelve grand pianos arrived from twelve different suppliers and a pipe organ so big it had to be carried by six men, by which point the road was jammed, traffic backed up two streets away, while fights broke out between enraged tradesmen. Expensive wares were smashed in the mêlée while other goods simply "disappeared". By the end of the morning central London was at a standstill.

Next to arrive were the vicars and chaplains each one requested to administer the last rites to someone at Mrs Tottenham's house. Dozens of domestic servants turned up for a job interview, along with private tutors, doctors, solicitors, undertakers, and even a few local dignitaries including the Lord Chief Justice, the governor of the Bank of England, the chairman of the East Indian Company, the Duke of Gloucester, and the Arch Bishop of Canterbury. Allegedly the Lord Mayor of London had to turn back because the streets to Mrs Tottenham's were impassable. Every available policeman was called to disperse the crowd which according to the *London Morning Post* was not cleared until, 'a late hour.'

Meanwhile Hook and some friends watched the madness unfurl in a rented room across the street.

To win his wager Hook had over the previous week, sent out around four thousand hand written letters, invitations, and advertisements to hundreds of people and businesses, all in Mrs Tottenham's name. (The Lord Mayor's letter stated that Mrs Tottenham had been summoned to appear before him but was confined to her room by ill health, and so requested that his lordship would do her the honour of calling on her.)

There followed a public outcry for the perpetrator to be caught and Hook laid low for a few days before embarking on a trip around England.

When he returned weeks later he found the incident had largely been forgotten. He had won his guinea and the 'Berners Street Hoax' was just another newspaper headline in history.

Chapter Nine

Music Hall

The biggest comedy star in Britain at the turn of the nineteenth century was the genius white-face clown, Joseph Grimaldi (1779-1837) whose extraordinary physical skills and comic improvisations were unparalleled.

He is widely regarded as the grandfather of modern comedians, the clown who elevated the pantomime comedian from village idiot to sharp witted anarchist, and his comic songs, interspersed with comic dialogue paved the way for future Music Hall comedians.

Grimaldi transformed the traditional English pantomime from a romantic tale into a comedy and was jointly responsible for establishing the pantomime as a fairy tale or nursery rhyme when in 1806 he and Tom Dibdon wrote *Harlequin and Mother Goose*.

British pantomime had no spoken dialogue before Grimaldi, he was the first performer to talk directly to the audience and have them partake in back-chat and sing-a-longs.

Charles Dickens edited the Grimaldi memoirs, a record of a traumatic childhood at the hands of a cruel and deranged father, the happiness he found through his beloved wife and son, and of the deep depression he suffered following their early deaths. The myth of the sad clown began when Grimaldi, in search of a cure for his melancholy visited a doctor:

The doctor said, 'Cheer yourself up, go and see Grimaldi.'
'Ah, there's the rub,' he sighed, 'You see, I am Grimaldi.'

At the time of Grimaldi's death in 1837 Music Hall entertainment was in its fledgling years, mostly impromptu gatherings of drinkers who told jokes, exchanged humorous banter, and partook in sing-a-longs.

No-one could have guessed that such auspicious beginnings would produce the most successful theatre entertainment ever in Britain, and the first theatre genre to be marketed as commercial entertainment for the masses.

The Industrial Revolution that began in the middle of the eighteenth-century enslaved and dehumanised millions of Britons. The revolution happened without rules or regulations and it was not until 1802 that the first Factory Act addressed the plight of the poor. Following laws meant that by the middle of the nineteenth century the ten-hour working day was established, with a half day Saturday, and a complete rest day on Sunday, which for the first time afforded the working classes regular leisure time.

Every Saturday afternoon workingmen collected their weekly wages and made for their local pub or tavern where ensconced in the Music Hall they could purchase apples and oranges, tripe and trotters, gin and beer, and enjoy impromptu entertainment.

The rooms were hot and stifling from the heat of gaslights and so many bodies crammed together, and thick smoke from tobacco pipes only added to the stench and seediness. In the corner a few upturned beer crates made for a makeshift stage for volunteers to lead the singing, of whom the most successful were paid in drinks until demand grew enough for them to charge a fee and become professional "turns" (sing-a-long entertainers going from one pub to another in the same evening).

In the 1840s Sam Cowell became the first star comedian of Music Hall, an innovator who decided to add patter between the verses of his songs, usually a running commentary to the events unfolding. In *Villikans And His Dinah* he joked that the daughter committed suicide by, 'drinking British brandy' before setting up the next verse:

'...now this is the most-melancholy part of it, and shows what the progeny was druv to in conskivence of the mangled obstropolousness and ferocity of the inconsiderable parient...'

Cowell was also the first international Music Hall star after American audiences went into raptures over him during a saloon tour in 1860. Sadly, like so many Music Hall comedians, alcohol led to his downfall and he died penniless four years later.

The upper-classes had their own version of Music Hall in the form of song-and-supper clubs where gentlemen wined, dined and were entertained by similar, though much less vulgar entertainment. They also had their private Gentlemen clubs, social gatherings, dinner dates, and grand balls where the jokers were the "society wits".

Wits like Theadore Hook, Jonathan Swift, and Reverend Sydney Smith, all of whom were regular guests at Victorian upper class social gatherings and dinner parties. No financial reward was sought but rather they looked to enhance their social standing and gain access to a higher grade of society which brought many advantages.

Wit is a Saxon word that originally signified wisdom, a *witte* was a wise man and the Saxon Parliament was called the *Wittenagemot*. By Elizabethan times a wit was someone who was considered clever and humorous in an impromptu manner.

Aristocratic Victorians considered witticisms to be superior to jokes, a joke was regarded as vulgar and detrimental to moral character while boisterous laughter was nothing short of an obscenity.

Correspondence is like small clothes before the invention of suspenders; it is impossible to keep them up. (Sydney Smith.)

It was wits like Smith that were largely responsible for the shift in attitude and despite reports to the contrary it was the Victorians who introduced the notion that making jokes, especially those of the drier, more cerebral sort, was socially acceptable, enjoyable even.

The high-brow and usually pretentious offerings of some self-professed "intellectual" joke collectors were not, as they so claimed, representative of the Victorians' sense of humour.

The 1842 *Jokes of the Cambridge Coffee-Houses* compiled by Shakespearian scholar and librarian at Jesus College, Cambridge, James Orchard Halliwell-Philips, is a collection of jokes and anecdotes he claimed were *the* most popular with upper class university types.

The jokes are dated from the seventeenth century to the time of publication and are advertised as, 'selected from various jest books' and, 'serve to show the state of this class of literature during that period.'

But they are far from reflecting the state of joke books during the period, the jokes being mostly from various Cambridge jest books, the result of which is a compilation of Latinised punch-lines and puerile puns:

A fellow of the college was chiding an undergraduate for talking too loud at dinner-time and told him, moreover, *vir sapit qui pauca loquitur*; and the other replies, 'Yes, *vir loquitur qui pauca sapit.*'

A Cambridge scull being asked how he got so much wit, being but a scull answered, 'where should wit be but in the scull?'

Toward the latter part of the book the jokes improve considerably, unsurprisingly considering they are from *Joe Miller's Jest Book* and joke collections of a M. S. Sloan:

Two soldiers at Plymouth, being comrades, the one was an economical and the other a very extra vagrant fellow. The former falling very sick and weak, his companion one morning very early, for the sake of his money, takes him upon his back and was going to bury him; but by chance his captain met them, and says, 'How now, Jack, what is that you have on your back so early in the morning?'

'Why, my comrade,' answered the fellow, 'he is stone dead and I'm going to bury him.' With which the sick man cries out as well as he could, 'I am not dead, indeed, noble captain.'

'Oh,' says the fellow, 'don't believe him, captain, don't believe him, for when he was alive, he was the hardenest lyin'est rogue in all the whole company, and doubtless he is as bad when he is dead.'

A gentleman who was very lame in one of his legs, without any outward show of anything, having sent for the surgeon, and he, more honest than ordinary told him it was in vain to meddle with it, for it was only old age that was the cause. 'But why then,' said the gentleman, 'should my other leg not be as lame as this, seeing that the one is no older than the other?'

The most popular joke cycle of the Victorian era was the "master and servant", and the *British Library Collection of Victorian Jokes* contains some real gems:

'Oh Mary,' said the mistress cutting short her conversation with her friends, 'will you run upstairs and bring the letter I left on my dressing room table.'
'Er, which one mum,' said the girl, 'the one about your brother's wedding or the letter from the vicar about the bazaar.'

'Darling,' said the lady of the house, 'I'm afraid cook has burned the bacon, you'll have to be satisfied with a kiss for breakfast.'
'All right,' said the husband, 'call her in.'

Lady Beaumont said to Lady Durham, 'I knew an artist who painted a cobweb so artistically that the maid spent several hours trying to get it down from the ceiling.'
'I don't believe it,' said Lady Durham.'
'Why not?' said Lady Beaumont. 'Artists have been known to do such things.'
'Maybe,' said Lady Durham, 'but not maids.'

The collection also gives an insight into the kind of jokes printed in Victorian magazines and newspapers, mostly mild breaches of social convention, social stereotypes, and puns:

He: 'I am a millionaire. Haven't I money enough for the both of us?'
She: 'Yes, if you are moderate with your tastes.'

'I have the best wife in the world,' said the henpecked husband, 'she always strikes me with the soft end of the broom.'

If all the seas dried up what would Neptune say?
I haven't got a notion.

A recently discovered notebook belonging to circus clown Tom Lawrence suggests that Victorians were fond of word-play jokes:

Bad husbands are like bad coals. They smoke, they go out, and they don't keep the pot boiling.

What is the difference between a rowing boat and Joan of Arc?
One is made of wood and the other is Maid of Orleans.

Lawrence's notebook, dated 1871 contains about two hundred jokes, monologues, and comic routines, and covers subjects such as ill-tempered wives, useless husbands, violent policemen, and the hard lot of the poor. The jokes are rather tame, with one notable exception:

Did you notice her bonnet? I gave her that... did you notice her dress? I gave her that... did you notice her black eye? I gave her that...

A circus ring was no place for drawn out narrative jokes, clowns were physical comedians who made occasional quips or one-line jokes in much the same manner as Music Hall comedians did between their song choruses.

The New London Jest Book, published in 1871, was compiled of mainly one and two-line jokes and quickly became a major source of material for Music Hall comedians:

A gentleman rode up to a public house in the country and asked, 'Who is the master of this house?'

'I am sir,' replied the landlord; 'the wife's been dead about three weeks.'

A lunatic in Bedlam was asked how he came there. He answered, 'By a dispute.'

'What dispute?'

The Bedlamite replied: 'The world said I was mad, I said the world was mad, and they outvoted me.'

Chapter Ten

Cartoon

Caricature jokes were well established by the nineteenth century with the British caricaturists William Hogarth (1697-1764), and James Gillray (1756-1815), who are widely acknowledged as the grandfather and father of etched political and social satire.

It was by enlarge satire aimed at the educated classes, that was until 1843 when caricature broadened its appeal, albeit inadvertently by the British satirical magazine, *Punch*.

Punch took its lead from numerous French satirical magazines, most notably *Le Charivari* which was first published in 1832 by Charles Philipoins (the first issue of *Punch* in 1841 was titled, *The London Charivari*). Its founders, journalist Henry Mayhew and the printer-engraver Ebenezer Landells decided from the outset that *Punch* would be a weekly magazine, 'without grossness, partisanship, profanity, indelicacy, or malice.'

Two years later the magazine took a satirical swipe at an exhibition intended to aid the selection of new paintings and murals for the Houses of Parliament, which at the time were being rebuilt after the fire of 1834. To be considered for selection artists made their submissions in the form of cartoons, which were then preliminary drawings for works of art; a painting, a fresco, or a tapestry.

Punch's entry for the Parliamentary exhibition was a series of drawings contrasting the exorbitance of government plans with the poverty of the poor which they ironically submitted as, "cartoons". Cartoon number one: *Substance and Shadow* by the artist John Leech depicted a group of ragged paupers puzzling at a gallery of opulently-framed portraits together with the caption: 'As they cannot afford to give hungry nakedness the substance which it covets, at least it shall have the shadow.

103

The poor ask for bread, and the philanthropy of the State accords - an Exhibition.'

Henceforth a cartoon was associated with pictorial satire and eventually with any humorous drawing.

Within a few short decades of its launch *Punch* was a shadow of its former self, more in tune with the rising aspirations of the middle classes. It was less likely to attack the Establishment and by the end of the century it *was* the voice of the Establishment (its first two editors were knighted), and though it made jokes about the upper and middle classes rarely were the victims wounded.

A Bishop said to a Page, 'Who is it that sees and hears all that we do, and before whom even I am but as a crushed worm?'

And the Page said, 'The Missus, me Lord.'   *Punch*, 1880.

In comparison *Le Charivari* and other French satirical magazines sustained a reputation for caustic wit while maintaining a healthy disrespect for political and religious leaders.

When a large scale anti-Christian offensive began in Europe in the 1870s and rationalists and freethinkers from the world of philosophy and science openly poked fun at religion and its apparitions and dogmas, it was the French magazines that led the way in cartoon satire.

In 1872 *La Collette* published a Paul Klenck cartoon of God in the guise of an old philosopher wearing rounded spectacles, his beard stained yellow by nicotine and beer, and his pockets stuffed with debunked railway bonds.

When the same magazine mocked the Immaculate Conception with a cartoon of the pregnant Mary knitting socks while a perplexed Joseph looked on, it earned its owners several months in jail. But the damage was already done, the cartoons characterized the loss of respect, both contractual and civil, for the image of God, Jesus, and the Virgin Mother and signalled the beginning of the separation in the West of state and religion.

Chapter Eleven

Why did the Chicken Cross the Road?

In 1847 an issue of the New York, *Knickerbocker* magazine printed the following:

Why did the chicken cross the road?
To get to the other side!

It was the first printed "why did the chicken cross the road", a joke that soon spread across the globe:

Why did the chicken cross the road?
To prove to the possum it could be done.

Why did the chicken cross the playground?
To get to the other slide.

In the introduction to his 1865, *The Jest Book* Mark Lemon praised the British sense of humour: 'A true Briton loves a good joke,' he wrote, 'and regards it as a thing of beauty, a joy forever.'

Lemon's collection is an eclectic mix of jokes and anecdotes, but its style is more modern than both *Joe Miller's Jests* and *Tom Brown's Jests*, and though its contents is perhaps overly non-contentious Lemon is to be admired for allowing the jokes to stand up for themselves at a time when a comic celebrity in the title virtually guaranteed sales:

A gentleman dining at a hotel, whose servants were "few and far between" despatched a lad among them for a cut of beef. After a long time, the lad returned and was asked by the faint and hungry gentleman, 'Are you the lad who took away my plate for the beef?'

'Yes, sir,' replied the lad. 'Bless me,' said the gentleman, 'how you've grown.'

'My notion of a wife at forty,' said Jerrold to his friend, 'is, that a man should be able to change her, like a bank note, for two twenties.'

The above was closer to truth than one might imagine. Changing a spouse was not uncommon, even selling one at market, a practise that began with the Anglo-Saxons. According to the *Annual Register* in April 1832 Joseph Thompson, a Cumberland farmer, went to Carlisle market whereupon he placed his wife on a large oaken chair and began his pitch:

Gentlemen, I have to offer, to your notice, my wife, Mary Anne Thompson, otherwise Williams, whom I mean to sell to the highest, fairest bidder. Gentlemen it is her wish as well as mine that we part forever. She has been to me only a born serpent. I took her for my comfort and the good of my home; but she became my tormentor, my domestic curse, a night invasion and a daily devil…

Joseph continued along much the same lines before coming to Anne's good points:

She can read novels and milk cows; she can laugh and weep with the same ease that you could take a glass of ale when thirsty. She can make butter and scold the maid; she can sing Moore's melodies, and plait her frills and caps; she cannot make rum, gin or whisky, but she is a good judge of the quality from long experience in tasting them. I therefore offer her, with all her imperfections, for the sum of fifty shillings.

After an hour of haggling Anne was sold to a Henry Mears for twenty shillings and a Newfoundland dog, and the register recorded that: 'They all parted in perfect good temper – Mears and the woman going one way, Thompson and the dog the other.'

The practise was still legal until at least the 1880s. Records show that in December 1884 the *All Year Round* listed twenty cases, complete with names and prices, which ranged from twenty-five guineas and a half pint of beer, to one penny and a dinner.

Lemon's *Jest Book* also gave us a glimpse of how the English viewed their fellow Britons at the time:

An affectionate Irishman enlisted in the 75th Regiment in order to be near his brother, who was in the 76th.

A Scotch pedestrian, attacked by three highwaymen, defended himself with great courage, but was at last overpowered and his pockets rifled. The robbers expected, from the extraordinary resistance they had experienced, to find a rich booty, but were surprised to discover that the whole treasure which the sturdy Caledonian had been defending at the hazard of his life, was only a crooked sixpence. 'The deuse is in him,' said one of the rogues, 'if had had eighteen pence I suppose he would have killed the lot of us.'

Sir Watkins William Wynne talking to a friend about the antiquity of his family, which he carried up to Noah, was told that he was a mere mushroom of yesterday. 'How so, pray?' said the baronet. 'Why,' continued the other, 'when I was in Wales a pedigree of a particular family was shown to me: it filled five large skins of parchment, and near the middle of it was a note in the margin: About this time the world was created.'

While Lemon's book was enjoying notable success in Britain the American newspaper, *The Oregonian*, printed the following joke in its April 12, 1872 edition:

107

Guest: Waiter, how comes this dead fly's in my soup?

Waiter: In fact, sir, I have no positive idea how the poor thing came to its death. Perhaps it had not taken any food for a long time, dashed upon the soup, ate too much of it, and contracted an inflammation of the stomach that brought on death. The fly must have a very weak constitution, for when I served the soup it was dancing merrily on the surface. Perhaps – and the idea only presents itself at this moment – it endeavoured to swallow to large a piece of vegetable; this, remaining fast in its throat, caused a choking in the windpipe. This is the only reason I could give for the death of this insect.

It started a joke cycle that lasted for over a century:

Waiter, what's this fly doing in my soup?
The backstroke, I think.

Two other food related joke cycles also emerged around the same time. The first began in America:

A bandaged accident victim was in the hospital and was being fed rectally through a tube. As a treat the nurse is giving him coffee this way, when suddenly through his bandages comes a muffled shout and attempts to shove the tube away from his buttocks. 'What's the matter?' says the nurse, 'Too hot?'
'N-n-n-o-o-o,' came the muffled cry, 'too much sugar.'

The joke cycle was created from the brief fad of feeding via the anus. *Feeding per Recturn* by Dr William Bliss was published in America in 1882 and promoted the practise of rectal dining as a healthy option. Jokes quickly followed, including:

A faithful butler is describing to the cook how their master, who is feeding rectally, has responded to the meals the cook has prepared for him that day. 'Did he like the fried brains?' the cook asks. 'So, so,' says the butler. 'What about the pig's trotter?' says the distraught cook. 'Well, he got it up him,' says the butler, 'but with no

108

great relish.' 'What about the baked cheese rolls,' says the cook, 'I was sure he'd like them?' 'Oh,' says the butler, 'he was mad about them. Yes, it certainly did my old heart a world of good to see the way his arsehole snapped at them.'

The second and more abiding food related cycle was the British "Cannibal" joke, which had been around since the turn of the sixteenth century but became more popular as the Empire extended into Africa:

At a cannibal wedding the caterer said to the chef, 'This is not what they meant when they said, toast the bride and groom.'

The word "cannibal" is dated at 1495 from a miss-recording by Christopher Columbus of the West Indian 'Carib' tribe. He wrote of a 'Canib' tribe who had recently abandoned a feast of human limbs, which he found simmering in small cauldrons and roasting on spits.

Two missionaries are caught by cannibals and both are stripped and put in the pot over the fire. As the water begins boiling the cannibals throw in various vegetables when one of the missionaries' notices that the other is giggling. 'What in Heaven's name are you laughing at?' he says, 'there's nothing funny here, we're about to be boiled up and eaten.' And the other sniggers, 'I just did number two's.'

Chapter Twelve

Erotica

Despite the high morals of Victorian upper-class society underneath the veneer of Christian respectability was a booming sexual sub culture in which prostitution, rape, buggery, and paedophilia was rife.

Erotic literature was big business, magazines sold "under the counter", and most included jokes. The best and most notorious of those erotic magazines was *The Pearl* which ran for eighteen months from 1879 and was edited and published in London by William Lazenby.

It was advertised as, 'A Magazine of Facetiae and Voluptuous Reading', and as expected its facetiae was of the adult kind:

An English lord taking a bath finds that the hot water has given him an erection. His butler sees this and says, 'Oh gracious, your lordship, shall I rally her Ladyship?'

'No Johnson,' says the lord, 'get my baggy pants. Maybe I can smuggle this one up to London.'

A prostitute said to a gentleman client; 'I've met some disgusting tricks in my time, but you are the most disgusting, dirty old man I have ever met.'

'Now, just you listen here, madam,' said the old gentleman, 'I've paid you, so I'll ask you to kindly keep a civil tongue in my arse.'

A Southern colonel determined to prove his gentlemanly ways and fine manners finds his daughter copulating with the Yankee guest in the wine cellar. 'Daughter', he chides, 'wheah is your manners? Wheah is your southern hospitality child? Arch your back more… and get that gentleman's balls offa that cold marble floor!'

Americans featured regularly:

An American attending a well-to-do banquet in London is surprised to notice that when the dowager breaks wind, one of the male guests rises and gallantly says, 'I beg your pardon!' The nicety of etiquette being explained to him, the next time the hostess broke wind the American leaps up and restraining the Englishman seated next to him, says, 'It's ok, this one's on me.'

As did the British aristocracy:

A French maid asked her mistress what the word 'fuck' meant and was told that it meant 'to serve'. At the next formal dinner, the maid announced to the Butler, 'James, fuck the duck.' And an English gentleman guest said excitedly, 'Oh, how jolly! Do you mind if I stick my prick in the mashed potatoes?'

At the time there were jokes made at the expense of Prince Albert's lack of English, much to the Queen's annoyance. *The Pearl's* contribution to the brief cycle went:

Victoria and Albert were dining in a plush West End restaurant and when the waiter asked for their order Albert said, 'Two rare steaks.'
'That's two bloody steaks, sir,' said the waiter.
'Quite right,' said Albert, 'two bloody steaks.'
And the Queen said, 'Yes, and plenty of bloody chips too.'

When the authorities shut down the magazine in 1881 Lazenby re-titled it *The Oyster*, which a year later was also banned only for it to resurface soon afterwards as *The Boudoir*.

111

At the other end of the spectrum were prose-chap books which date back to the beginning of the eighteenth century and were some of the earliest literature written specifically for ordinary Britons.

The editor's note in Robert Hays Cunningham's collection described chap books as literature written by the people, for the people, and proposed that, 'every district had its proportion of local geniuses who had a gift above their fellows in the matter of story-telling.'

In 1889 Cunningham published *Amusing Prose Chap-books*, a two-volume definitive collection of chap books chiefly of the last century that included comical tales of Robin Hood, Dick Whittington, and Dr Faustus, plus the jest books, *The Merry Tales of the Wise Men of Gotham; The Mad Pranks of Tom Tram: Son in Law to Mother Winter;* and *The Penny Budget of Wit and Package of Drollery*, the latter a rare dialect laden Scottish joke book:

A Highlander who sold brooms went into a barber's shop in Glasgow to get shaved. The barber bought one of his brooms, and after shaving him asked the price of it. 'Tuppence,' said the Highlander.

'No, no,' said the barber, I'll gie ye a penny, and if that disna satisfy ye, ye can take yer broom again.'

The Highlander took it, and then asked what he had got to pay. 'A penny,' said the barber.

'I'll gie ye a bawbee,' said the Highlander, 'and if that disna satisfy ye, ye can put on ma beard again.'

Scottish joke books were published for a wide market and jokes usually carried only the merest hint of Scots accent. The 1803 *Glasgow Magazine of Wit* contains more than five hundred jokes and not a trace of a Scottish accent in any of them:

A gentleman having a pad that started and broke his wife's neck. A neighbouring squire told him he wished to purchase it for his wife to ride upon. 'No, no,' says the other, 'I will not sell the little fellow, because I intend to marry again.'

One Scottish chap book bucked the trend and despite being written in thick Scottish brogue had notable success both in England and America.

The Laird of Logan was compiled some twenty years earlier but for reasons unknown was not released until 1889. It was edited by John Donald Carrick, William Motherwell, and Andrew Henderson who claimed the collection to be: '... a sort of embodiment or concentrated essence of the floating facetiae and indigenous wit and humour of the western and north-western districts of Scotland.'

A Scottish crofter's wife went into labour in the middle of the night and the doctor was called out to assist the delivery. The doctor handed the crofter a lantern and said, 'Hold this high so I can see what I'm doing.' Soon, a baby was born but the doctor said, 'Och, dinna be so keen to put doon the lantern, there's another wee bairn coming.' Sure enough, within minutes another baby was born, the doctor said, 'Na, dinna put doon the lantern yet, there's another one besides.' When minutes later a third baby arrived, the crofter turned to the doctor and said, 'Doc, do ye no suppose it could be the light that's attracting them?'

The book consists of five hundred and sixty-five jokes attributed to various characters, the principal being Hugh Logan, the Laird of Logan (1739-1802); others include the Reverend James Robertson of Kilmarnock; Will Speir, son of the Laird of Camphill, Ayrshire; and William Cameron, alias Hawkie, described as a, 'Scottish Diogenes, and the greatest street orator of our day'.

Hawkie's Politics:

'I am neither,' said our public lecturer, 'a Tory nor a Radical; I like middle courses, gang ayont that, either up or doon, it disna matter – it's a wreck any way ye tak it.'

The Last Debt plays on the mean Scots stereotype:

An old man about to bid his last adieu, had his friends called round him, when he was desired by his wife to tell what debts were owing to him: 'Tam, there's Tam awn me five shillings for mutton.'

'Oh,' says the wife, 'to see a man at his time o' day, and just guan to close his last account, hae the use of his facilities, just carry on James.'

'Ay, and Stuart, ten shillings for beef,' and interrupts the wife, 'What a pleasant thing to see a man dee'in and sensible to the last! Any mair James, only don't distress yourself.'

'And Robert, a crown for a cow's hide.'

'Ay,' quoth the wife, 'sensible yet, weel James, what else was ye gawna say?'

'Ney mair,' quoth James, 'but I'm owin' Jock Tamson twa pounds in balance o' a cow.'

'Hoot, hoot,' quoth the wife, 'He's ravin' now, he's just tattrin, dinna mind any mair he says.'

The canniness of a Scots wife is displayed in *Before Elders' Hours*:

'If I'm no home from the party tonight at ten o' clock,' said a husband to his better half, 'don't wait up for me.'

'That I won't,' said the wife, 'I'll come for you.'

He returned at ten precisely.

"Stupidity" jokes are aimed at the people of St. Mirren:

As the Paisley steamer came alongside the quay at the city of the Seestus, a denizen of St Mirren hailed one of the passengers, 'Jock! Jock! Distu hear, man? Is that you or yer brither?'

Chap books remained popular until the end of the Victorian era, beyond which they were unable to compete with the growing number of cheaper magazines and newspapers.

Toward the end of the century a great number of jokes from French and Russian compilations found their way into British joke

114

books. The following from *The Pearl* was originally printed in an anonymous 1883 French volume entitled, *Histoires Naturelles*:

A little boy at the Paris zoo said to his nurse, 'What's that?' And the nurse replied, 'That's the elephant's trunk.'
'No, not that – that!' the boy insists. 'That's the elephant's tail.' said the nurse. 'No,' said the boy, 'that thing right there!'
'Oh,' said the nurse, 'that's nothing.' And a bystander tipped his hat and said, 'Mademoiselle is blasé.'

The most plundered French collection was *Kryptadia*, twelve volumes of erotic folk tales, anecdotes, and jokes that originated in numerous European countries.
The series, published in France and Belgium between 1883 and 1911 was founded by Isidor Kopernicky and Friedrich S Krauss, and edited by the French and Italian folklorists, Gaston Paris, E Rolland, Henry Gaidoz, E-Henri Carnoy, and Giuseppe Pitre, all of whom remained anonymous to protect their positions on the companion yearbook, *La Tradition*. Translations from *Kryptadia* include:

A boy told his parents that he saw his sister and her music teacher kissing and then taking off their pants. 'Well, what happened then?' the mother urged. 'I know not,' said the boy, 'I figured they were going to shit in the piano, so I left.'

Newly-weds are in bed in a small hotel when a travelling merchant mistakes their bedroom door for the toilet. He begins rattling the locked door handle, 'What do you want,' cries out the bridegroom. 'You know what I want,' said the merchant, 'If you're not using both of them holes I want one.'

Kryptadia also contains the first printed European jokes featuring thief tricksters who take on false identities with names such as, 'Who-Shit?' or 'Kick-My-Arse', the idea being that when the victim gives chase he calls out, 'Hey, Who-Shit?' or, 'Ho, Kick-My-Arse'.

115

Onlookers either engage him in trading insults or kick his arse which allows the tricksters to escape.

Similar jokes appear in the 1865 *Russian Secret Tales* by Aleksandr Alfanasyev, posthumously published in 1872, and again in Paris in 1897 where it was translated and re-titled, *Stories from Folklore Russia*, though the Russian tricksters have the Arabic and Latin names, Cacabo and Cacavi, suggesting the jokes have at least two other sources.

Russian Secret Tales is a mixture of regular jokes and those featuring famous characters of Russian folklore like the fictional Poruchik (Lieutenant) Dimitry Rzhevsky, the straightforward talking cavalry officer:

Natasha Rostova attends her first formal ball and dances with Pierre Buzukhov: 'Pierre there is grease on your collar.' And Buzukhov says, 'Oh my, how could I miss such a terrible flaw in my uniform,' and he retreats in shame. Then, she dances with Kniaz Bolkonsky and tells him: 'Kniaz, isn't this a spot of sauce on your tunic?' and Bolkonsky says, 'I am devastated' and faints. Finally, she is dancing with Rzhevsky: 'Poruchik,' she says, 'isn't that mud on your boots?'

'No,' says Rzhevsky, 'it's shit, don't worry it will fall off when it dries.'

And real-life officer and Red Army hero, Vasily Ivanovich Chapayev and his aide-de-camp Petka:

'I flunked my history exam, Petka,' said Vasily Ivanovich, 'they asked me who Caesar was, and I said, it's a stallion from our seventh cavalry squadron.'

And Petka said, 'It's my fault, Vasily Ivanovich. While you were away, I re-assigned him to the sixth.'

In 1888 America produced its first great joke book, *The Stag Party*:

An Irish immigrant new to New York embarrasses his Americanised brother by urinating in public on lower Broadway. 'Now, Pat ye don't have to be doing that. All ye have to do is knock on any door and ye'll be allowed to use the toilet.' A few days later Pat again is called short and when he knocks on a door a hand comes out with a beer-growler and fifteen cents, and a voice says, 'One quart, please.' Afterwards Pat goes to his brother and says, 'Jaysus, Mick, why didn't I come here sooner? To think I pissed away a fortune back in Ireland.'

The famines in Ireland during the nineteenth century saw more than four million Irish emigrate to England, Scotland, America, Canada, Australia, and New Zealand and as immigrants at the bottom of the economic ladder they were ripe for dim-witted jokes. From *The Stag Party*:

An Irishwoman went into a New York store, 'How much are your fish Mr Goldstein?' she asked. 'Eight cents a pound, Mrs O'Brien', Goldstein told her.

'I'll take two,' said Mrs O'Brien, 'how much will that be?'

'Vell, let's see,' said Goldstein, 'eight pounds, eight times eight is eighty-eight... tell you vot, Mrs O'Brien, take them for seventy-five cents.'

'Ah now, thank ye Mr Goldstein,' said Mrs O'Brien, 'yer always good to the Irish.'

The Stag Party is a joke book under the guise of a fictitious meeting of the gentleman-only, *Chestnut Club* whose purpose according to their King, Mr Bird is to: 'throw off the yoke. To be cussed. To say naughty words. To simulate a lack of virtue for the time and imagine we are as wicked as can be. It is the law of this club that when a member is called upon for a story, joke, or song he shall at once respond, or pay a round of drinks.'

Bird also reminds members that the jokes must be, according to club rules, "old chestnuts". Mr Hitchcock's contribution:

117

When out on the road the other day I struck several new men at a country town up in Wisconsin. We had all filed in together, and one after another registered. The names of the others were: Alcock, Babcock, and Hancock. As we registered in turn a smile began and slowly broadened as one after another the names were written. At the rear of the gang was a small, black-eyed Hebrew. He looked at the register, turned his head on one side, waved his hand a la horizon and said: 'Vell, shentlemen, I belong to dot femily mineself.'

'What is your name?' I asked.

He said, 'My name is Kuntz.'

The book contains the first published version of the infamous Timbuktu joke:

In a schoolroom during recess a young lady teacher said to a boy pupil, 'My boy, can you write a verse of four lines putting in the word Timbuktu twice and still make sense?' The boy wrote as follows:

Tim and I a-hunting went
On the plains of Timbuktu.
We found three maidens in a tent,
I bucked one and Tim bucked two.

Then the perplexed, innocent young teacher asked, 'Did you get it in twice?'

And the boy said, 'No, I didn't, but Tim did.'

As one might expect at a stag party, sex jokes abound:

A fellow checked into a Western hotel and as he left the front desk casually said, 'Oh, could you send me up a whore?' The proprietor's wife was so offended and incensed that she demanded her husband throw him out. But the owner was a mild man and did not want any confrontation.

'Fine,' his wife said, 'I'll do it' and she stormed up the stairs. Within minutes her husband heard a great commotion; screaming, cursing, breaking furniture, and then silence. After a few minutes the guest appeared at the bottom of the stairs battered, bloody and bruised. 'Well,' he said, 'that was a tough old broad you sent up, but I fucked her, yup, God-damn-it, I fucked her!'

American author Herman Koerner's *Beleaguered: A Story of the Uplands of Baden in the Seventeenth Century* published in 1898, contained the line: 'I have sent for you for two reasons, General. First, because I have good news and bad news...'.

Did Koerner inspire "Good News/Bad News" jokes? Highly debatable, and likely coincidence that in a relatively short time the line became a joke set-up:

A secretary walked into her boss's office and said, 'I'm afraid I've got some bad news.'

And her boss said, 'Penny, why do you always bring me bad news? Try to be a little more positive.' 'Ok,' she said, 'good news, you're not sterile.'

There are several permutations of the "good news/bad news" joke. When it was first created it was simply the teller relaying good news followed by bad news that invalidates the former:

A man who had to have his leg amputated woke up in hospital and asked the doctor how the operation went. The doctor said, 'I have bad news and good news. The bad news is we took off the wrong leg. The good news is the other one's getting better.'

Relatively quickly came variations such as, "That was the good news?":

A doctor said to a feller, 'We got your test results back and the good news is that you have twenty-four hours to live.'

'What?' cries the feller, 'That's the good news? What's the bad news?'

And the doctor said, 'I forgot to call you yesterday.'

119

"Good news that needs no bad news because the set-up reveals it all":

Doctor: 'The good news is they are naming a disease after you.'

"Bad news and worse news":

A doctor told a patient, 'I have bad news and worse news.'
And the patient said, 'What's the bad news?'
And the doctor said, 'The bad news is that you have one month to live.'
'Oh my God,' cried the patient, 'what's the worse news?
'It's February.'

And finally:

A policeman knocked on the door of a house and when the woman answered he said, 'Mrs Jackson, I've got some good news and bad news. Your husband has been seriously hurt in a car crash.'
'Ok,' she said, 'give me the bad news?'

In 1898 the first magazine dedicated entirely to jokes was published, the New York, *Madison's Budget*. It sold for a dollar and was advertised as: 'A cyclopaedia of comedy material for Vaudeville artists, masters of ceremony etc., containing original monologues, sketches, minstrels first-parts, sidewalk patter, wise cracks, revue and burlesque bits...'

Have you heard the one about the cowboy who didn't know heads from tails?
You should see his scalp collection.

A Scotsman wrote an angry letter to the editor of *Madison's Budget* saying that if any more Scotch jokes were printed in his paper he'd quit borrowing it.

120

As promised in its blurb *Madison's Budget* proved invaluable to Vaudeville comedians, and many took "inspiration" from its jokes.

The word *Vaudeville* is a corruption of French *voix de ville* which literally translates as, 'voices of the town'.
In the early 1800s the *Theatre de Vaudeville* in Paris presented comic dialogue between players during the interludes of operas and billed them as *Pieces en Vaudeville*. Vaudeville was also used to describe mini theatrical trifles like *French Opera Comique* and short plays, Mozart titled some of his mini operas as *Vaudevilles*, as did Chekhov his one act plays.
The term was adopted in America toward the latter part of the nineteenth century by theatre owners who wanted to distance their family entertainment from the bawdy bars and saloons that also presented Variety but had a reputation for wild, drunken audiences and wanton women. Prior to Vaudeville, theatres were no better than their saloon counterparts, and not only offered Variety entertainment but also alcohol, food, gambling, and prostitutes.
The shows mostly consisted of singers, Music Hall comedians, and Minstrel entertainers, the latter a mixture of music and comedy. Minstrelsy was the first form of musical theatre that was purely American.
Minstrelsy began in 1828 after white entertainer Thomas Dartmouth, stage name Thomas "Daddy" Rice, during a tour of Ohio, blackened his face with burnt cork and impersonated a crippled Negro slave he had seen working in a stable. He performed a song and dance he called, *Jim Crow*:

Come and listen all you gals and boys
I'se jist from Tuckyhoe,
I'm gonna sing a little song,
My name is Jim Crow.
Fist on de heel tap, den on the toe
Ebry time I wheel about
I jump Jim Crow.
Weel about and turn about
En do jist so,

121

Ebry time I weel about
I jump Jim Crow.

Rice was an overnight sensation and quickly became American Variety's biggest star, inspiring dozens of white, blackface entertainers across the country.

In the wake of Rice's success songwriter Daniel Decatur Emmett and three other white musicians devised a program of singing and dancing accompanying themselves with bone castanets, fiddle, banjo, and tambourine. Their *Virginia Minstrels* made their public debut in New York in 1843 and their enormous success saw the rise of countless imitators.

Such was the popularity of Minstrelsy that the following year the *Ethiopian Serenaders* played at the White House for the President and his family and friends. By the 1850's ten theatres in New York alone presented Minstrel entertainment exclusively, which by then incorporated comic skits and a stump orator, the latter a character who aspired to impart great wisdom but only revealed his ignorance by his outrageous malapropisms.

Ah done caught one of d'niggers weez play cards wi, cheatin'. De boss sez we shoulda ostracised him. Dats what ah wanted to do but I didn't hab no razor wid me.

One of the first black performers to become a blackface minstrel was William Henry Lane, the man who created tap dancing. Known as Master Juba he began blacking-up in the mid-forties and his unique dancing style made him a much in demand act.

Other black musicians and entertainers followed Juba's lead, though as black men had to declare themselves as "real coons". Bizarre as it now seems, black performers added burnt cork to blacken their already dark skin and took on the more perverse comic caricatures and racial stereotypes of their white counterparts.

The cultural legacy of Minstrelsy is quite a complex one for fans of Vaudeville. The portrayal of a black man in grotesque make-up may be considered detestable today, but Minstrelsy laid the foundations of American show business. Ragtime, Jazz, and Blues music, stand-up, double act, and sketch comedy all are indebted to Minstrelsy.

Comedy double talk was invented by minstrel troupes who interspersed songs with dialogue between the middle man, Mr. Interlocutor, and the two end men, tambourine player Mr. Tambo, and bones player, Mr. Bones. The double act of Tambo and Bones was responsible for establishing quick-fire gags as a standard element of Vaudeville humour:

Tambo: Say, Bones, I done fooled de Railroad Company.
Bones: How you done that?
Tambo: Bought me a round ticket den didn't use de return.

Douglas Gilbert in his 1940, *American Vaudeville: It's Life and Times* said of American Variety prior to Vaudeville: 'The audiences, all male, were none too bright, a mental condition hardly improved by alcoholic befuddlement. Jokes had to be sledge-hammered home. The days of personalities, subtlety, wit, expert dancing, and superb technique were yet to come.'

American Variety entertainment changed dramatically in 1881 when Tony Pastor, owner of the *New Fourteenth Street Theatre* in New York advertised his show as, 'Unblushing Entertainment, a Variety show that wives, sisters and sweethearts would find acceptable'. He called it, 'Vaudeville'.

Pastor's small theatre gave birth to American Vaudeville, but the men responsible for its form and ultimately its incredible success were Benjamin Keith and Edward Albee. Together they came up with the idea of a continuous Variety show which they first introduced at their *Bijou Theatre* in Boston, a continuous show running from late morning to late evening, five or six complete performances a day whereby people could sit down at any time and leave when they got to the part where they came in.

The format proved so popular that by the beginning of the twentieth century there were over two thousand Vaudeville theatres across America.

Chapter Thirteen

Ruthless Rhymes

While Vaudeville was sweeping across America in the mid-1880s, British Music Hall was entering its Golden Age.

The old pub style halls were being replaced at an incredible rate by large, ornate theatres, a circuit of which covered the length and breadth of Britain and were packed six nights and two afternoon matinees a week, fifty-two weeks a year.

The comedians had long since established themselves as audience favourites, though in truth they were singers who told an odd joke or added some comic patter between song verses. That was until the late 1880s when Dan Leno decided on a unique approach and became the first comedian to put all credence on his comic patter. And what patter it was:

...Kissed her right before me face. Well, I never, upon my word, I never heard a kiss like that since I was vaccinated... it came so sudden on me that, for the moment, I didn't know whether I'd had a shave that morning or not... you know, there's no person more fond of a kiss than I am, between meals, but if you'd heard this kiss you would have lost your eye sight... it sounded for all the world like a man, who had a train to catch, trying to eat a plate of hot tripe and onions with a fork...

Leno was born George Galvin in Somerset Town, London in 1860 to Johnny and Louisa Wilde, a comic duo that played the lowest grade halls.

During his teens he was part of a double act with his older brother until 1880 when the *Princess Palace Music Hall* in Leeds held a "Champion Clog Dancer of the World" competition and Leno, fresh from winning a shoulder of mutton in a similar competition at

Wakefield, entered and won which kick started a solo career that took him to the pinnacle of his profession.

After five years in the northern halls as the 'Celebrated Irish Comic Vocalist and Clog Dancer, Dan Leno', he made his first London appearance at *Forrester's Music Hall*, Mile End, soon after which he dropped the Irish gimmick and the clog dancing.

The decision only to enter and exit on a song chorus was bold and innovative, but for Leno it was all about the jokes:

There's a bit of money come into our family and we can't tell who is really entitled to it, and of course none of us like to take it, not knowing who it belongs too, well, as a matter of fact they won't let us… But it's through my stepfather, you see when my Dad died, dear old Dad, I can see him now, he used to come home from work, once a year, he was a hot cross bun maker… He used to sit me on his knee and pat me on the shoulder, well not always on the shoulder but I was his son so he could pat me where he liked… but it was through our stepfather that we can't find who this money belongs too, you see my stepfather married twice and when he married our second mother, my brother and I we were away at the time, my brother who's dead now, he died of hydrophobia, he had false teeth and took them out and put them in his tail coat pocket and bit himself…

However, very few Music Hall comedians followed Leno's lead of placing the onus on their jokes rather than their songs. Jokes were an aside for most comedians, something to fill the introduction or bridge of a song, and not until Music Hall had run its course and change was forced upon comedians did they alter their approach.

In 1898 the writer and poet, Jocelyn Henry Clive Graham, a k a Harry Graham (1874-1936) released *Ruthless Rhymes for Heartless Homes*, a magnificently dark "children's" book.

Graham was a distinguished English military officer and published his *Ruthless Rhymes* under the pseudonym Col. D. Streamer, a reference to his regiment.

125

Baby in the cauldron fell,
See the grief on mother's brow,
Mother loved her darling well,
Darling's quite hard boiled by now.

Following in the wake of *Ruthless Rhymes* were American, "Little Willie" jokes, the earliest of which were blatant copies of Grahams':

Little Willie, in bows and sashes,
Fell in the fire and got burned to ashes;
In the winter, when the weather is chilly,
No one likes to poke up Willie.

Graham's original:

Billy, in one of his nice new sashes,
Fell in the fire and was burned to ashes;
Now, although the room goes chilly,
I haven't the heart to poke poor Billy.

But Little Willie soon had his own rhymes and like Graham's involved much murder and mayhem:

Little Willie hung his sister;
She was dead before we missed her.
Willie's always up to tricks,
Ain't he cute? He's only six.

The ghoulish quality of Little Willie rhymes created the metaphor, to give someone "the Willies".

A regular feature of Graham's and Little Willie rhymes were dead babies. Graham's, *Calculating Clara*:

O'er the rugged mountain's brow
Clara threw the twins she nursed,

And remarked, 'I wonder now,
Which will reach the bottom first?'

Little Willie:

Willie, with a thirst for gore,
Nailed the baby to the door.
Mother said with humour quaint,
'Willie dear, don't spoil the paint.'

Many folklorists believe the origins of "dead baby" jokes that were incredibly popular in the 1960s came from Graham's *Heartless Rhymes* and "Little Willie" jokes, and both are generally regarded as the first "sick" joke cycles.

Chapter Fourteen

The British

The Australian colonies became a nation in 1901, the jokes, specifically those on its citizens and their lack of decorum remained unchanged:

An Australian was visiting the Vatican with his mates and declared loudly, 'Hey, look at all these crummy murals...' and was overheard by an Italian priest who popped his head out of the confession box and said, 'This is-a-de-Sistine Chapel. These are de-most-a-beautiful paintings in-a de-world. You must appreciate a-them properly, so I will personally give-a-you-a conducted tour.'

'Ah, good on yer mate,' said the Australian, 'but don't rush, finish yer shit first.'

Remote outback farms gave rise to bestiality to jokes, perpetuated by Australians themselves:

A Melbourne court was trying a man for having sex with a goat. The prosecutor asked the main witness what he saw. 'Well,' said the witness, 'I was walking along and saw this goat eating grass when this feller, him there yer honour, sneaked up from behind, unbuckled his belt, dropped his pants, and pulled the goat up to him. Then there was a lot of shaking and then that feller lets out a loud grunt, he then let go of the goat and dropped to his knees. The goat then turned around and started licking his penis.' And the judge said thoughtfully, 'Yes, a good goat will do that...'

But by far the most popular jokes told by Australians were, "Pom" jokes, Pom being a derogatory term for an Englishman:

A Pom visiting Australia was walking back home from the pub with his new cobber, Oz, when they come across a sheep with its head caught in the fence, 'Just a minute, mate,' said Oz, and dropped his pants, got down on his knees and proceeded to get stuck up the sheep. When he finished he turned to his Pom mate and said, 'Fancy a go?'

'Don't mind if I do,' said the Pom and promptly dropped his pants, got down on his knees, and stuck his head in the fence.

The joke relationship between the English and Americans was forged during the Victorian era and continued in much the same vein in Edwardian times. Americans generally regarded the English upper-class male as aloof and dim, while the English thought all American males were uncouth and dim:

An Englishman is told by an American that skin condoms are best because they are thinner and can be washed and used again. A few weeks later the Englishman bumps into the American and complains: 'They were all right, you know, thinner and all that, but I got a very rude note from laundry.'

An Englishman gives an American a riddle to solve: 'What is it that is hard, and long, and leaks?' The American smiles, but the Englishman says, 'No, it's not what you're thinking, it's a fountain pen!'

Back in America he decides to impress some ladies at a dinner party and asks, 'What's hard, and long, and leaks?' The women all raise their hands in horror, but the American says, 'No, it's not what you're thinking, it's not a prick, it's a fountain pen!'

Having been duly chided and forced to apologise the American plots his revenge and at the next dinner party he asks the same ladies, 'What's hard, and long, and leaks?'

They collectively groan and say, 'Yes we know, it's a fountain pen!' and he says, 'No, it's a prick!'

129

British stereotypes were well and truly established by the twentieth century:

An Englishman, Irishman and Scotsman were playing a round of golf and their wives were caddying for them. On the third hole the English wife tripped on a mole hill and her skirt flew over her head to reveal that she was not wearing knickers. 'What the hell?' the Englishman screamed, 'You're embarrassing me, why on earth aren't you wearing knickers?' And the wife said, 'Darling, you don't give me enough housekeeping, and so I make sacrifices and…' 'All right, all right, here, here's half-a-crown,' said the Englishman, 'go and buy some knickers.' A few holes later the Irishwoman trips and falls and the same thing, no knickers, 'Beejaayses!' cried the Irishman, 'cover yerself woman why in St. Patrick's name are you not wearing knickers?' 'Well, Dermot,' she said, 'on the little you give me for housekeeping, I can't afford knickers.' 'Ok,' said Dermot, 'I'm sorry love, here's half-a-crown go and buy yerself a pair.' Another few holes later the Scottish woman tripped, and her dress flew over her head and revealed that she too was without knickers. 'Och, woman,' screamed Jock, 'you should be ashamed, look at the state of you.' And his wife said, 'Well, what can I do? You're so tight I canna be affording luxuries like knickers. But if you give me half-a-crown I'll be glad to go and buy a pair.' Jock thought for a second and then said, 'Never mind, here's a comb, tidy yourself up a bit.'

Scots told jokes about their own meanness, but when a joke featured the English the Scot inevitably became the trickster:

An American tourist was so taken with Angus's collie dog he asked if he could buy him. 'Nae,' said Angus, 'I could'nae part with Frazer.' Just then an Englishman came by and was also smitten with the collie and he too offered to buy the dog. 'Ten shillings,' said Angus and the deal was done and the Englishman walked off with the dog.
    The American said, 'Hey, I thought you said that you wouldn't sell your dog.'

'Nae,' said Angus, 'I did'nae say that, I said I could'nae part with him. Yon Frazer, well, he'll find his way back in a few days, but the Atlantic Ocean, that's a bit too much even for him tae swim.'

Irish jokes remained extremely popular. The incredibly successful 1908, *Mr. Punch's Irish Humour* portrayed the usual stereotype:

Paddy got home one night only to be met by his neighbours who told him that his wife had been in a terrible accident. He ran to the hospital and said to the nurse in charge, 'How is she? Can I see her?'
The nurse shook her head solemnly and said, 'I'm sorry, I'm afraid you're too late.'
'Oh, right,' said Paddy, 'no problem, I'll come back in the morning.'

In America at the beginning of the twentieth century some Irish jokes were aimed instead at other ethnic minorities. The Irish joke cycle did not die out, far from it, but due to the Irish gaining skilled positions and moving up the social ladder they were no longer perceived as the only fools and were often replaced by newer immigrants such as Scandinavians, Poles, and Chinese:

A Swedish housemaid tells the lady of the house that the master of the house caught her by the washtub and 'yumped' her.
'What do you mean, Helga?' shrieked the lady. 'Ay mean he fooked me, at the washtub, he fooked me good!'
'What did you say?!' screamed the lady. 'Ay say, tank you, Mr. Carson.'

A Polish teacher asked his pupil, 'How much is seven and seven?'
'Ten,' said the Polish pupil.
'No,' said the teacher, 'but I'll mark you as passing, seeing as you only missed it by one.'

American ethnic jokes tended to vary depending on location; Irish and Italian were the main butt in Eastern states, while in the Mid-West it was Scandinavians, "Bohunks" (Hungarians and South Slavs), and Polacks (Polish). In the West stupidity jokes were told mostly at the expense of immigrant miners and railroad workers, particularly Chinese:

An army officer's wife has come to visit him at his post in the West where he has been stationed for several months. In the morning his Chinese valet wakes her by slapping her on the ass, and says, 'All light, missy, time fo' blekfast, then you go home.'

A wife of a railroad foreman has a Chinese serving boy who keeps embarrassing her by walking into her bedroom while she is dressing and so insists that he knocks before entering. He never again embarrasses her, but he also never knocks, and when she queries him he answers, 'Velly simple, before me come in, me look frough keyhole, if you no dlessed, me no come in.'

Though the Chinaman was not always the butt of the joke:

The cowboys decide that their New Year's resolution is not to tease the Chinese cook anymore, and all troop to the chuck wagon to apologise for the tricks they have played on him over the year. 'No pull China-boy's pigtail no more?' he says. 'No John,' says one cowboy, 'no more pulling pigtail.'
'No put sand in China-boy's bed?' he says. 'No, no more sand in bed or anything else,' the cowboy promises, 'from now on we're gonna treat you right.'
'Velly good,' says the cook, 'and me promise no pissee in coffee no more.'

Chapter Fifteen

Freud

In 1905 Sigmund Freud published *Jokes and their Relationship to the Unconscious*, a significant work for the joke, not least in that it encouraged telling jokes purely for fun, and in doing so gave the serious Edwardian upper classes permission to lighten up and appreciate jokes as much as they did witty repartee.

The book is in three parts, Analytic, Synthetic, and Theoretical. The Analytic begins with a synopsis of earlier theories on wit and joking, followed by a psychological classification of jokes based on such features as wordplay, brevity, word displacement, errors of thought, and double meanings, which Freud demonstrates through numerous examples:

Hirsch-Hyacinth, a Hamburg lottery agent and curer of corns boasted of meeting the rich Baron Rothschild saying, 'I sat next to Solomon Rothschild who treated me just as if I were his equal, quite famillionaire.'

On being introduced to his prospective bride the suitor was unpleasantly surprised, and drawing aside the marriage agent he reproachfully whispered to him, 'Why have you brought me here? She is ugly and old. She squints, has bad teeth, and bleary eyes.'
'You don't have to whisper,' said the agent, 'she's deaf too.'

An elderly gentleman showed his devotion to a young actress by bestowing lavish gifts. Being a respectable girl, she took the first opportunity to discourage him by telling him that her heart was already given to another man. The gentleman said, 'Oh, I never aspired as high as that.'

Freud also analyses joke tendencies, both contentious and non-contentious. He believed that a contentious joke works when the conscious allows expression of thoughts that society usually suppresses or forbids altogether.

Non-contentious jokes he considered relatively harmless, but was also keen to point out that non-contentious does not necessarily mean poor and gave the following as an example of a good non-contentious joke:

A horse dealer in recommending a horse to his client said, 'If you mounted this horse at four o'clock in the morning you will be in Monticello at six thirty.' And the client said, 'What will I do in Monticello at six thirty in the morning?'

The Synthetic part is Freud examining the pleasurable tendencies of jokes, and why we enjoy them as a social process. He proposed that pleasure could be derived from telling jokes that contain feelings of hostility, aggression, cynicism, or expressing sexuality, which bypass our internal censor and that such jokes give us a tremendous sense of relief, like letting off steam, or as Freud put it, 'Laughter through discharge'.

He also acknowledged other sources of pleasure from jokes including recognition, nostalgia, topicality, and the simple enjoyment of nonsense and playful jokes:

A Jewish gentleman embarking upon a long journey entrusted his daughter to his friend, begging him to watch over her chastity during his absence.

When he returned some months later he found that his daughter was pregnant.

'But how is this possible?' said his friend.

'Where has she been sleeping?' the father asked.

'In the same room as my son,' his friend replied.

134

'How is it that you allowed her to sleep in the same room with your son after I had begged you so earnestly to take good care of her?' remonstrated the father.

'Well,' said the friend, 'there was a screen between them. There was your daughter's bed and over there was my son's bed and between them stood the screen.'

'And suppose he went behind the screen, what then?' asked the father.

'Well, in that case,' said the friend thoughtfully, 'it might be possible.'

'What is this: It hangs on the wall and one can dry his hands on it?'

Answer: 'A towel.'

'No, it is a herring.'

'But for mercy's sake, a herring does not hang on a wall.'

'But you can hang it on a wall.'

'But who wants to dry his hands on a herring?'

'Well, you don't have too.'

He concluded the Synthetic part by discussing why people joke together, looking at social cohesion and social aggression. Freud considered jokes not only to be a means of taking pleasure from the psychic process but also as a, 'social process' which he believed often reveals more about social life at a given time than its people can.

In the final part Freud connected his theories on jokes and joking with his dream theories and their relationship with the unconscious, saying: 'Frequently they [dreams and jokes] are not at the disposal of our memory when we look for them, on the other hand, they often appear unsolicited and at places in our train of thought where we cannot understand their presence.'

In jokes and dreams Freud observed how often things are condensed and displaced and are represented indirectly or by their opposites.

135

From this Freud concurred that jokes and dreams share a common origin in the unconsciousness and that both outwit our inner censor. There is however, one critical difference, in that jokes are meant to be understood, in fact it is crucial to their success, whereas the meaning of a dream often eludes even the dreamer.

Freud also gave his thoughts on the different types of Jewish jokes: 'Jewish jokes made up by non-Jews are nearly all brutal buffooneries in which the wit is spared by the fact that the Jew appears as a comic figure to a stranger. The Jewish jokes that originate with Jews admit this, but they know their real shortcomings as well as their merits, and the interest of the person himself in the thing to be criticised produces the subjective determination of the wit-work which would otherwise be difficult to bring about. Incidentally I do not know whether one often finds a people that makes merry so unreservedly over its own shortcomings.'

By way of example Freud quotes two "scnorrer" jokes as ones typically told by Jews [A scnorrer is a poor Jew who relies on a rich Jewish benefactor]:

A schnorrer who was a regular Sunday-dinner guest at a certain rich man's house appeared one day with a young stranger who prepared to seat himself at the table.

'Who is this?' demanded the host.

'He became my son-in-law last week,' replied the scnorrer, 'and I have agreed to supply his board for the first year.'

A scnorrer implored the help of a wealthy baron for a trip to Ostend where he asserted the physicians had ordered him to take sea baths for his health.

'Very well,' said the baron, 'I will assist you, but is it absolutely necessary that you go to Ostend, the most expensive of all watering-places?'

'Ah sir,' said the scnorrer, 'nothing is too expensive when it comes to my health.'

136

Freud elevated the joke to a position of high seriousness, a subject for polite and intellectual conversation, and challenged the negative attitude of the upper-class Edwardians toward joking, and in championing jokes gave them permission to enjoy them as a source of simple pleasure.

Chapter Sixteen

World War One

The outbreak of World War One in 1914 created several new joke cycles, the army medical being one of the first:

A young lad was being examined by the army doctor who told him, 'Now, we want a urine sample.' The lad looked puzzled, 'I mean,' said the doctor, 'I want you to pee in one of those bottles on the shelf there.' And the lad said, 'what, from here?'

At his medical the young soldier dropped his pants and the army doctor said, 'Blimey, you've not got much down there.'
And the soldier replied, 'Well, we're only gonna fight them ain't we?'

Wartime jokes fell into three distinct camps: official patriotic jokes, favoured by political and military leaders; jokes that poke fun at the military hierarchy and its values and express a strong desire to get back to civilian life, which were not favoured by political and military leaders; and jokes that mock and deride the enemy, which were approved by all:

> The First Division went over the top - Parlez-Vous.
> The First Division went over the top - Parlez-Vous.
> The First Division went over the top
> To circumcise the Kaiser's cock,
> Inky-dinky Parlez-vous!

Bless 'em All was initially not on the approved list:

Bless 'em all - Bless 'em all
The long and the short and the tall,
Bless all the Sergeants and W O ones,
Bless all the corporals and their blinkin' sons...

The composer, Fred Godfrey explained to the *Daily Mirror* in 1941 why the song was not approved: 'I wrote *Bless 'em All* while serving in the old R.N.A.S. in France in 1916. And, furthermore, it wasn't, "Bless".'

The excellent French joke book, Perceau's 1913, *Histoires d'Hommes et de Dames* was a favourite with both French and British troops:

A widowed army officer expresses his astonishment that anyone can remarry after being married to such a charming wife. He explains that he has had a portrait of his former wife painted for him, and has made a hole in it, 'just where you suppose', and makes love to the portrait while giving himself the illusion of still possessing his wife. 'Yes,' replied his orderly, who overheard the conversation, 'but the colonel has forgotten to tell you that he makes me put my arse behind the picture!'

An English soldier and a French madam are having sex on the beach at night. 'Is it in?' he asks. 'No,' says the woman, 'it's in the sand.'
'Now, is it in?' he says.
'Yes,' she replies, 'it's in.' A few moments pass, and the man says, 'I don't know, I think I'll try it in the sand again.'

A wife learns that her husband has made advances to the maid and that he plans to come to her bed that night. So, she replaces the maid whom she sends on a pretence errand to the other side of Paris. That night she has sex like she has never had sex before, and when she is finally exhausted and can take no more she decides that is the

139

time for her revenge. She jumps from the bed, lights the bedside lamp and says triumphantly, 'I'll bet you're surprised!'

'Ah, sure is, Ma-am, ah sure is,' says her Negro servant.

Many wartime jokes were updated versions from previous conflicts, the following has been translated into at least a dozen different languages:

A young soldier panicked during a ferocious battle and ran for cover some distance from the fighting. He was crouched down behind a wall when he felt a hand on his shoulder.

'What are you doing here?' a voice boomed, 'think of your regiment, your comrades. Go back there a do what you know is right.'

Pulling himself together the young soldier stood up and said, 'Yes, sorry mate, you're right.'

'Mate! Mate!' bellowed the voice, 'I am your commanding officer.'

'Oh, sorry, sir,' said the soldier, 'I didn't realise I'd run back this far.'

J. Y. F. Cooke's 1906, *Stories of Strange Women*, contained the short story, *When the Vestilinden was Lost*, a heart rendering tale of how the only descendant of a noble family took the final minutes on a sinking ship to consummate his affair with a young cabin-girl before throwing her onto the last departing lifeboat while he went to his certain death. By 1916 it had been re-written:

The Vestilinden was returning to England and on the ship was an army Major who had been paying particular attention to a pretty young nurse, and everyone on board was talking about the progress of the affair. When a violent storm hit the ship and swept the lifeboats overboard, the major poked his head onto the bridge and asked the Captain, 'Are we in any danger, sir?' As the weather grew increasingly worse the Major again returned to the bridge, 'are we in any danger, sir?' and this he did three times until the Captain finally reacted furiously, 'Danger? We are in very serious danger, sir, why are you bothering me at a time like this? Are you afraid, Major? Is that it, sir, you're afraid?' And the Major said, 'No, not at all Captain, but I was just thinking that if the ship were going down I ought to profit by my last five minutes and fuck that nurse.'

There were literally dozens of humorous, "Trench Newspapers" available during the war, which basically fell into two categories, those like the *Wipers Times*, which was exclusively for soldiers, and others like *Blighty* which was for soldiers and civilians.

The *Wipers Times*, or *New Church Times*, or *Kemmel Times*, or *Somme Times* depending where the 12th Battalion Sherwood Foresters was at the time, was created by Captain F J Roberts and Lieutenant Jack Pearson while they were stationed at the ruins of Ypres, Belgium ("Wipers" reflects the difficulty British soldiers had with the pronunciation of the town). The first editorial introduction in February 1916 read:

Having managed to pick up a printing outfit (slightly soiled) at a reasonable price, we have decided to produce a paper. There is much that we would like to say in it, but the shadow of censorship enveloping us causes us to refer to the war, which we hear is taking place in Europe, in a cautious manner.

We must apologise to our subscribers for the delay in going to press. This has been due to some unwanted visitors near our printing works during the last few days, also to the difficulty of obtaining an overdraft at the local bank.

Any shortcomings in production must be excused on the grounds of inexperience and the fact that pieces of metal of various sizes had punctured our press. We hope to publish the "Times" weekly, but should our effort come to an untimely end by any adverse criticism or attentions of our local rival, Messrs Hun and Co., we shall consider it an unfriendly act, and take steps accordingly.

The paper included jokes, cartoons, comic rhymes, but the best humour came from the "Letters Page" contributed by the soldiers themselves:

141

Sir, may I draw attention to the fact that the gas mains of the town seriously need attention. I was returning from the Cloth Hall Cinema the other night when a big leak broke out on the Rue de Lille. It was only by promptly donning my gas-helmet that I was able to proceed on my way.

Signed: A Lover of Fresh Air.

Sir, on taking my usual morning walk this morning, I noticed that a portion of the road is still up. To my knowledge the road has been in this state for at least six months. Surely the employees of the Ypres Corporation can do better than this.

Signed: Early Riser.

Servicemen dealt with horror of war with dark humour and a sense of the absurd, the "DSO Award" (Dick Shot Off) being just one example. Royal Flying Corps fighter ace, Major Mick Mannock regularly joked about, 'Flamerinoes' and 'joining the sizzle brigade', until his worst fear was realised and he was shot down in flames.

The darkest and surely most distressing World War One joke was a collective one from a battalion of French soldiers in April 1917 at the Chemin des Dames after they were ordered to prepare for what they knew to be a futile offensive.

As the soldiers set out across open wasteland towards the waiting German machine guns, they bleated like sheep.

> What passing bells for these who die as cattle?
> Only the monstrous anger of the guns.
> Only the stuttering rifles' rapid rattle
> Can patter out their hasty orisons.

Anthem of Doomed Youth by Wilfred Owen.

Chapter Seventeen

Stand-Up Comedian

Throughout the war the music halls offered the British people a few hours of escapism, but when hostilities ceased in 1918 Music Hall took its final bow.

Music Hall had always been in a state of flux and since the 1890s its true spirit survived only in the back rooms and annexes of the tavern halls. Lewd comedians, drunken chairmen, and equally drunken audiences, that was Music Hall, a world away from the twentieth century plush all seated Variety theatres with their alcohol-free auditoriums and printed programmes.

Variety entertainment catered for all ages and all social classes, and from the end of World War One and for thirty years thereafter Variety theatres were where the British masses flocked to see live entertainment.

Variety also produced the first British stand-up comedians, a new style joker that was borne out of American Vaudeville.

Joe Cook is considered by many to be the greatest of all Vaudevillians, a one-man circus who billed himself as:

Master of all Trades. Introducing in a fifteen-minute act; juggling, unicycling, magic, hand balancing, ragtime piano, violin playing, dancing, globe rolling, wire walking, and talking. Something original in each line – Some Entertainment!

His talking was indeed, some entertainment:

I will now give an imitation of three Hawaiians. This is one (whistles), this is another (mimes playing ukulele) and this is the third (marks time with his foot). I could imitate four Hawaiians just as easily, but I will tell you the reason why I don't. You see, I bought a horse for fifty dollars and it turned out to be a running horse. I was offered fifteen thousand for him and I took it. I built a house with the fifteen thousand and when it was finished my neighbour offered me one hundred thousand dollars for it. He said my house stood right where he wanted to dig a well. So, I took the hundred thousand dollars to accommodate him. I invested it in peanuts and that year there was a peanut famine, so I sold the peanuts for three hundred and fifty thousand dollars. Now why should a man with three hundred and fifty thousand dollars bother to imitate four Hawaiians?

Vaudeville comedians like Cook were all round entertainers who dressed in loud suits and hit their audience with a myriad of skills, which at very least was singing, dancing, and telling jokes. But in the early twenties one comedian tried a different approach. Dressed in fashionable evening wear he casually sauntered onto the stage and began making quips, humorous observations, jokes, and talking to the audience as if they were old friends. He was Frank Fay, the first stand-up comedian.

Born Francis Anthony Donner in 1891 in San Francisco to Irish Vaudevillians, Fay adopted his stage name in 1916 when he became half of a vocal/comedy double act, Dyer and Fay. Soon afterwards he went solo and within two years had established himself as an entertainer who sang, danced a soft-shoe, recited comic monologues, and cracked the odd joke.

He made his New York debut at the prestigious *Palace Theatre* in 1919 which is testimony to how highly rated he was, but after creating a new type of comedian he blazed a trail for others to follow, and by the time he returned to *The Palace* in 1925 he was the headline act.

A booking at *The Palace Theatre* was the pinnacle of any Vaudevillian's career and only a select few ever played more than one week at a time there. In 1925 Fay played ten consecutive weeks, and at eighteen thousand dollars a week, Vaudeville's highest ever paid entertainer.

That same year the musical *No, No, Nannette* by Vincent Youmans and Irving Caesar had the popular *Tea for Two* in its score. Fay put it into his act:

(Fay Singing) Tea for two, and two for tea...
(Speaking) Ain't that rich? Here's a guy that has enough tea for two, so he's going to have two for tea, notice he doesn't say a word about sugar!
(Singing) Picture you upon my knee...
This guy just owns one chair! Tea for two, me for you, and you for me, alone... so here's the situation; the guy has one chair, but enough tea for two, so he has two for tea. What if anyone else shows up? He shoots 'em?
(Singing) Nobody near us, to see us or hear us...
Who'd want to listen to a couple of people drinking tea?
(Singing) We won't have it known dear that we own a telephone...
Oh, so this guy's too cheap to get another chair, but he has a telephone and he won't tell anyone about it...

Fay was never a populist and always carried an air of casual arrogance, but fame gave him extra attitude, and some. At a court case when asked his profession he replied, 'The greatest comedian in the world.' When his attorney asked why he would say such a thing, Fay answered, 'Why? I was under oath.' When he married the actress Barbara Stanwyk it gave rise to the joke:

Who's got the biggest prick in Hollywood?
Barbara Stanwyk!

In 1929 Warner Bros. cast him as the master of ceremonies in its most expensive movie to date, *The Show of Shows*, after which he starred in a succession of bland stage musicals and forgettable films.

The downward spiral continued until 1944 when Fay was chosen to play Elwood P. Dowd in the original Broadway production of *Harvey*, written by American playwright Mary Chase.

Harvey was a gentle comedy, about a gentle man with a drinking problem who kept company with a large imaginary rabbit. Fay was not the first choice for the role but received lavish praise for his performance which helped the play to a Pulitzer Prize for drama that year. However, when the stage show was turned into a Hollywood movie James Stewart was given the lead and Frank Fay, the father of stand-up comedy, drifted into obscurity.

Chapter Eighteen

Radio and Film

Britain won the war but for most it hardly felt like a victory, and the supposed heralding of a new dawn for the British people proved to be a time that promised much and delivered little.

While the upper classes partied through the "roaring twenties" life was tough for the poorest, and an economic depression together with high unemployment created an atmosphere of pessimism and gloom.

Yet somehow the Variety theatres thrived and despite competition from radio and films the twenties marked the beginning of its Golden Age.

Radio began as a commercial medium in 1922 when the British Broadcasting Company was formed by a consortium of manufacturers of radio sets. Five years later it became the British Broadcasting Corporation, publicly owned and funded by the sale of Receiving Licenses.

Early BBC programmes were mainly light music recitals and concerts, while comedians shied away from radio, afraid of giving away their live act. Comedians could, and many did, use the same act for decades secure in the knowledge that the live circuit was so extensive that by the time they returned to a theatre the audience would have long since forgotten their act.

Unable to attract the star comedians of the day the BBC delved into the less professional world of concert parties and made household names of comedians like Fred Spencer, Ronald Gourley, Jack Duncanson, Norman Long, and John Henry whose quiet and intimate Yorkshire drone proved perfect for the airwaves:

My pal Joe Murgatroyd comes from Yorkshire the same as I do. Of course, I am a Yorkshireman, you know. Oh yes, a lot of people think I'm an Oxford man, but I'm not. No, I'm a tyke... Joe comes from Heckmondwyke. That's in Yorkshire you know... it's near Cleckheaton. Oh, he's a very clever fellow. It was Joe that found out when you're hanging pictures it's a good thing to put a drop of oil on your thumb nail, and then the hammer slides off easier... He knows all about politics too. He was telling me the other day that there's only one man gone into the House of Commons with the right idea, and that was Guy Fawkes....

Henry's accent was the exception rather than the rule, in the mid-twenties a *Pronunciation Committee* was formed by the first BBC Director-General, Lord Reith who was determined to keep unwelcome vowels from broadcasts.

Reith was a blend of Scottish Calvinism, snobbishness, and arrogance, and one who believed that the Corporation's responsibility was to give listeners what was good for them rather than what they might want or even like.

Eventually he was persuaded to include a few Variety programmes, but *The Valve Set*; *The Indefinites*; and *Variety* were broadcast live from an empty studio and were predictably cold and lifeless. However, when the BBC proposed the same type of show in a Variety theatre with a live audience, managers formed an alliance to prevent any broadcasting from their theatres.

In 1933 a BBC Variety Department was created which resulted in more comedy on air and produced the first British radio comedy star in Oliver Wakefield, "The Voice of Inexperience":

You know, actually there a really very few subjects which I am qualified to and I actually find myself on the horns of a dilemma and it's not a particularly comfortable place to find oneself because a dilemma as you know has a very hard tooth, ehm horn and inhabits the frozen regions of northern Scotland and a very hardy animal the Scot is, existing almost entirely on haggis which is their national fish, ehm dish, a great nation the Scotch, real mixers, they never say when, ehm die, they go round having a dock with Doris and a wee buff of the bairn, of course I don't quite know what a dock is but Doris seems to get it...

148

While radio continued to be regarded as a threat to live Variety, films were not. The first purpose-built cinema in Britain opened in 1909 and within five years there were four thousand throughout the country with a combined audience count of around seven million.

Films were considered a novelty and some Variety theatre managers added short comedy films to their bills, a format that became known as *Cine-Variety*.

There was, initially at least, no objection from the acts, after all, how could silent black and white films compete with colourful live performances? A belief that began to wane as first the French and then the Americans produced the greatest silent movies ever made.

The jokes in films were physical, slapstick, although written jokes occasionally appeared in the subtitles, added after shooting which could, and often were changed or updated for later releases. The American *Biograph* movie, *The Toledo Blade* subtitled lead actor Fred Mace joking about the English:

London's a strange place... I was going into a tea shop on the Strand when I saw the notice, Lyons Brand Here. Well, you know the Strand isn't the place for wild animals, so I went inside and had a cup of tea. I told the girl I wanted a spoon, she said, 'Alright, I'll come and sit with you when the shop's empty.'

In 1926 Warner Brothers Studio released *Don Juan*, the first film to have a synchronized musical accompaniment which it followed a year later with the feature length, part talking, *The Jazz Singer*, and in 1928 made the first all-sound feature film, *Lights of New York*.

Sound changed everything for film comedians. Sound ruined the old jokes. Slapstick is unreal, and surreal. When words were added to slapstick, when the comedians talked, they became sensible, and sense and slapstick do not mix. It was not as funny. When the great film comedians like Buster Keaton, Harold Lloyd, and Charlie Chaplin spoke their comedy was greatly diminished.

The sole beneficiaries from the silent era were Laurel and Hardy, perhaps because their comedy was never entirely dependent on sight gags but on their characters and their relationship with each other.

149

Films were suddenly the main competition for live Variety, and the advent of sound meant Cine-Variety was especially tough on comedians, particularly if the film had a loud soundtrack. Most theatre managers helped by placing microphones in the footlights, allowing comedians the aid of the newly invented Public-Address system.

Regular Variety theatres quickly followed suit and installed PA systems of their own which made a significant difference to comedians who no longer had to belt out every joke and could add more finesse to their performance.

Perhaps the PA systems encouraged comedians to tell more jokes, certainly by the end of the twenties most Variety comedians while not exactly stand-up comedians in the Frank Fay mould, placed more credence on their jokes and patter.

Comedians like Billy Bennett and Dick Henderson, the latter a small rotund man who dressed in an ill-fitting suit, too-small bowler hat, and held a large cigar between his thumb and forefingers. In between an opening and closing song he cracked a succession of one-liners:

She came right up to me and looked into both of my eyes, and I looked into her one… Mind you, I didn't really mind her only having one eye, what I really took exception too was her teeth, not that I do in the ordinary course of events, but I did to hers because they belonged to her sister, and her sister has a bigger mouth than her...

Billy Bennett has the dubious distinction of inventing the trick of tagging his punch-lines with, 'Bum-bum!' either shouting it himself or having the drummer hit the bass drum twice (In America it turned into a snare drum roll and rim shot).

He was surreal before surreal entered the English language, in Bennett's world a Scotsmen broke his neck trying to lick medicinal whisky from his back, another broke his fingers telling jokes to a deaf person, while a postman had to turn his legs up at the bottom because his feet had worn away. Bum-bum!

In 1928 the definitive compilation of filthy limericks was published, *Some Limericks* by Norman Douglas.

The term limerick is most likely a reference to the City or County of Limerick in Ireland and a traditional Irish nonsense verse parlour game going back to at least the mid-nineteenth century. The game included the sung refrain, 'Will you, or won't you come up to Limerick?'

The first documentation of, 'limerick' as a description of a short poem was in the 1898 *New English Dictionary*.

Limerick verses are five-line rhyming jokes with the punch-line on the last line, a form made popular by Edward Lear, the thirteenth Earl of Derby who published his *Book of Nonsense* in 1855:

> There was a young person of Smyrna
> Whose grandmother threatened to burn her,
> But she seized the cat
> And said, 'Granny burn that,
> You incongruous old woman of Smyrna.'

Unsurprisingly bawdier versions were written, collected and published, all containing most of the same limericks, but what made Douglas's collection superior was his added commentaries:

Number 1:
> There was an old girl of Kilkenny,
> Whose usual charge was a penny;
> For half of the sum
> You might roger her bum –
> A source of amusement for many.

Douglas: Kilkenny, a slumberous old town famed for its cats and monastic ruins, is not the kind of place to harbour people of this profession. Puzzling over the matter, and scrutinizing the text more closely, I find that the lady is described not as *of* Kilkenny but as *from* there. I conclude, accordingly, that in youth she found her way from the green fields of Leister into some Dublin establishment, like many another country girl; and that it is her activities in the capital which are here commemorated. Be that as it may, nobody can complain of her charges.

The same year Douglas's controversial collection was published *The Joker* was released as a weekly paper. It was typical of British comic papers at the time, a mixture of adolescent jokes and terrible puns. The following is an extract under the heading: *Chirpy Chatter and Perky Patter*, a conversation between the fictional double-act, Bright and Gay:

'Hallo Bright, you look as if the world is treating you unkindly.' – 'It is, I tripped over the curb a moment ago and a lump of the world hit me in the eye. Made my eyes water it did' – 'That's because you've got water on the brain' – 'I've got no such sandwich' – 'Then, how do you get a flow of ideas?' – 'When my head swims.'

Chapter Nineteen

Knock, Knock!

Southern journalist, raconteur, and anthologist Irvin S. Cobb said in his joke book, *Tall Talk from Texas*: 'If this collector of jokes were asked to name the three stories that are told oftener than any others the answer would be that the three are all Negro jokes.'

Cobb had been a war correspondent in France during World War One and admitted that during his time there he had become a great admirer of American black soldiers. Nevertheless, his numerous 1920s best-selling joke books perpetuated the stereotype of the cowardly Negro.

'How dat Sambo? You says you was at de battle of Bull Run when I sees you at New York on de same night!'

'Yes Julius, you did for sartin. You see, our colonel says, boys strike for yer country and yer homes! Well, some struck for der country, but dis chile he struck for home.'

Cobb's 1923, *A Laugh a Day keeps the Doctor Away* included several "Gallows" jokes featuring Negroes, stark, astonishingly brutal:

It befell in the old days that a mob one night took a Negro out of a county jail in Southern Kentucky and carried him across the line into Tennessee and there hanged him at the roadside. As he dangled they riddled him with bullets and then kindled a fire under him with intent to destroy the body.

By the light of the mounting flames somebody saw something stirring in a brush pile, close by the scene of the execution. He kicked the brush away and dragged out an old coloured man, who had been on his way home when he saw the lynchers coming. He had deemed it part of prudence to take cover immediately. But as luck would have it, he had gone into retirement at the very spot where the mob halted to do its work.

Men poked big guns into his face and swore to take his life if ever he dared reveal what he had that night beheld. The old man protested that the whole thing was purely an affair of the white folks, in which he had no concern or interest. He was quite sure that by daybreak of the following morning all memories of the night would be gone from his mind. The leader of the mob felt it incumbent to press the lesson home to the consciousness of the witness. Still casually cocking and uncocking a long pistol, he flirted a thumb over his shoulder toward the gallows-tree and said: 'Well, you know that black scoundrel yonder got what he deserved, don't you?'

The old man craned his neck about and gazed for a moment upon the spectacle. 'Boss,' he said fervently, 'it looks like to me he got off mighty light.'

Black Minstrel comedians on the Vaudeville circuit were popular and accepted to a point, white audiences enjoyed Minstrel humour but would not tolerate a black man speaking directly to them. Black comics told their jokes to each other, or when working solo as if they were thinking out loud or talking to someone in the wings.

The only places where black comedians could speak directly to an audience was in the "Dark Houses", low grade venues for black audiences on what was known as the "Chitlin" circuit.

Dark House comedians were the first black professional entertainers to indulge in authentic African-American humour. They were assertive and graceful, and they told "lies".

'We didn't call them jokes at the time,' recalled song and dance man Sammy Davis Jr, 'we called them lies… that nigger sure can lie, was a common phrase.'

They were the first black stand-up comedians, and the first Americans to feature the black man as a trickster:

The boss suspects his black butler of stealing his cigars and shouts to him loudly in the next room, 'Samuel, who's been stealing

154

my cigars?' No answer. 'Samuel, who's been stealing my cigars?' the boss shouts even louder, but still no answer. So, he goes into the next room and confronts the butler. 'Samuel, didn't you hear me speaking to you just now?'

'No sir,' says Samuel, 'must be something wrong with the acoustics.'

'Is that so,' says the boss, 'I tell you what, you go into the next room and say something, and we'll see if I can hear you.' The butler goes into the next room and shouts at the top of his voice, 'Some flat-faced son of a bitch has been screwing the ass of ma wife!' He then returns to the other room. 'Did you hear me, sir?' he asks. 'You're right, Samuel,' says the boss, 'couldn't hear a word, here, have a cigar.'

Black comedians also played venues booked by the *Theatre Owners Booking Association* who supplied Variety acts for a circuit of third rate theatres that were also exclusive to black artists and black audiences.

The co-operative was formed in 1907 by F. A. Barrasso, a Memphis based Italian businessman who owned several run-down theatres and who, together with a few other white theatre owners created their own a small circuit. At its peak in the mid-twenties there were more than forty *TOBA* theatres across America.

Bad conditions, low wages, late night curfews, and various other "Colour Laws" earned *TOBA* the acronym, 'Tough On Black Asses'.

It was tough, but it was in those third-rate theatres and Dark Houses that American black comedy took its first tentative steps away from Minstrelsy and toward a folksy, southern Negro style which paved the way for the future smooth, hip, flamboyant, urban black comedians.

Vaudeville managers eventually allowed a select few black comedians to drop the blackface, comedians like Tim Moore, Pigmeat Markham, Mantan Moreland, Jodie Edwards, Bill 'Bojangles' Robinson, and Stepin Fetchit.

Civil rights groups later criticised those comedians for playing, "Uncle Tom" for the white man, but just as black musicians before

155

them gained acceptance and changed the musical taste of America, minstrel comedians like Bert Williams cautiously but deliberately changed the image of the black entertainer and subtly altered and toned down the more grotesque antics of Jim Crow.

Williams described his stage persona as: 'a shiftless Darky to the fullest extent, his fun, his philosophy. Show this artless Darky a book and he won't know what it's about. He can't read. He can't write. But ask him a question and he'll answer it with a philosophy that's got something':

Feller axed me, 'Are your neighbours honest?' I said, 'Sure dey is.' And de feller say, 'So why you keep a loaded shotgun near your hen coop?' I said, 'Dats to keep 'em honest.'

During the twenties in northern American states, and in New York especially, jazz music was the catalyst for the first sphere of social interaction in which racial barriers were challenged.

There was a significant advancement for African American entertainment in New York during the Harlem Renaissance of the late 1920s, a time when Black artists' literature, art, and music came to the fore in the Harlem district which quickly changed from a predominantly European immigrant neighbourhood (it was named after the Dutch town of Harlem) to an almost totally black one.

Harlem was where people of all colour could experience African-American culture, all-black revues, the coolest jazz music, and authentic black humour. Harlem theatres and clubs placed no restrictions on their comedians, they to their audiences and told black jokes:

A black hobo arrived at the better part of the Negro section in a southern city. Seeing a prosperous looking woman seated on a front porch, the hobo, dropped to his knees and began to eat grass.

'Man,' cried the woman, 'what you's doin' there?'

'I is eatin' ma-am,' said the hobo, 'I is dat hungry I is eatin' de grass.'

'You po' man,' said the woman, 'now, you jes come around to the back door, won't you?' And the hobo followed her till she

156

stopped at the back of the house and pointing to her lawn said, 'De grass is a lot longer here.'

While black comedians were making small inroads on the Vaudeville circuit an extraordinary number of Jewish stand-up comedians had already established themselves as headline acts.

Between 1880 and 1920 over two million Jews from Eastern Europe came to America, and by the turn of the twentieth century the Lower East Side of New York had synagogues, Yiddish book stores, Jewish eateries and grocery stores, and Jewish theatres.

Jewish Variety shows were a counterpoint to Vaudeville, Jewish acts for Jewish audiences, which meant that the great Yiddish comedians, and there were many, never achieved recognition outside of their own community.

The earliest Jewish comedians working on the regular Vaudeville circuit spoke with a thick European/Jewish accent and were so popular that Hebrew masks were sold in theatres so that people could mimic the comedians at home. The jokes mostly encompassed Jewish stereotypes:

A Jewish son said to his fader, 'Fader, may I have fifty cents?' and de fader said, 'forty cents! Vot you vont thirty cents for?'

The following generation of Jewish comedians like Eddie Cantor, Milton Berle, and Jack Benny distanced themselves from the dialect-laden speech and though they often played up to a comic Jewish stereotype they were not overtly Jewish.

At the beginning of the 1920s radio stations sprung up across America and the programme sponsors quickly realised that jokes sold products and were keen to sign the hottest Vaudeville comedians, however, like their British counterparts, American comedians were afraid of giving away their act. So, radio stations came up with the novel idea of employing joke writers, which meant the comedians kept their live act while gaining national exposure on air.

Radio shows were initially recorded live in front of an audience that was instructed to remain silent throughout the broadcasts for fear that any laughter or applause would distract the home listeners. That was until the early thirties when comedian Eddie Cantor delivered an ad-lib that sent the audience into fits of laughter. Listeners at home, far from being distracted, were delighted and their positive feedback resulted in the broadcasting of live radio shows to "live" audiences.

Live shows do have drawbacks however, as *Pepsident* sponsors of *The Bob Hope Show* soon discovered when Hope ad-libbed a response to Dorothy Lamoure after she told him to meet her, 'in front of the pawn shop,' and he said, 'Okay, you can kiss me under the balls!'

In 1934 Rolfe Arrow, a newspaper columnist for the *Hee Haw News* in Iowa, included in an article:

Knock, knock!
Who's there?
Rufus.
Rufus who?
Rufus the most important part of your house.

It was the first printed "knock, knock" joke, a joke cycle that caught on quickly, and just as quickly irked other columnists. Two years later an *Associated Press Newspaper* article in the August edition of the *Titusville Herald* roundly condemned the joke with its headline: *The Latest Nutsy Parlour Game!*

'What's this?' has given way to knock, knock as a favourite parlour game. Gone apparently are the days when the more serious minded settled down to a concentrated spar with jigsaw puzzles, anagrams, intelligence tests, and similar intellectual pursuits.'

While in the Heywood, *Reading Times* Hal Broun wrote:

Knock, knock!
Who's there?
A gang of vigilantes armed with machine guns, leather straps and brass knuckles to thump the breath out of anybody who persists in playing this blame-fool knock, knock game.

Knock, knock soon went global; a German version from the mid-thirties:

Knock, knock!
Who's there?
The Gestapo
The Gestapo who-oh shit!

It has been suggested that Shakespeare was the originator of the knock, knock joke. His drunken porter in *Macbeth* cries out, 'Knock, knock' and replies to himself, 'Who's there?' But without a punch-line we cannot credit Shakespeare as the creator, although there are Shakespeare Knock, knock jokes including: Who's there? Toby. Toby who? To be or not to be... Mandy who? Man delights not me; no, nor women either... Otis who? Oh, 'tis foul in here...

A more likely source is the popular parlour game from at least as far back as the late nineteenth century, called, 'Do You Know'. Writing in the *Oakland Tribune* in 1900, reporter Merely McEvoy wrote how he remembered from his boyhood:

Do you know Hiawatha?
Hiawatha who?
Hiawathagood girl until I met you!

Henry Betts in his 1929, *The Games of Children: Their Origin and History* proposed that knock, knock is a variation on the Victorian children's game, "Buff" whereby a child would thump a wooden staff on the ground and shout:

Knock, knock!
Who's there?

159

Buff.
What says Buff?
Buff says, Buff to all his men and I say, Buff to you again.

Betts proposes that the game got more sophisticated as children began inventing more sophisticated answers to, 'Who's there?'

While knock, knock was annoying some journalists "Little Audrey" was inspiring others.

The Little Audrey [Smith] joke cycle originated in America at the early part of the twentieth century, a fictional character and the main protagonist in macabre jokes:

Little Audrey and her grandma were standing on their front porch watching the men pave the street. There was a cement mixer, a steam roller, and all kinds of things to watch. All of a sudden grandma saw a quarter out there in the middle of the street and she dashed right after it, but as she went to pick it up along came the steam roller and rolled her out flatter than a sheet of theme paper. Little Audrey just laughed and laughed, because she knew all the time it was only a dime.

In 1937 she went international when Australia erected its first animated sequence neon sign, 'The Skipping Girl' to advertise the products of Nycander's Vinegar Brewery in Abbotsford (now a suburb of Melbourne). Colloquially she became known as, 'Little Audrey' and Australians were so taken with her that Little Audrey joke competitions were held by various newspapers throughout forties and fifties.

Little Audrey was playing with matches and her Mama said, 'You better not do that.' But Little Audrey was awful hard headed, and she kept right on playing with matches, and after a while she set the house on fire. It burned right down to the ground. Mama and Little Audrey were looking at the ashes, and Mama said, 'I told you so! Now young lady, you are really going to catch it when your Papa

160

comes home.' Little Audrey just laughed and laughed, because she knew all the time that her Papa had come home an hour early and had gone to bed for a nap.

Little Audrey was sitting on the corner just crying and crying when along came a cop, who said, 'Little Audrey, why are you crying?' And Little Audrey said, 'I've lost my Papa!' And the cop said, 'Why Little Audrey, don't cry, there's your Papa right across the street leaning against that bank building.' Little Audrey was overjoyed and without even looking she ran across the street, and a big two-ton truck ran over Little Audrey and killed her dead. The cop just laughed and laughed, because he knew all the time that wasn't Little Audrey's Papa leaning against that bank building.

In 1947 *Paramount Pictures* released the first of many Little Audrey animated cartoons, while the introduction of Tiny, her African-American friend made the *Little Audrey Comic Book* the first integrated comic book series without racial stereotypes.

Chapter Twenty

Stand-up Comic

Variety comics were the first British stand-up comedians, the first out-and-out joke tellers who boldly announced: 'Two fellers talking in a bar... Did you hear the one about?... Here's one...' and then lived or died on the strength of their punch-lines.

Ted Ray in his autobiography, *Raising the Laughs* said the notion to change his style came to him in the early thirties, he thought, 'Just be human. Stroll onto that stage in an ordinary suit, just as if you'd walked in from the street.'

Ray became a quick-fire gagster and a star name who headlined Variety bills and fronted his own radio shows. He weaved jokes into credible everyday events:

I went to a restaurant the other day and I recognised the waiter as an old comedian I used to work with, I said, well, you've come down in the world, working in a dump like this. He said, 'Yes, but I don't eat here.' Well, he brought me a salad and I called him back, I said, do you know I've found a button in my salad? He said, 'It must have come off while I was dressing it.' I finished the meal and he said, 'Well, how did you like it?' I said, it wasn't bad really, except for the sweet, and that was terrible. He said, 'What did you have the apple fritter or the jam roll?' I said, I don't know but it tasted like glue. He said, 'It was the jam roll, the apple fritter tastes like putty'.

Theatre and cinema managers soon took advantage of the new style solo comedians, those requiring only a stage and a microphone. When a cinema showed a full-length feature film the projector at some point overheated and had to be switched off. When that happened cloth curtains would be brought down in front of the screen and a comic would work in front of them, telling jokes until the projector cooled down and the film could restart. Those comics were known as, "Lantern Coolers".

Similarly, during a Variety show when a change of scenery was needed or props setting, cloths would be lowered, and a comic would stand on stage and tell jokes until the next scene was ready to begin. They were called, "Front Cloth Comics".

Variety managers and agents would inquire of a comic, 'Can you just stand up there and tell jokes?' Eventually, 'Can you do stand-up?', and those who could were stand-up comedians.

Many great comedians served their apprenticeship as front cloth comics, including the "Cheeky Chappie", the incomparable Max Miller (1894-1963), the first to take risqué material to the limit, the first "Blue" comedian.

"Off-colour" was an Americanism meaning, 'not clean, stained', a term used to describe the comedy of Burlesque comedians, but Miller thought the term too negative while black or dark comedy is something different entirely, so he chose the colour blue. He always offered his audience a choice, jokes from the *White Book* or jokes from the *Blue Book*. Inevitably they chose the latter:

'Ere did you hear about the eighteen-year-old girl who swallowed a pin but didn't feel the prick until she was twenty-one?

Miller was a pioneer in so many ways, the first blue comic, the first to make the milkman, coal man, rent man, and window cleaner the butt of infidelity jokes, and the first to give women their own sexual independence:

I went home the other night, now there's a funny thing... I said to the wife, hello mother of three, she said, 'Hello father of two,' no, listen... There's a fella standing there, not a stitch on! Can you imagine that lady? How's your memory, girl? He hasn't got a stitch on, I said, who's this? She said, 'Don't lose your temper, Miller, don't go raving mad.' I said, I'm only asking a fair question, who is

163

it? She said, 'He's a nudist and he's come in to use the phone.' Now, there's a clever one from the wife, ey?

He began his career in summer concert parties that played *al fresco* on the lawns at Brighton. Outdoor entertaining was tougher than in a theatre, comedians not only had to grab the attention of passers-by but had to turn them into an audience. Rather than act like some town crier Miller coaxed them to come closer, like he had a secret to tell, a method he kept throughout his career: 'Come 'ere, no listen, I want to tell you something, no, shush, you won't believe this, come 'ere...'

He also originated the much-copied technique of not quite finishing a joke, breaking off before the punch-line and letting the listener's mind do the rest:

I started courting a fan-dancer, to marry her, that was my plan. Now it's all off with the smashing fan-dancer, she fell down and damaged her... now, there's a funny thing...

In May 1929 he made his debut at the premier Variety theatre in Britain, the *London Palladium*, two years later he appeared on the *Royal Variety Performance*, and by the mid-thirties was commanding a weekly fee of fifteen hundred pounds plus a percentage of the box office. An incredible feat considering it was all on the strength of his live shows. He was an occasional guest on radio programmes, but it was not his forte, it was too intimate a medium, Miller was used to big auditoriums and radio made his performances sound aggressive and overly harsh. On top of which the BBC censors restricted him, he was banned several times, most famously for telling an unscripted joke, which fortunately the engineer managed to fade out before the outrageous punch-line was delivered:

I was walking on this mountain pass when I saw this beautiful blonde coming towards me with not a stitch on, not a stitch on, I didn't know whether to block her passage or toss me self-off...

164

Max Miller continued to headline London theatres until 1959 when a heart attack forced him into semi-retirement. His final theatre appearance was in Folkestone the following year, followed shortly afterwards with one parting shot at notoriety when at the *Black Lion Hotel* in Patchem he recorded an LP for *Pye Records* entitled, *That's Nice Maxie* which was promptly banned by the BBC.

The solution to jokes being eaten up by radio performances was finally resolved in 1938 when *Bandwagon* became the first British radio program to not only have a resident comedian, Arthur Askey, but also a resident joke writer, Vernon Harris, although for some time neither Harris or any other comedy script writer was credited as the BBC wanted listeners to think that the comedians were making up the jokes as they went along.

The success of *Bandwagon* encouraged the BBC to experiment with more comedy shows such as, *Variety Half Hour; Theatre of Varieties; Up with the Curtain; 'Appy 'Arf 'Our*; and the exceptional, *It's That Man Again* starring Tommy Handley.

ITMA as it was known, first aired in 1939 and its characters, catch phrases and quick paced lunacy paved the way for other surreal programmes such as *Round the Horn* and *The Goon Show*.

Tommy Handley had a quick mind and a gift for always being word perfect even as he sped through complicated arrays of non-sequitur play on words, various puns, or just plain gobbledegook. On a Variety stage Handley was a good comedian, on radio he was exceptional:

Well folks it's nice to be back in this part of the world again, and to see all the old faces full of anticipation and extra strong peppermints... I'm staying in a lovely hotel here, or rather it's a pub, it's called the Announcers Annexe... a pound a week all in, find your own food and sleep next door... I've got a lovely room, overlooking nothing, from my window I can see Oxshott, Bagshott, Bullford, Hookham, Cookham, and F-arnhum.

165

British television meanwhile was in its infancy, it had been broadcasting regularly for a few hours nightly since 1936, however, the BBC regarded itself as a public service, a responsibility it took very seriously and typically produced programmes that were conservative and dull, besides which, BBC executives believed television to be a novelty that the public would soon tire of.

As it happened the public had no time to tire of it because the government pulled the plug in September 1939, citing that its signal interfered with the frequencies of the highly secret radar system which would be vital in the impending war with Germany.

Chapter Twenty-One

World War Two

Long before the start of World War Two, Europeans were familiar with "Italian cowardice" jokes, which began in the 1890s after Italy attacked Ethiopia and suffered a humiliating defeat.

Prior to World War One, Italy signed a triple alliance with Germany and Austria-Hungary as a defensive strategy, but when its allies began attacking other countries they refused to be part of the offensives. When they did join the war in 1915 it was to fight *against* Austria-Hungary, and despite heavy losses they were ultimately victorious over the Imperial army.

Jokers chose to overlook Italy's brave and honourable stance and focussed on its changing sides. Like most joke cycles it would have eventually died out, however the constant failures of the Italian army sent by Mussolini to assist General Franco in the 1936-9 Spanish Civil War kept it well and truly alive:

Three officers of Franco's army were watching the progress of the battle, one was Italian, one was German, and the third Spanish. The German looking through his binoculars said with some horror, 'But they're fleeing, our friends are fleeing, look, look, the Italians are running away!'

'Let me see,' said the Italian officer somewhat agitated. And as he peered through the binoculars, his face, troubled before began to clear, until a large smile broke out, and with a broad gesture of his free hand cried out, 'Yes, they are fleeing, but proudly, like lions.'

At the beginning of World War Two, Mussolini knew that Italy was ill prepared for war yet still he entered the conflict in league with the Germans, but when Sicily fell, and the first air raids hit

Rome, Italy switched to the side of the allies. The Greco-Italian conflict of 1941 did little to help their cause either:

During the Greek-Italian war a badly wounded Greek soldier was captured by the Italians, the Greek was dressed in a red uniform which confused the Italian general; 'Why are you wearing red?' the general asked the Greek. 'Well,' said the Greek, 'I am bleeding all over, I am badly hurt, and I don't want to give you Italians the satisfaction of seeing my blood.' And with that the Greek died. The Italian general thought for a moment then said, 'What a splendid idea, I'll order brown trousers for my soldiers.'

German jokes were common prior to World War Two, particularly Nazi jokes, first told by comedians in German cabaret clubs.

German Cabaret was performed in small intimate halls where the shows were a mixture of short sketches, comic songs and monologues, all linked by an emcee who interacted with the audience and told topical jokes. The emcee comedians were occasionally satirical, but sex and sexuality jokes were much more prominent and covered subjects such as prostitution, homosexuality, and lesbianism, subject matter other German entertainments shied away from. For a short while however, the Nazi's focussed the comedians' attention.

One night shortly after the Nazi's came to power in 1933 a group of Nazi officers attended the Berlin *Catacombs Cabaret Club* where the star comedian was Werner Finck. When introduced the comedian walked onto the stage, raised his arm in Nazi style salute, and as the soldiers stood in returning the salute Finck said, 'That is how deep we are in the shit.'

Another night when he spotted Gestapo officers in the audience Finck asked, 'Am I going too fast for you?' and later joked that should it rain on a forthcoming Nazi parade all Jews in the vicinity would be shot.

Munich comedian Weiss Ferdi brought onstage large photographs of Hitler, Goering and other Nazi leaders, and thinking out loud said, 'Now should I hang them, or line them up against the wall.'

168

The jokes were not tolerated for long and after a brief flirtation with Cabaret as a method of feeding party ideology to audiences by mixing humour with Nazi propaganda, the Nazi's banned political jokes and social satire altogether which effectively killed off Cabaret as a form of satirical entertainment.

The Nazis banned Jews from performing altogether and fearing the worst most Jewish comedians fled abroad. The lucky ones found safety in England or America, but those who emigrated elsewhere in Europe were later captured by agents of the expanding Reich and sent to concentration camps.

Many Jewish comedians produced cabaret shows at the camps, Rabbi Erich Weiner, a prisoner at Theresienstadt in Czechoslovakia said that the comedians, 'strengthened their [the prisoners] will to survive as well as infused their power to resist.'

Telling jokes in Germany during the Nazi regime was dangerous, the Nazis outlawed any jokes aimed at their party or party members, declaring them, 'treacherous attacks on the state' which in effect meant that telling an anti-Nazi joke was an act of treason, an accusation cited to remove any dissidents and one evoked on literally thousands of occasions. Catholic priest Josef Muller was executed for allegedly telling his parishioners the following joke:

A German soldier was fatally wounded, an army chaplain asked him if he had any final wish, 'Yes,' said the soldier, 'place a picture of Hitler on one side of me, and a picture of Goering on the other side. That way I can die like Jesus, between two thieves.'

The indictment against Muller was, according to party line: 'one of the vilest and most dangerous attacks directed on our confidence in our Fuhrer. It is a betrayal of the people, the Fuhrer, and the Reich.'

A young Berlin munitions worker and widow of a fallen German soldier, Marianne Elise Kurschner was also executed after she was found guilty of telling the joke:

Hitler and Goring are standing atop the Berlin Radio tower. Hitler says that he wants to do something to put a smile on Berliner's faces. 'So,' Goring says, 'why don't you jump?'

East Germans told *Flusterwitzes* (whispered jokes):

A man is running down a Berlin alleyway when he is stopped by his friend who asks, 'Why are you running so hard?'
'Haven't you heard?' he says, 'It's illegal to have three balls!'
'But surely you have two,' his friend replies.
'I do,' says the man, 'but the Gestapo cut them off first and count them afterwards.'

Hitler bragged that he would have Britain on its knees by August 1940, when the month came and went, and Germany had not invaded Britain it created a new joke cycle. The following is Czechoslovakian:

Do you know why daylight-saving time has been prolonged this year? Because Hitler promised that before the summer is over, he and his army will be in England.

The Nazi's ordered all metal in Czechoslovakia to be melted down and sent to Germany for munitions, including metal statues:

Do you know that when the Nazis confiscated the statue of Moses, Hitler sent an urgent wire that this statue be transported to Berlin without being melted down? Moses was the only individual who could advise the Fuehrer how to get across the English Channel.

An Italian joke from the same cycle:

It was late 1940 and Hitler called Mussolini on the phone. 'Benito, aren't you in Athens yet?' And Mussolini replied, 'I can't hear you Adolf, you must be ringing from a long way off, presumably London.'

170

In Britain during early stages of the war the army medical joke cycle resurfaced:

An army doctor was examining a new recruit and as he cupped his testicles he said, 'Don't worry it's perfectly normal to get an erection in a situation like this.' And the recruit said, 'I haven't got an erection.'
'No,' said the doctor, 'but I have.'

Meanwhile BBC Radio comedians were given new directives, forbidden topics included the Home Guard, Sergeants and Colonels, Fire Guards, illegal marketing of goods, and any derogatory remarks about Spam. An innocuous Tommy Trinder joke went:

I was walking down Whitehall and a passer-by asked me, 'Which side is the war office on?' I said, ours I hope!

The joke was cut from a radio show because it was thought that it would lower morale.

Variety had its final hurrah during the war; there was little unemployment in Britain, people were either sent to fight, drafted into munitions, or worked down coal mines, and though wages were reasonably good, food, petrol, and luxury items were in short supply. Audiences flooded to the theatres where comedians like Max Miller helped them laugh in the face of adversity:

Do you like these black nights ducky? Do you like 'em, lady? No, they're nice, ain't they? I don't care how dark it is, I don't care, I like it! All dark and no petrol! I don't want any petrol, I didn't ask for any, I don't... Before the war I used to take 'em out in the country, it's any doorway now, 'ere...

When America joined the war in December 1941 Tommy Trinder quipped that its GI's (private soldiers) stationed in Britain were, 'Overpaid, oversexed, and over 'ere'. A GI joke cycle quickly ensued:

171

She wears GI knickers, one Yank and they're off.

GI's responded saying that British soldiers were, 'Underpaid, undersexed, and under Eisenhower', and had their jokes at the expense of the British:

A GI hated the food set before him in a London restaurant and barely touched it before pushing the plate away. The indignant waiter chided him saying, 'Aren't you ashamed to waste so much food? Don't you know that food will win the war?'
'Could be,' replied the GI, 'but who's going to get the Germans to eat here?'

Soldiers on leave was another popular joke cycle:

A cockney airman arrived back from his twenty-four-hour leave dripping wet, soaked head to toe. 'Blimey,' said one of his mates, 'is it still raining in London?'
'No,' said the airman, 'when I got home the wife was in the bath.'

A young English soldier and his girlfriend wanted to get married quickly as he was leaving for the front line in forty-eight hours. The couple knocked on the door of the local Vicarage and asked the Vicar to do the honours. 'Impossible,' said the Vicar, 'even a special license would take too long.'
'Well,' said the soldier, 'couldn't you just say a few words to tide us over the weekend?'

The monthly *Der Gag Bag* was the first American joke magazine to focus solely on the war in Europe. The first edition in 1939 portrayed Hitler on its front cover as a ventriloquist with his doll, 'Mein Chump', while the back cover had a 'pin the tail on the donkey' game with the donkey's bum in the image of Hitler.
Its popularity was only exceeded by *Yank Magazine* which began printing after America entered the war and was aimed specifically at Americans serving overseas. It quickly gained a circulation of over

two and a half million making it the most widely read magazine in U. S. military history.

Bennet Cerf's 1943, *Pocket Book of War Humour* was also a favourite of the American troops:

Two Russian ski-troopers are talking, and one says to the other, 'What's the first thing you are going to do when you get home?' And the other replies, 'Do you really have to ask?'
'Ok,' says the first, 'what's the second thing you're going to do?' And the other says, 'I'm going to take my skis off.'

Bennett Cerf (1898-1971) was a New York journalist and publisher who had successfully fought government censorship in the 1933 landmark court case, *United States V One Book Called Ulysses*, after which his Random House company published the first unabridged version of the classic James Joyce novel.

Aside from being a highly regarded publisher of quality literature, and one whose close friends included the eminent authors William Faulkner, John O'Hara, and Eugene O'Neil, Cerf was an avid collector of jokes and in 1944 released his second collection, *Try and Stop Me*, followed a year later by *Laughing Stock*, the latter mostly concerned with marital troubles:

'I simply got to divorce this woman,' the disconsolate man explained to the court. 'She insists on keeping a pet goat in our bedroom. The smell has got so terrible I just can't stand it no more.'
The judge shook his head. 'That sounds bad,' he admitted, 'but couldn't you just open a window?'
'What?' cried the man, 'and let all my pigeons out?'

Cerf also included some excellent Scottish jokes which he credited as being from the earlier *499 Scottish Stories for the price of 500* by American business analyst F. C. Forbes:

An Aberdonian walked into a high-class restaurant, dined well, and, paying the check, pushed a penny toward the efficient waitress.

173

She looked at the picayune tip, registered dissatisfaction and declared, 'Even the champion miser of Aberdeen tips us tuppence when he eats here.' The unabashed Aberdonian waved his hand and announced dramatically, 'Gaze on the new champion.'

Over the following twenty years Cerf compiled and published numerous joke books including, *Anything for a Laugh*; *Shake Well Before Using*; *Laughter Incorporated*; *Good for a Laugh*; *The Laugh's on Me*; and *Laugh Day*. In retirement he said that of all the numerous awards he received during his career, he was most proud of those given to him by the humour magazines, *The Yale Record* and *The Harvard Lampoon*.

World War Two ended in 1945, but for decades afterwards Italians remained the main butt of cowardice jokes, though in post war Britain the French were a close second:

An English feller arrived at Calais in 1947 and a French border officer asked to see his passport, 'Oh I'm sorry,' said the feller, 'I didn't think I needed it yet.'

'You have been to France before?' the officer asked condescendingly. 'Oh yes,' said the feller.

'Then you should know that you must have your passport ready for inspection.' The officer barked.

'Yes, it's just that the last time I was here I didn't show my passport,' the feller said.

And the officer shook his head and said, 'Oh, monsieur your memory is mistaking you, you always have to show your passport...'

'No, I assure you that the last time I was in France I did not,' the feller insisted.

'Ok, monsieur,' sighed the officer, 'and tell me where and when and how you arrived in France and did not have to show your passport?'

'Well,' said the feller, 'it was 1944, Juno beach, D-Day, and I couldn't find a fucking Frenchman to show it too!'

174

The French responded in their own inimitable fashion:

A French girl was depressed when her lover did not return to her at the end of the war, so she stripped naked and threw herself into the Seine. A man passing by saw her and jumped in the river and pulled her to the riverbank. But she was already dead. The man went off to find a gendarme. In the meantime, another man came by and saw the naked girl, so he lay next to her and started making advances, and as she did not resist he started to make love to her. When the other man returned with a gendarme he was horrified, 'Monsieur,' he cried, 'stop, stop, she is dead!' And the man jumped up and cried, 'Oh, sacre bleu, I just thought she was English.'

Nazi jokes lingered:

After the war the new German government appointed a Minister for de-Nazification, whose task it was to weed out Nazi's and those with Nazi sympathies who held government posts. A couple of years after his appointment he spoke at a large political rally telling them about his achievements: 'In the first year the de-Nazification programme eliminated two hundred Nazis. In the second year we eliminated two thousand Nazis, and last year we eliminated two hundred thousand Nazis. And this year we shall eliminate two million Nazis, and when we have eliminated all the Nazis in Germany we shall eliminate the Nazis in POLAND, FRANCE, ENGLAND... AND THEN THE WHOLE WORLD!'

A new German joke cycle was on their perceived lack of humour:

This German comic said to his audience: 'My dog has no nose. I know what you're thinking. How does it smell? It doesn't, but it has good ears and a pair of fully functioning eyes that compensates for it... My mother-in-law is so fat that she wears clothes in extra-large sizes... A horse walks into a Munich beer house and the barman says, 'Why the long face?' and the horse does not respond because it is a horse.'

175

Yet one must concede that the German version of the joke is far superior:

A barman walks into a stable and the horse says, 'Why the short penis?'

British war veteran jokes proved durable:

A woman asked a veteran, 'So, did you fight in the war?'
'Yes,' he replied.
'Were you ever hurt?' the woman pressed.
'Yes,' said the veteran, 'I was shot in the Dardanelles.'
'Oh, dear,' said the woman, 'are they still painful?'

Rationing began at the start of the war and remained for fifteen years, as did the jokes:

A woman asked her grocer for a cauliflower and the grocer said, 'Sorry, there's no cauliflowers.'
The woman said, 'Oh, you mean there's no cauliflowers for us working classes, but I bet if Lord or Lady Muck came and asked you'd have one.'
'Look missus,' said the grocer, 'There's no cauliflowers.'
'No, of course there isn't,' said the woman, 'but I bet if that floozy from number twenty-two comes in and asks, oh, I'll bet there would be cauliflowers then.'
'Alright,' said the grocer, 'let me ask you something. How do you spell dog, as in dogmatic?' And the women said, 'd-o-g'.
'Good,' said the grocer, 'and how do you spell cat, as in catatonic? And the women said, 'c-a-t'.
'And how do you spell fuck, as in cauliflower?' said the grocer, and the woman confused replied, 'But, there is no fuck in cauliflower.' And the grocer said, 'That's what I've been trying to tell you, THERE'S NO FUCKIN' CAULIFLOWER!'

However, the most enduring and surely the cruellest was the Holocaust cycle:

176

Do you want to hear a great Holocaust joke?
No, my granddad died at Auschwitz
Oh, was he gassed?
No, he got drunk one night and fell out of the Watchtower...

The World War One, *Blighty* had been reissued in 1939 as a shilling magazine that featured jokes, cartoons, and pin-up photographs of bikini clad young women.

The Blighties page of the December 1949 edition is an example of the type of jokes it contained:

A chef reports that some exotic tinned fish has come on the market that tastes like rubber.
Nothing like making your sardines stretch!

In 1958 *Blighty* became *Blighty Parade* and within a year *Parade*, a nude glamour magazine in which jokes were relegated to the odd saucy cartoon.

The fifties saw a boom period in the sale of British adult joke magazines, with the likes of *You've Had It*; *This Is It*; and *Basinful of Fun* all of which featured the usual joke suspects of foreigners, nagging wives, mother-in-law's, dumb blondes, big bosomed secretaries, leering drunks, along with ever more revealing female pin-ups.

Taking advantage of more liberal times in the 1960s were joke magazines like *Carnival*; *Laugh Magazine*; and *Funny Half Hour*, the latter of which featured many jokes originally in the Victorian erotic magazine, *The Pearl*, including:

A woman was worried because she had two green spots between her legs, so she went to see the doctor.
'Madam,' said the physician, 'you are married to a gypsy?'
'Yes,' exclaimed the woman.
Well,' said the doctor, 'tell your husband that his ear rings aren't real gold.'

Chapter Twenty-Two

American Wit and Humour

Nat Schmulowitz (1899-1966) considered jokes to be, 'the small change of history' and believed they had, 'detected and exposed the impostor and saved man from the oppression of false leaders.'

A son of Polish immigrants who ran a Speakeasy and Nickelodeon in San Francisco, Schmulowitz became a lawyer who gained fame defending the silent movie comedian Roscoe "Fatty" Arbuckle in the early 1920s. (Arbuckle was accused of murdering a young starlet at a drunken orgy and though acquitted without, the judge said, 'a stain on his character', a smear campaign by the press ensured the comedian's career never recovered).

Schmulowitz was also the most prodigious collector of jokes in history, and was owner of a great many rare books, pamphlets and magazines of humour that came in thirty-five different languages and covered a span of four centuries. The numerous rarities and out-of-print works included various editions of Joe Miller, Nasreddin, and Bracciolini.

On April Fool's Day, 1947 he donated his collection to the San Francisco Public Library, and to this day the *Schmulowitz Collection of Wit and Humor* remains the largest single collection of jokes in the world.

Two years after Schmulowitz's generosity, the excellent *Encyclopaedia of Wit, Humor, and Wisdom* was released, compiled by the American humourist Leewin B. Williams.

Williams had published a similar, though considerably smaller collection in 1938, his *Master Book of Humorous Illustrations* which was popular during wartime, but his encyclopaedia is a meatier joke book, containing almost four thousand jokes and humorous

178

anecdotes that the author had collected from the turn of the century to the book's release in 1949.

Subject matter covers most conventional aspects of American life and Williams boasts that, 'no dirt or smut' is within. That it has countless ethnic, racist, and sexist jokes is merely a sign of the times:

Ike and Rachel took baby Moses to the concert and were told by the attendant that unless the child kept quiet they would be given their money back and made to leave. Halfway through the concert Ike turned to Rachel and whispered, 'Vell, what do you think?'

'Terrible,' whispered Rachel. 'Ok,' said Ike, 'pinch the baby.'

The magistrate asked the accused, 'What induced you to strike your wife?'

And the husband replied, 'Well, your honour, she had her back to me, the broom was handy, and the back door was open, so I thought I'd take my chance.'

The oldest are Wild West jokes:

A rancher rode to see the doctor in town. 'Doc,' he said, 'something's awful wrong with the wife, her mouth is set, and she can't speak.'

'Oh,' said the doctor, 'it sounds like she's got lockjaw.'

'Lockjaw, well I'll be,' said the rancher, 'well, if you're doing your rounds next month, call in.'

Two old settlers, and confirmed bachelors sat in the backwoods. The conversation drifted from politics to cooking. 'I got one of them new-fangled cookery books but never could do a thing with it.'

'Too much fancy work in it, eh?' the other replied.

'You said it!' said the first, 'Every one of them recipes began, take a clean pan, and that settled it for me. (A later version gained the topper: I ain't had a clean plate since the dog died).

179

A 1951 New York joke book warned potential buyers, 'Prudes won't think it's funny'. *Over Sexteen* quickly became an international best seller, as did its follow up, *More Over Sexteen* and the remaining volumes in a series of seven.

Its editor, J M Elgart informed readers: 'In "originating" the old jokes, we devoted our time, intellect, and kleptomania to recapture the heights (or depths) of the original. To coin a word, it is HUMORISQUE, earthy hilarity that runs the gamut of humour from S to X.'

The jokes and cartoons in the *Over Sexteen* series are quite tame by today's standards, but were at the time extremely risqué and went as far as a publisher could without attracting the attention of American State censors:

First Fisherman: I hear you went fishing with a girl last week.
Second Fisherman: Yes, that's right.
First Fisherman: Catch anything?
Second Fisherman: Don't know yet.

King Farouk had been ousted as the head of Egypt by the powers that be. We can only assume that this did not please him very much. Nevertheless, while in exile, he summoned his legal aids and instructed them as follows: 'To show the people that I carry no grudge and bear no malice, I wish to donate a million dollars to the founding of a university in Egypt. There's but one condition. It must be named after me. I want it to be called, FAROUK U'.

Chapter Twenty-Three

The Green Book

When television began broadcasting again after the war the BBC re-enforced its strict rules on joke types with its infamous *Green Book*, a guide for radio and television producers.

Jokes about religion and royalty were already banned, as were ones about prominent politicians, but the *Green Book* went much further with an absolute ban on jokes about: Lavatories; effeminacy in men; immorality of any kind; suggestive references to honeymoon couples, chamber maids, fig leaves, prostitution, ladies underwear (for example, 'Winter draws in'), animal habits (for example, 'Rabbits'), lodgers, and commercial travellers; and extreme care should be taken in dealing with or jokes about pre-natal influences (for example, 'His mother was frightened by a donkey').

Most comedians followed the regulations, although Max Miller was suspended from radio after an unscripted joke about a man having an eye test:

'That's funny,' this feller said to the optician, 'every time I see F, you see K'.

Post war radio Variety shows sounded old hat, particularly when compared to the likes of *Band Wagon*; *ITMA*; and the hilarious mini-sitcom about the dysfunctional Glum family, *Take It from Here*:

Pa Glum: 'Ron, rush upstairs and fetch me your mother's toothbrush. I've got me new suede shoes on and I've trod in something.'

Then along came two shows that eclipsed all; *The Goon Show*, devised, co-written and starring Spike Milligan; and *Hancock's Half*

Hour written by Ray Galton and Alan Simpson, and starring Tony Hancock. *The Goons* and *Hancock* transformed radio comedy from what had been essentially, radio Variety, to pure radio comedy.

Terence Milligan was born in Ahmednagar, India in 1918 where he lived until Ministry of Defence budget cuts brought his family back to London in 1933.

Teenager Milligan was a fan of jazz music and a proficient ukulele player and crooner, and after winning a local singing competition was engaged as a singer in a local dance band, *The New Era Rhythm Boys*.

'In 1939 I was invited to partake in World War Two,' is how he described his call up to the army, and it was during his training at Bexhill-on-Sea that he acquired the nickname, "Spike" from his fellow trainees.

At the time the *Popeye* cartoon strip, written and drawn by E. C. Segar featured the Goons, 'The Goons tickled my sense of humour,' Milligan said, 'and any soldier I thought an idiot I called a Goon.'

After being wounded in action he drifted through numerous low ranked military jobs before embarking on a showbiz career playing in troop concert parties with the musical comedy act, *The Bill Hall Trio*.

On his return to England in the late forties, Milligan began pitching jokes to the BBC and impressed enough to be hired as a comedy script writer for *The Derek Roy Show*. When he proposed *The Goons* as a comedy series the BBC were not persuaded, but Milligan persisted and in 1951 they agreed on the condition that it was called, *Crazy People*, an attempt to make it more palatable by connecting it to the popular Variety comedians of *The Crazy Gang*.

Milligan gathered a cast of four; himself, Peter Sellers, Harry Secombe, and Michael Bentine for what was initially an unconnected and random sequence of jokes and short comedy sketches, such as the Tutankhamen one below:

Bentine: I can see him!
Milligan: Look! King Tutankhamen.
Sellers: Stop!

182

Bentine: What is it?
Sellers: We're too late.
Bentine: You mean...
Sellers: Yes. He's dead!

The second series was re-titled *The Goon Show* and Milligan decided to give each episode some semblance of a plot, though in Milligan's world anything was possible; Napoleon's piano was rowed across the English Channel, an army canteen flew, and after the duty 'constabule' was knocked out by a hand basin, 10 Downing Street was stolen: 'And when I come three... er, too... the building had gorn...'

The Goon Show ran for nine years and became a cult phenomenon, but Milligan had wanted his Goons to be much more satirical. The BBC shied away, 'Frightened out of their fucking jobs,' he complained to Pauline Scudamore, author of *Spike: A Biography*, 'Sellers could do any voice of any politician in the land, the Queen included and that made us lethal.'

Tony Hancock served his comedy apprenticeship in the years leading up to the war as an amateur concert party comedian in Bournemouth. During the war he had a stint in the RAF Gang Show after which he was one of the resident comedians at the infamous *Windmill Theatre*, London, where he performed between strip-tease acts.

When he landed the part of tutor to the ventriloquist doll, Archie Andrews in the hugely popular radio show *Educating Archie* (yes, a ventriloquist on radio) it elevated him to national stardom and in 1954 Hancock was given his own radio series, *Hancock's Half Hour.*

Hancock's writers Ray Galton (born 1930) and Alan Simpson (1929-2017) met in 1948 while both were recovering from tuberculosis at the Milford Sanitorium in Surrey. They formed a comedy scriptwriting partnership that culminated in numerous award-winning television series' including *Hancock, Steptoe and Son*, and *Comedy Playhouse.*

In the wake of the huge success of *Hancock's Half Hour* radio series came the inevitable television series, which made Tony Hancock the first television star comedian.

Hancock had a genius for painting scenes of physical comedy with only the slightest inflection of his voice, and his instinctive ability to derive laughs from what lesser comedians would consider an innocuous line was uncanny, even after he took to reading his lines from cue sheets, as he did for the famous *Blood Donor* episode:

How much do you want then? ...A pint? Have you gone raving mad? Oh, you must be joking, I don't mind giving a reasonable amount, but a pint, that's very nearly an armful, I'm not walking around with an empty arm for anybody...

Hancock's Half Hour ran concurrently on radio and television for three years, but as listening figures fell and viewing figures grew the decision was taken to drop the radio show, at which point Hancock decided to drop his co-stars, leaving himself the lone performer in the renamed, *Hancock*.

In 1961 Galton and Simpson wrote Hancock's first film, *The Rebel* which got mixed revues, and the comedian inexplicably fired his writers. From then on Hancock's career spiralled downwards and over the following seven years he cut away from his agent, colleagues, and friends, seeking solace in alcohol until 1968 when the troubled star committed suicide.

Galton and Simpson were members of the writer's agency non-profit co-operative, *Associated London Scripts* which involved most of the leading radio and television comedy writers of the fifties and sixties.

Comedian, actor, and scriptwriter Eric Sykes originated the idea in the early fifties and he and Spike Milligan persuaded other new comedy writers to join, eventually over thirty of them, including John Antrobus, Terry Nation, Johnny Speight, and Dennis Spooner. Those rather wonderful joke writers of *ALS* were largely responsible for taking British radio and television comedy into the modern era.

184

In 1961 Galton and Simpson became the first television scriptwriters to be given their due when they were included in the credits for the television series, *Comedy Playhouse*.

Not that it changed public perception much, as Ray Galton explained: 'English people would think that the only reason writers were employed was because Hancock hadn't got time to write his own stuff. It didn't occur to them that he couldn't write his own stuff, and without us he wouldn't have stuff to do. I still have to say to people that Hancock's view was, "You're the writers, you write it; I'm the actor, I'll perform it." And he did not add anything. But people do not believe that. Even now if a newspaper wants to use a gag from one of our shows, they don't credit us, they attribute it to Hancock or Steptoe.'

In the late fifties a journalist asked comedian Rob Wilton if he believed Variety was dead; 'I wouldn't be surprised,' Wilton said, 'it was very ill when I was in Barnsley a few weeks ago.'

The increasing popularity of television severely curbed British cinema audiences, but it was nothing like the devastation it wrought on Variety.

Audiences had been steadily declining throughout the fifties and long before the end of the decade they slumped to an all-time low. In a final effort to attract customers managers offered nude shows and rock 'n' roll acts, which only served to alienate family audiences further.

Denis Norden wrote in his 2008 semi-autobiographical, *Clips from a Life*: 'Looking back on it, Variety was really an inter-war phenomenon. In essentials, it came to an end on the third of September 1939. While it lasted, it was the most consistently successful and fulfilling family entertainment this country has known. After the war, it died of television, nude shows and the indifference of the young.'

The joke owes much to the Variety comics and their Vaudeville counterparts, for it was they who brought it to its modern form, they were the first professional, out-and-out joke tellers.

185

They also came up with the comic's, "rule of three", that is grouping jokes on the same subject into sets of three, and like a boxer, jab, jab, punch:

Some advice for men my age: Never pass a bathroom, don't trust wind, and if you get an erection, use it, even if you're on your own.
Vaudeville comic, George Burns.

Chapter Twenty-Four

American Stand-up Comedy

The 1930s Depression killed off live Vaudeville and forced many of its entertainers into early retirement. Stand-up comedians however found work aplenty in nightclubs, cabaret rooms, holiday resorts, and since the 1940s the hotel-casino lounges of Las Vegas, perfect venues for quick fire gagsters like Henny Youngman:

I've been in love with the same woman for over forty years, if my wife ever finds out she'll kill me...

A host of American/Jewish comics like Youngman, Milton Berle, and Jack Benny became household names in the post-Vaudeville era, and it was they who were instrumental in providing a secular cultural identity, not of Jews as religious people, but of Jews as *funny* people.

In the late fifties a new generation of Jewish comedians broke onto the scene, comedians like Mort Sahl, Jackie Mason, Woody Allen, and Lenny Bruce who were some of the first comedians to ignore the traditional set-up, punch-line formula of a joke. *Monty Python* member Eric Idle, described Mort Sahl as, 'the first alternative, observational stand-up comedian.' Sahl's humour was caustic, satirical, and intellectual:

Liberals feel unworthy of their possessions, while Conservatives feel they deserve everything they've stolen...

He was an alternative to the conventional suited, bow-tie joke tellers, opting to dress in casual slacks and Ivy League sweaters while adopting a more conversational style of stand-up.

John F. Kennedy became a fan, and a friend, not that it excluded him from Sahl's jibes, which came back to haunt him after the

President was assassinated and he was effectively blacklisted by the powerful players in the showbiz industry.

It remained that way for some time until the counter culture generation of the late sixties rediscovered him. Sahl picked up right where he had left off:

Richard Nixon! Would you buy a used car from this guy?

When Lenny Bruce died of a morphine overdose in August 1966, *Time* magazine called him: 'A leading outpatient of the sick comic-school,' and said that, 'he viewed life as a four-letter word and, with gestures commented blackly on it.'

Lenny Bruce the comedian is all too often overshadowed by Lenny Bruce the legend, focussing on his expletive language, police arrests, and drug abuse, but he was a breath-taking comedian, daring social commentator, and the founding father of modern stand-up comedy.

'Lenny paved the way for all of us,' said comedian Red Foxx, 'but you've got to remember one thing... heroes ain't born, they're cornered.'

Bruce started out as an innocuous comic impressionist in the early fifties before working as emcee in seedy Los Angeles strip clubs which liberated him and allowed him to experiment and create humour from whatever came to mind during his sets.

Bruce wrote in his autobiography, 'I could just wheel and deal for hours, and the same people started coming every night, and there was always something different, and it would really drive them nuts. I had a whole bagful of tricks that I'd developed in the burlesque clubs. There was already this "in" thing with all these musicians who had heard of me, but the controversy that actually did, let's say, "make" me was the bit I call, Religious, Inc.'

Religious Inc. features a gathering of religious leaders eager to hear the latest marketing reports from Reverend Roberts. The meeting is interrupted by a phone call from the newly elected Pope John to whom Roberts must explain the problems they are experiencing with the civil rights movement in the south:

188

... they're bugging us again with that dumb integration, no, I don't know why they want to go to school either... yeah that school bus scene, well, we had to give them the bus, but there's two toilets on each bus... they're bugging us, they say get the religious leaders, make them talk about it... I know it, but they're getting hip, yes, no, they don't want no more quotations from the bible they want us to come out and say things, they want us to say, let them go to school with them...no, I did the walking on the water and snake into the cave, they don't wanna hear that jazz anymore, and that stop war, every time the bomb scare, yeah, they keep saying, thou shalt not kill means that and not amend section A... yeah, of course they're communists...

Bruce turned off his internal censor and ran with any idea that popped into his head, literally creating jokes in the moment. But being a free-flowing comedian meant that sometimes the jokes failed, and when that happened Bruce admitted as much; 'I wasn't very funny tonight, sometimes I'm not. I'm not a comedian, I'm Lenny Bruce.'

His humour mostly fixed on race hate and bigotry, religion, and challenging the prevailing attitudes to sex, drugs, and language.

He upset the status quo, and he needed to be silenced. The 1965 John Magnuson's, *Performance* film captures Bruce opening his act with the line: 'I have been on television, mostly newsreels...'. At the time he had been arrested nine times in four different American cities, banned from performing in Australia, and refused re-entry into Britain.

Initially he held his own and early arrests and court appearances merely became part of his act, but as time went on and the arrests and court cases stacked up, club owners, afraid of losing their license, ceased to book him. Bruce became a comedian without a stage.

The arrests and subsequent trials together with a worsening drug addiction wore him down until he became a sad caricature of himself. In 1966 promoter Bill Graham gave Bruce a gig supporting Frank Zappa and the Mothers of Invention at the legendry Fillmore Auditorium in San Francisco. 'I was not really a fan,' said Graham, 'but I felt he was being denied his rights. What I wanted to present was a combination of talent and a martyr, a man who was truly fighting for his sanity and fighting for his life.'

Lenny Bruce the quintessential hipster comedian played his last performance to a hippie rock crowd, slouching around the stage in a deranged manner while conveying the torment of a broken mind. The crowd laughed, at him, not with him. Six weeks later he was dead.

Comedians rarely change anything, Bruce was the exception. His five-year battle with the law and self-proclaimed protectors of public decency helped bring down barriers to free speech in America which enabled the following generation of comedians to speak openly without fear of reprisal. He was more than a comedian, he was Lenny Bruce.

Throughout the sixties the American media complained bitterly about an epidemic of "sick" humour that they claimed was infecting the country. Lenny Bruce was the comedian they took most exception too, but as they no doubt heaved a collective sigh of relief over his death, along came a joke book that raised their hackles again, the 1968, *Rationale of the Dirty Joke* by Gershon Legman (1917-99).

Legman (real name not a pseudonym) was an avid joke collector and joke analysist of the Freud school who believed that jokes disclosed infinite aggressions, especially male aggression towards women, and were he said, 'essentially an unveiling of the joke teller's own neuroses and compulsions.'

He was already a cult figure in New York, he inspired the sixties slogan, "Make Love, Not War" (what Legman actually said was, 'We shouldn't be killing, we should be fucking'), allegedly invented the vibrator, and was the infamous editor of the psychoanalytic quarterly magazine, *Neurotica*.

After graduating from Pennsylvania High School in the late thirties Legman settled in New York where at the age of twenty-three he published his first book: *Oragenitalism: An Encyclopaedic*

190

Outline of Oral Technique in Genital Excitation, Part 1, Cunnilinctus. Unsurprisingly, the book did not impress the authorities and after his publisher's office was raided Legman fled the state.

His follow up book, *Love and Death* was a fierce polemic on violence as the real pornography of the age which Legman was forced to self-publish and mail copies to customers. When the U.S. Postal Service accused him of sending illicit material in the mail and cut off his deliveries Legman, who by this time had his own FBI File, left the country for France, taking with him his vast collection of folklore, limericks, comic anecdotes, and jokes.

Rationale of the Dirty Joke is Legman's transcriptions of his vast joke collection, some sixty thousand variants, almost all of which are dated and traced to their origin. (This author is greatly indebted to Legman, not least for the origin of many of the jokes in this book.)

The first volume of *Rationale* is categorised under, "clean" dirty jokes, with relatively mild themes such as, nervous brides, phallic bragging, Water Wit, and infidelity:

A doctor is caught in bed with a farmer's wife and explains that he is only taking her temperature. The farmer cocks his shotgun and says, 'Well, I guess you know what you're doing doc, but when you take it out that thing better have numbers on it.'

The first collection also includes jokes from various countries and reveal more about a country, its social problems and its people than any official party line:

A customer asked a saleswoman in a Moscow department store, 'Don't you have any shoes here?' And the saleswoman said, 'No, we don't have any electrical goods. No shoes is on the next floor.'

The second volume, published in 1975 under the title, *No Laughing Matter* contained the "dirty", dirty jokes and covers subjects like prostitution, disease, castration, and homosexuality:

191

Two travelling salesmen discover the hotel has only one room available, and that with a double bed, so they agree to share a bed together. They're lying in the dark when one says to the other, 'Don't answer now, but are you by any chance sucking me off?'

When Legman died in 1999 the *New York Times* facetiously described him as a, 'self-taught scholar of dirty jokes'. But Legman was passionate about jokes and their cultural importance, and if the history of folklore is a history of human thinking then jokes need to be collected, recorded, and published, and who better than someone who considered the joke worthy of serious psychoanalytic study?

The American media was right about one thing, "sick" joke cycles were rife during the sixties, in Britain as well as America.
The American, *The Best of Sick Jokes* by Max Rezwin in 1962, featured the first printed "Mummy, mummy" jokes:

Mummy, mummy granddad's going out.
Well, throw some more gasoline on him.

Part of the sick cycle and probably the most controversial were "Dead Baby" jokes, told mostly by adolescents with the intent to shock and outdo one another for grossness:

What's the difference between a truck load of dead babies and a truckload of bowling balls?
You can't unload bowling balls with a pitchfork.

It was proposed by some that dead baby jokes reflected societal changes and guilt caused by the new contraceptive pill (available since 1960). When abortion was made legal in Britain in 1967 and in some states in the U. S. in 1970, it also became part of the joke cycle:

Mummy, mummy what's an abortion?
Ask your sister.
But I don't have a sis...

192

"Wind-up Doll" jokes also began in the sixties, initially a non-contentious cycle that originated in Los Angeles where the jokes were aimed at Hollywood celebrities and American politicians:

The Eisenhower Doll; you wind it up and it does nothing for eight years.

Soon it was part of the sick joke cycle. In 1962 Jack Wohl and Stan Rice produced: *Dolls My Mother Never Gave Me*:

The Muscular Dystrophy Doll; you wind it up and it falls down.

Least contentious of the sick cycle were "moron" jokes, briefly popular in the thirties but more so in the late sixties and seventies. It spread worldwide and endures today where it is especially popular in India:

Moron-ji and his wife are drinking in a coffee shop and Moron-ji says, 'Drink quickly.' His wife asks, 'Why?' and Moron-ji says, 'Because it says, hot coffee five rupees, cold coffee ten.'

Moron-ji was asked the eternal question: What came first the chicken or the egg? Moron-ji laughed and said, 'Uh Yaar, whatever you order first will come first.'

The sixties produced other less contentious joke cycles, if not less offensive to those who were the butt, some more durable than others. Hippie jokes were relatively short lived:

Standing at a bus stop a feller turned to the person next to him and said, 'Look at that teenager over there, the one with the long hair smoking the strange smelling cigarette. Is it a boy or a girl?'
'It's a girl,' came the reply, 'she's my daughter.'
'Oh, I'm sorry my dear,' said the feller, 'I would never have been so forward if I'd known you were her mother.'
'I'm not, I'm her father.'

193

The anarchic schoolboy, "Little Johnny" also came to the fore in the mid-sixties:

A teacher asked the class for a sentence using the word 'contagious'. Stephen stood up, 'Please Miss, last year my brother had measles and I wasn't allowed near him cos my Mum said it was contagious.' Then Mary stood up, 'Please Miss, my Nan says there's a bug going around, and it's contagious.'
'Well done,' said the teacher, 'anyone else?'
Little Johnny stood up, 'Please Miss, the feller next door is painting his fence with a two-inch brush, and my Dad said it'll take the contagious.'

Little Johnny at Sunday school and the teacher is telling the story of Lot. 'And God told Lot to take his wife and flee from the city,' says the teacher, 'But Lot's wife looked back, and she was turned into a pillar of salt.'
'Wow!' says Johnny, 'So, go on, what happened to the flea?'

The cycle was popular in numerous countries including Russia, where "Little Vavochka" made life difficult for his teacher, Marivanna:

The teacher draws a cucumber on the blackboard and asks, 'Children who can tell me what this is?' Little Vavochka raises his hand, 'Please Marivanna, it's a cock!' Shocked to tears the teacher runs out of the classroom. After a short while the principal storms in and shouts: 'All right, what did you do now? Which one of you brought your teacher to tears? And who drew that cock on the blackboard?

The "Light Bulb" cycle was originally created from a "Polack" joke in the late sixties:

How many Polacks does it take to change a light bulb?
Three – one to hold the light bulb and two to turn the ladder.

194

The joke cycle proves to be as adaptable as it is abiding:

How many sex therapists does it take to screw in a light bulb?
Two, one to screw it in and the other to tell him he's screwing it the wrong way.

The decade also saw 'Gay' became synonymous with homosexual. It was first adopted by American West Coast homosexuals as a positive word to describe themselves, prior to which derogatory words like, 'fruits', 'queers', and 'fairies' were most prevalent:

A Bronx teenager said to his tough Sicilian father, 'Pops, Johnny says I'm a queer.'
And his father said, 'Yeah, well punch him in the face.'
'I can't,' said the son, 'he's so cute.'

The word, 'gay' originally meant, 'happy, carefree,' which in the eighteenth century in England became a slang word that implied prostitution and living on one's wits.
'Gay' meaning homosexual, was first used in the 1920s and thirties and is present in the works of Noel Coward and Gertrude Stein, amongst others.

Predictably the sixties Women's Liberation Movement also created a joke cycle:

History remembers Emily Davison who threw herself under the King's horse and became a martyr for the suffragette movement. But nobody remembers her husband who didn't get his dinner that night.

The first feminist movement in England went hand in hand with the campaign for the abolition of slavery and child prostitution. Barbara Leigh Smith and friends began meeting in the 1850's at Langham Place in London to discuss the needs of women, focussing largely on education, employment, and marital law.

In 1867 the infamous "Ladies of Langham Place" became the *London Society for Women's Suffrage* which published the monthly journal *Englishwoman's Review* for similar groups around the country. A joke that appears in numerous nineteenth century joke books goes:

'Where,' asked the woman-suffrage orator, 'would man be today if it were not for women?'
And a voice answered from the gallery, 'Eating strawberries in the Garden of Eden.'

The first wave of feminism began with the Suffragette movement at the beginning of the twentieth century which in 1919 gained suffrage for women in America and in Britain for women with property over the age of thirty.

The second wave of feminism in the sixties gave women a reputation as men haters, but most sixties feminists were cool, groovy, and fun, and they did not burn their bras!

At a protest rally against the Miss America beauty contest in 1968 a group of feminists produced a live sheep and crowned it Miss America before tossing their high-heels, bras, girdles, and curlers into a, "Freedom Trash Can", the contents of which they did initially intend to burn, but the police advised against it as they were on a wooden boardwalk. However, when a journalist for the *New York Post* mentioned this and called the protestors, 'bra-burners' the rest of the American press picked up on it and the myth was born.

Sixties feminists were concerned with issues of equality and discrimination, and the phrase and concept of "Women's Lib" was invented by women who became active in business and politics, and who demanded equal access to a university education and a career. Such demands inevitably gave rise to lesbian and "dyke" jokes:

One lesbian said to the other, 'Now, let me be frank...' and the other said, 'No, I want to be Frank, you be Ernest.'

The word lesbian originated in the late nineteenth century from the Greek *lesbios*, from the Greek island of Lesbos, home of Sappho who expressed affection for women in her poetry.

Dyke was first coined in the1940s from the American *bulldyke*, a word used to describe a female of masculine appearance or manner, which later became a generic word for lesbian.

But dyke jokes were not the only ones to emerge in the sixties. There were plenty of sexist jokes with men as the butt:

A woman was in swinging London having a fantastic time shopping in the summer sales and picking up bargain after bargain; shoes, a sweater, a dress, until in one boutique a sales clerk shouted, 'Is there a Mrs Smith in the shop, I have an urgent phone call.' She rushes to the phone and a female doctor tells her, 'Oh, thank God we finally tracked you down. I'm sorry but your husband has been in a terrible accident and is in a critical condition...'

The woman told the doctor that she'd be there as soon as possible. But then as she was about to leave the boutique she realised that she was cutting short the best day's shopping of her life, so decided to get in just a couple more purchases before heading to the hospital. She ended up shopping the whole morning, then suddenly remembering her husband she jumped into a taxi and raced across to the hospital where she was met in the corridor by a female doctor who glared at the number of shopping bags she carried. 'You finished your shopping, didn't you?' the doctor said, 'I hope you're proud of yourself because while you were having a good time for the last three hours your husband was in the intensive care unit. Well, I can tell you it will be your last shopping trip because for the rest of his life your husband is going to need round the clock care and as from now you are his nurse.'

And as the woman broke down and began to sob uncontrollably the doctor laughed and said, 'I'm joking. He's dead. What did you buy?'

Once upon a time there was a beautiful princess who was happy and contented and in love with the world. One day out walking she came upon a frog who told her: 'I was bewitched, I am really a

197

handsome prince, and if you kiss me, I shall become so again, and we shall be married, and I will be King, and you will be my Queen and you will have my children, and we shall live happily ever after.

That night as the princess dined on a repast of lightly sautéed frog's legs in a white wine sauce, she smiled, looked down at her beautiful dish and said, 'I don't fucking think so.'

A honeymoon couple went to Blackpool and on the beach decided on a donkey ride. The wife's donkey got stubborn and refused to budge so she whispered into its ear, 'That's once'. The donkey still refused to move so again she whispered into its ear, 'That's twice.' When the donkey still wouldn't budge she said, 'That's three times' and took out a gun and shot the creature dead.

The husband said, 'My God, love, that's a bit extreme! Was that really necessary?' And the wife, smiling, linked his arm and as they started out along beach she whispered in his ear, 'That's once…'

The above is from the 1330, *El Conde Lucanor* by Don Juan Manuel, and also in Straparola's 1553 *Piacevoli Nottid*, though on both counts the wife is the complainant.

Sexist jokes against women have been told for thousands of years, but for one comedian in the mid-sixties the jokes proved costly.

In his nightclub act Woody Allen ridiculed a generic comic wife, referring to her as 'Quasimodo', joking that he gave her an electric chair for her birthday, and while holding up a picture of her and a house, said, 'She's the one with the shingles.' On an *NBC Television* show, he joked, 'My first wife lives on the Upper West Side and I read in the newspaper the other day that she was violated on her way home. Knowing my first wife, it was not a moving violation.'

The put downs were relentless and received huge laughs, but Allen's ex-wife, Harlene was not impressed and compiled a dossier of his comments, quips, and jokes, including the one about rape and a moving violation. She then filed a million-dollar lawsuit for defamation of character.

Allen maintained that they were 'just jokes' and Harlene was being oversensitive. Harlene responded by raising the lawsuit to two million dollars.

Woody Allen would have been the first comedian to be sued for his jokes had he not settled out of court, a settlement that included an agreement that he would stop telling jokes about his ex-wife.

Chapter Twenty-Five

Race

For all the furore over sick joke cycles there was no public outcry about race jokes. In America the targets were African-Americans while in Britain the butt of race jokes was usually those of Asian and Caribbean origin. Few questioned their noxious nature, they were "just jokes" and ethnic minorities appeared to take them as such.

In 1963 Dr Charles Winick revealed in his *American Imago* that of the thirteen thousand and eighty-four current jokes being told by ninety-two comedians in New York, the two main subjects were sex and race, seventeen percent about sex and eleven percent about Negroes.

"Elephant" jokes were not included in Winick's calculations despite many believing that they were cloaked racist jokes. They started out quite innocently in the early fifties:

Why do elephants wear shoes with yellow soles?
So that you can't see them when they float upside down in the custard.

Have you ever seen an elephant floating upside down in custard?
No.
There you go then…

By the sixties there were elephant trading cards and elephant jokes appeared regularly in newspaper columns throughout America. There was however, a darker side to the joke, the elephant being a euphemism for a black man:

Why does an elephant have four feet?
It's better than six inches.

How can you tell when an elephant is in the bath with you?
By the smell of peanuts on his breath.

The last joke an alleged reference to the intrusion of black people into the most intimate areas of white people's lives, the black man portrayed as a sexual threat, a notion originally perpetuated by white slave owners to divert attention from the fact that many regularly raped their black slave women.

"Rastus" jokes were considered the least truculent of race jokes, first created at the beginning of the twentieth century. By the 1960's Rastus was popular both in America and Britain:

Rastus and a rich white Texan were crossing a bridge one night and both desperate to relieve themselves agreed to do so off the side of the bridge and into the water below. After a few seconds the Texan said to Rastus, 'My, that water's cold.'
'Uhum,' said Rastus, 'deep too.'

Rastus was a generic, derogatory name for a black man, likely rising from the black deacon, Brer Rastus in the popular *Uncle Reamus* books written by Joel Chandler Harris in the 1880s.
Despite never being a common black name (an 1870 census reported only four black people named Rastus in the entire U. S.), by the turn of the century Rastus was established as a major character in race jokes
He was a stereotype of an ever upbeat black man, one who became a familiar comic character in Minstrel shows; fictional works such as *Adventures of Rastus Brown in Darktown* (1906); in popular songs like *Rastus, Take me Back* (1909); on radio; in early films, most notably the Rastus "shorts" with titles like *How Rastus Got His Chicken* and *Rastus Runs Amuck*; and in jokes:

Rastus' wife, Liza sent him to the doctor because of his inability to perform in bed. Three hours later Liza goes looking for him and finds him on a street corner all dressed up in fancy duds.

Liza said, 'Rastus! What you doin' here in yuh best duds on a street corner?'

And Rastus said, 'Liza, ah done went to the doctor, and he said ah was impotent. I figured, Rastus if you is impotent, you gotta dress impotent.'

In the context of Rastus jokes, Liza was usually his wife:

Rastus and Liza were sitting on the porch and Liza says, 'My, dees flies are sure annoyin' me tonight.' And Rastus says, 'Dem flies are called bum, bum flies, on account dey fly round a cow's behind.'

And Liza says, 'Rastus! Are you sayin' dat ma face is like a cow's behind?'

'No, I ain't,' says Rastus, 'but you sure can't fool dem bum, bum flies.'

In the late fifties the entertainer, writer, and talk show host Steve Allen said in a magazine article that American society, 'Would not permit the emergence of black comedians who were the equivalent of Bob Hope, much less any that were the equivalent of Mort Sahl and Lenny Bruce.'

Allen then pointedly asked how it was possible for black comedians to be as successful as their white counterparts when they could not talk directly to a white audience.

Everything changed when black comedian Dick Gregory shot to fame after appearing at the Chicago *Playboy Club* in 1961.

From the beginning of his career Gregory said that he vowed to, 'go up there as an individual first, and a Negro second,' an approach that was severely tested in the small nightclubs of Chicago during the late fifties where he schooled himself in dealing with the inevitable racist heckles.

Normal comebacks he decided were impractical; a black man putting down a white man would turn the audience against him, while ignoring the insult risked losing command of the room. Instead he casually informed the audience that a clause in his contract stipulated that he would receive fifty dollars from the management every time someone called him, 'Nigger' and that he appreciated it

202

because he needed the extra money. Initially his sets were made up of innocuous one-liners:

Just my luck, I bought a suit with two pair of pants and burnt a hole in the jacket...

The Playboy was his biggest booking to date and the show started badly, as Gregory related in his autobiography, *Nigger*: 'The audience fought me with dirty, little insulting statements, but I was faster, and I was funny, and when the room broke it was like the storm was over. They stopped heckling and listened.'

The *Playboy* manager signed him to a three-year contract and within a year he was a national star with a string of television appearances behind him.

'From the moment he was booked into the *Playboy Club*,' wrote *Newsweek*, 'Jim Crow was dead in the joke world.'

The timing was perfect, white Americans had gotten used to seeing on television angry black men demonstrating for equal rights, facing fire hoses, police dogs and baton waving police officers, so a quiet unassuming black man who dressed well, talked smart and was funny, was a welcome relief.

Baseball is very big with my people. It figures. It's the only way we can get to shake a bat at a white man without starting a riot.

Gregory was the first black American stand-up comedian to break into mainstream entertainment, but his jokes were not "black" jokes. Prominent black American novelist, Richard Wright (1908-60) defined the following as an authentic "black" joke:

The Secretary of the National Society for the Advancement of Coloured Persons, a white gentleman, is on his way home from the Long Island train station late one afternoon, when he feels the need to take a leak. He holds it for a few blocks because there are people everywhere, but the pain gets harder to bear with every step. Suddenly he notices an old Negro raking leaves by the curb, and so he says to him, 'Pardon me, my good man, you seem to be doing an excellent job of raking those leaves. I'd like to give you a job on my estate – double the salary you're getting now.'

'Why, that's wonderful,' says the old Negro.

'Yes, and does your wife do housework?' the secretary asks.

'Why, yass, a little now an' then,' says the Negro.

'Fine,' says the secretary, 'she gets whatever you're getting now, and you can both live over the garage – it's a four-room apartment we had fitted up for our son. He's in college now. So, when can you start?'

And the Negro says, 'Anytime you want boss, but tell me something. While you is talking to me boss, you ain't by any chance pissin' up my leg, is you?'

American musicologists and folklorists had researched and documented black music, blues and jazz, its roots and connection to African culture, but not until the sixties was there a serious study of black humour.

At the beginning of the decade folklorist Roger D Abrahams took up residence in Camingerly, a black ghetto in Philadelphia where he studied black humour and in 1963 published his findings in *Deep Down in the Jungle*.

Abrahams was the first to cover urban rather than rural Negro folklore, ghetto folklore, and the jokes he recorded were the type told by black people, about black people, folklore that had previously been ignored:

One day a preacher was walking across a bridge. He was the kind of preacher that always cussed a lot. He was walking across the bridge and he heard the train coming and as he turned around he done slipped and hit the side of the bridge. Hanging on the bridge, he looked down to see the water below, so he started praying, he said, 'Lord, don't let me fall into this water.' Just then his left hand slipped, and he was just hanging on by his right hand, and still praying, 'Dear God, don't let me fall into the water, I promise I'll never say another cuss word.' Then his right hand slipped, and he fell into the water.

Water only came up to his knees.

Preacher said, 'Ain't this a damn shame, I done all this damn praying, and this damn water only up to my motherfucking knees.'

A black travelling salesman asked if he could stay the night at an old black farmer's house. The old man agreed but as there was only one bed he'd have to share it with him and his daughter. The old man slept in the middle, with his daughter on one side and the salesman on the other.

After a couple of hours, the daughter says to the salesman, 'Come on over', but the salesman was afraid the old man would wake up. 'My Daddy's an awful sound sleeper,' says the daughter, 'pull a hair out of his ass, you'll see.'

So, the salesman pulled a hair out the old man's ass, and the old man just went right on snoring. So, then the salesman went on over and gave the daughter what she wanted.

After a while the daughter says, 'Come on over again.' The salesman was not so keen this time, but she got him in the notion, and so he pulled another hair out the old man's ass, and sure enough the old man just kept on snoring. The salesman went on over and gave the daughter what she wanted.

The third time the daughter says, 'Come on over again' the salesman didn't want to, 'We better leave well enough alone,' he said, but again she got him in the notion. So, finally the salesman jerked another hair out the old man's ass, but this time the old man woke up. 'Look,' he said, 'I don't mind you fucking my daughter, but I do mind you using my ass as a tally-board!'

Deep Down in the Jungle set a precedent for scholarly publishing of American folklore. It is a pioneering body of work that covers jokes, insults, dozens, anecdotes, and toasts. It is a fascinating insight into the humour shared by black men in social groups at the poolroom or bar, or on a street corner where "passing speech" or "dozens" was common:

'Man, why you want to look at me like that?'
"Cos, you is ugly"

205

'I'm ugly? You got a nerve to call me ugly.'

"Look boy, you so ugly that the stork that brought you here should be locked up by the FBI"

'Look here man, you wuz so ugly when you wuz a baby that your mother had to put a sheet on your face, so sleep could creep up on you. And your girl, your wife ain't no cuter."

'Wait a minute. Don't you talk about my wife.'

"Your wife is ugly. Me and your wife went out to get a drink and have a good time and she wuz so ugly she had to put on sneakers to sneak up on the drinks. She looked like something I used to feed peanuts too at the zoo."

'You callin' my wife, ugly?'

"No, I ain't saying she's ugly, I just saying she ruined. Now, I don't know where she wuz when they were giving out looks, she must have been hiding down in the cellar somewhere, and you, when they wuz giving out looks you must have been playing craps. You look like you been slapped in the face with a sack of razor blades."

It is likely that these verbal jousting contests between black males known as, "dozens" (possibly from the Saxon word, doze, meaning to stun or overwhelm someone), derived from Ghana.

African tribes had for centuries periodically held insult contests in which one tribe member would go head to head with a neighbouring tribesman, or sometimes entire tribes competed against one another. The wit of the insult was thought to exert magical influence, but usually the contests ended in violence.

Prof. Robert C Elliot's 1960 book, *The Power of Satire: Magic, Ritual, and Art* details insult contests in Hawaiian, Eskimo, Greek, Arab, Italian, Irish, and Ashanti (central Ghana) cultures.

"Dozens" contests began in America and the Caribbean islands between male black slaves as a substitute for physical fights at a time when violence amongst chattel slaves was a property crime that carried heinous consequences. Contestants had to be self-controlled, verbally agile, and mentally tough.

Dozens, sometimes called "capping" is still a rite of passage amongst young American black males who often target their opponent's family. In its simplest form its, "Yo Momma" jokes:

206

Yo Momma is so fat she had to be baptised at Sea World.

Yo Momma is so old she farts dust.

Yo Momma so stupid when they shouted, 'Order in court', she asked for fries and a shake.

Despite many making the breakthrough into American mainstream entertainment, black comedians did not tell jokes from a black person's perspective. They erred on the side of caution, they had been on the peripheral for so long they figured, why run the risk of alienating white America again?

Then along came the hybrid genius that was Richard Pryor. Candid and confessional, indignant and indigenous, he became the most important figure in the history of black stand-up comedy. The first comedian to point out the differences between white and black, and the first to publicly make white people the butt of his jokes:

I remember tricks used to come through our neighbourhood. That's where I first met white people. They come down through my neighbourhood to help the economy, nice white dudes, 'Hello little boy, is your mother home? I'd like a blow job.' I wonder what would happen if niggers go through a white neighbourhood doin' that, 'Hey man, is yo momma home? Tell the bitch we wanna fuck.'

He was born in 1940 and raised in Peoria, Illinois where his family ran a bar and a whorehouse. There he lived amongst characters he described as, 'an assortment of relatives, neighbours, whores and winos, the people who inspired a lifetime of comedic material.'

Pryor started out as a clean cut, regular gag comic, perfect for television. Instantly likeable, well groomed, with an act consisting of a light mixture of physical impressions, non-threatening one-liners, and harmless spoofs of ghetto life:

I heard a knock on my door and I said to my wife, there's a knock on the door, and my wife said to me, 'That's peculiar, we ain't got no door'...

He soon became frustrated: 'I was doing material that wasn't funny to me,' he said in his 1995 autobiography, *Pryor Convictions*, 'It was Mickey Mouse material and I couldn't stomach it anymore... I don't understand it myself. I only knew that my days of pretending to be as slick and as colourless as [Bill] Cosby were numbered. There was a world of junkies and winos, pool hustlers and prostitutes, women and family screaming inside my head, trying to be heard. The longer I kept them bottled up, the harder they tried to escape. The pressure built until I went nuts.'

In September 1967 at the *Aladdin Hotel* in Las Vegas he walked onstage, stared at the crowd for an unerring minute, sighed and asked himself out loud: 'What the fuck am I doing here?' He then left the stage.

After three years of experimenting in front of often nonplussed crowds Pryor made a triumphant comeback. His 1974 album *That Nigger's Crazy* spent a year on the Billboard Chart and won the Grammy Award for Best Comedy Recording:

Cops put a hurtin' on your ass man, y'know they really degrade you, white folks don't believe that shit, they don't believe they degrade you, 'Aw come on, those beatings, those people were resisting arrest, I was told it was harassment of police officers'... cos police be living in your neighbourhood see, and you be knowing them as Officer Timpson, 'Hello Officer Timpson, going bowling tonight? Nice Pinto you have, haha'. Niggers don't know them like that, white folks get a ticket, get pulled over, 'Hey officer glad to have been of help to you.' Nigger got to be talking like, 'I... AM... REACHING... INTO... MY... POCKET... FOR... MY... LICENSE', cos I don't wanna be no motherfuckin' accident...

'He is creating a new style of American comedy,' wrote *Time Magazine* that same year, 'which must be observed and heard at the same time in order to be completely understood and appreciated.

Pryor is certain of one thing. He is proudly, assertively a Nigger, the first comedian to speak the raw, brutal, but often wildly hilarious language of the streets.'

There was no equivalent black comedian in Britain, there was not even the equivalent to Dick Gregory or Bill Cosby, neither of whom indulged in authentic black humour, but at the same time neither told race jokes.

In Britain, social club comics, white and black, told racist jokes as a regular part of their act, and audiences laughed. After all, they were "just jokes", right?

Chapter Twenty-Six

Club Jokers and Satire

In post Variety Britain most comedians earned their living on a vast circuit of Working Men's Clubs and in such an abject environment there emerged a new style of stand-up comedian, the hard hitting, quick-fire, gag man.

Social clubs proved a much tougher proposition than Variety theatres and Variety comedians suddenly found themselves competing with boisterous boozers, slot machines, bingo, and pies.

Scottish comedian Billy Crockett remembered how the arrival of hot pies at the club door could kill an act: 'Oh, but clubs were hard to play. You used to go on in some clubs and they were all drinking and talking to one another and then someone would shout, "The pies are coming", and you were left talking to yourself.'

The history of Working Men's Clubs runs parallel with the trade union movements and social reforms of the late nineteenth century when reformers strove to improve the lot of the working man and limit the exploitation of women and children in the mines, mills, and factories of industrial Britain.

The Reverend Henry Solly worked tirelessly on behalf of the working classes and recognised the need for places where working men could meet for a social drink and enjoy their leisure time.

The first Working Men's Club was established in Brighton in 1849, the influence of which was felt throughout the country and similar clubs sprung up across Britain. Instigated by Solly and Rev. David Thomas and supported financially by benefactors Lord Brougham and a W. M. Neil, the Working Men's Club and Institute Union (CIU) was formed in South Shields in 1862, a national union promoting the benefits of social clubs for the working man.

In 1898 Kettering WMC in Northamptonshire became the first club in the country to add a "Concert Room" to its premises, complete with stage and began booking semi-professional concert parties (a troupe of Variety performers) which proved so popular that most other clubs followed their lead.

During the twentieth century the number of social clubs steadily grew, accelerated in the 1950's by the creation of huge government housing estates that sprang up across Britain, every one of which had at least one social club, but more often several. By the end of the decade there were more than four thousand affiliated social clubs in Britain.

The housing estates accommodated the working classes and were the responsibility of local councils. Council houses needed maintaining so tradesmen and non-skilled workers were employed, council workers, who quickly acquired a "work-shy" joke cycle:

This feller applies to the local council for job and a council foreman sees on his application that he has been in the armed forces and was forced to leave on medical grounds. 'A land mine blew my testicles off,' the ex-soldier explains.

The foreman says, 'Well, you're due a break so you're hired. Start Monday, the hours are eight to four, so we'll see you about ten o'clock.'

'Ten o'clock?' says the feller, 'but you just said that the hours were eight to four.'

'This is the council,' the foreman says, 'for the first two hours we sit around scratching our balls. No point you coming in for that.'

While the Variety circuit thrived, social clubs could only book semi-professional acts, but the demise of Variety meant its professional artists were suddenly available which led to a vast increase in concert room numbers. Clubs responded by building bigger concert rooms.

'When the big clubs came into being everybody had to play them,' explained Roy Hudd, 'there was no other work. To see some of the great theatre acts struggling in those plastic palaces against drinking, talking and heckling was a sad spectacle.'

Some comedians however, found their niche in social clubs, like the bawdy Scot Hector Nicol:

211

There was this feller sitting there, and he had a baldy heed, he wez a baldy… next chap come in and baldy rubbed his heed and he sez, 'This just feels like ma wife's arse', and the boy rubbed it an all and sez, 'Aye, so it does.'

Les Dawson became the first star comedian nurtured in social clubs where his verbal flights of fancy stood him apart from the more aggressive gag man:

An excess of the grape caused me to drift towards my front door like a bank of fog. As I fumbled in my pocket for the key which opens the portal to my heavily mortgaged Wimpy Valhalla, the door was quite violently flung ajar to reveal the formidable hulk of female pestilence, who for some ten nerve jangling years had shared my name…

In his autobiography Les Dawson compared the club comic to a 'human sacrifice', referring specifically to the nightly battles with hecklers, who considered taking on the comedian as part of the evening's entertainment. In response club comedians armed themselves with a stock collection of heckler jokes:

Save your breath, you're going to need it for your blow-up date… Stand next to the wall, it's plastered as well… There's a bus due soon, be under it…

Some encouraged hecklers. 'No comedian is any good without hecklers,' claimed Bernard Manning, 'because they help create the atmosphere.'

Bob Monkhouse disagreed. Monkhouse was a well-known theatre and radio comedian, a first-rate comic and joke writer who was well respected both in Britain and America. Club audiences cared little for reputation.

His first experience of a social club was in the late fifties at Ridgeway in Hammersmith which he described in his 1993 autobiography, *Crying with Laughter*: 'I opened with a song I hoped was a funny parody of *The Alphabet Song*, a hit record by Perry

212

Como and the Fontaine Sisters: A - I'm adorable, B - I'm so beautiful, and a man shouted, 'C - You're a cunt!' And that was the end of my act.'

Monkhouse was more suited to the far less hostile atmosphere of cabaret clubs.

My wife and I just moved into a little village, very tightly knit community I think we're the first new residents in centuries and we were just unpacking when a neighbour came around to welcome us, then he said, 'I'd like you to meet my wife and sister', and there was just the one woman standing there.

When Harold Clark, the owner of the *Palace Theatre* in Hull transformed his small Variety theatre into a theatre restaurant in 1958 and renamed it the *Continental Palace* it gave rise to hundreds of cabaret clubs across the country.

Privately owned cabaret clubs were run in similar fashion to social clubs, not in competition but as late-night options. British Licensing laws meant that regular pubs and clubs had to close at ten-thirty, whereas nightclubs remained open until the early hours and offered food, drink, and entertainment.

In stark contrast to the social club cimics satirical comedians came to the fore at the beginning of the sixties, and though there were no British equivalents of Mort Sahl or Lenny Bruce it did produce for the first time in the country, University type comedians, ones who offered a contrariety in style and content to their club counterparts.

It was a brief satirical boom ignited by four young university students and their ground-breaking small revue, *Beyond the Fringe*.

Spectacular revue is glitzy and glamorous, all singing, all dancing productions, small revue on the other hand is compact, fast paced with minimal scenery, costume design, and lighting.

Typical of small revue jokes is the following from Noel Coward's 1924, *London's Calling* which included the sketch, *Growing Pains* in which an English aristocrat attempts to instruct his son on the facts of life:

Boy: Why are you so nervous, Papa?
Papa: I am not nervous, Herbert, but that which I have to tell you is rather delicate and ahm… rather difficult.
Boy: What is it you want to tell me Papa?
Papa: Well, my boy… ahm… well… er, hum… there's no Santa Claus!

Herbert Farjeon's version added a topper:

Papa: And, by the way, I shouldn't tell your brother, not just yet.
Boy: I see… does mother know?

By the fifties small revue appeared dated. Cambridge medical student Jonathan Miller who himself had starred in a couple of promising shows, *Out of the Blue* and *Between the Lines* told author Humphrey Carpenter for his 2000, *That Was Satire That Was*: 'They were still on the rump of the old tradition, there was still an awful lot of stuff with people walking on in Blazers and flannels and boaters, and singing songs about Proctors and, "Going down for the last time" and punts, and things of that sort… there were satirical, rather biting little sketches, which were written by people like Freddy Raphael, but still cast in an old fashioned, rhyming verse form.'

Miller and three fellow students rejuvenated small revue with their pioneering show at the 1960 Edinburgh Festival.

Now the largest festival of its kind in the world the Edinburgh Festival began in 1947 as a celebration of the performing arts. However, due to the increasing amount of theatre companies performing unofficially, and rather than try to police them, the Festival Fringe was created to accommodate the rogue companies.

The director of the Edinburgh Festival during the fifties was Robert Ponsonby who throughout his tenure had grown increasingly frustrated by the fact that the unofficial productions were much more creative and exciting than the official events, and that the Oxbridge undergraduates were year after year stealing the limelight.

214

In 1960 he tried to book the American jazz star, Louis Armstrong but when the deal fell through his assistant, John Bassett suggested they produce their own revue. The title they came up with was *Beyond the Fringe*, implying that the show was better and *beyond* whatever the Fringe could produce.

Bassett first enlisted Dudley Moore, an Oxford graduate and the pianist in Bassett's own jazz band. Moore was already a proficient cabaret artist whose act combined music and comedy.

His next signing was Alan Bennett who had impressed Bassett in a University cabaret and in the 1959 Oxford revue, *Better Late* at the Edinburgh Fringe.

Jonathan Miller already held a medical degree and was studying to become a neurophysiologist. He also had a reputation as a first-rate comedy writer and performer. In 1953 while still in his final year at school, Miller appeared on the BBC radio show *Under Twenty Parade* and a year later received critical acclaim for his starring role in the *Footlights* revue, *Out of the Blue* which ran for three weeks in London's West End.

Over the next couple of years, he performed regularly in cabaret and was a guest on various radio and television shows, including *Sunday Night at the London Palladium* and the BBC's, *Tonight* programme where he performed his *Death of Lord Nelson*:

But what were his dying words? There is some historical doubt about this. Some people say that Nelson said, kiss me, Hardy, in which case a young cabin boy would have been dispatched up on deck to fetch Captain Hardy... Admiral's compliments, sir, Captain Hardy, sir, he says you're to come below and kiss him...

When he agreed to be part of the venture Bassett asked Miller if he could recommend a final member and without hesitation he said, 'Peter Cook.'

Cook was born in 1937 in Torquay, Devon which made him the youngest of the newly formed troupe, and like Miller was well known at Cambridge University for his sharp comic mind and excellent mimicry. One of his creations was the character Grole who spoke in a monotone voice. A sketch written by Cook featuring

215

Grole was bought for the 1959 revue, *Pieces of Eight* starring comic actor Kenneth Williams.

Grole, seated in a train carriage with a cardboard box on his knees addressed a man opposite: 'I've got a viper in this box, you know...' impressing on the man that it is a viper and not an asp.

'Cleopatra had an asp, but I haven't, I don't want one either, I'd rather have the viper myself, not that they're cheaper to run, if anything the viper is more voracious than the asp; my viper eats like a horse.'

"Like a horse?"

'Oh yes, I'd like a horse, I've got nothing against horses, I could do with a horse, mind you, you'd never get it into this box...'

Beyond the Fringe opened on Monday, August 22 at the *Royal Lyceum Theatre* to a half full auditorium, but the wildly enthusiastic crowd ensured that the rest of the week was sold out, after which the company agreed that the show should have a London run of some kind.

After a triumphant week at Cambridge at the end of April the following year and a badly received week at Brighton, *Beyond the Fringe* opened on May 10, 1961 at the *Fortune Theatre* in the West End of London as a stop gap for a few weeks while the revue playing there, *And Another Thing* was revamped.

The critics were unanimous in their praise. Michael Frayn in *The Guardian* described the show as, 'the official opening of the Satirical Sixties', while Kenneth Tynan's review in the *Observer* entitled, *English Satire Advances into the Sixties* began: 'Future historians will thank me for providing them with a full account of the moment when English comedy took its first decisive step into the second half of the twentieth century.'

Beyond the Fringe ran for a year at the *Fortune* with the original cast, after which substitute actors took over before it transferred to the *Mayfair Theatre* in 1964 where it played for another two years. The original cast meanwhile played the *John Golden Theatre*, New York for two incredibly successful runs in 1962 and 1964.

Following the second New York run the team dissolved, Cook and Moore continued in comedy, Bennett went on to become one of the great comedy dramatists of British stage and screen, while Jonathan Miller became an opera director.

Beyond the Fringe was an important milestone for British comedy, not only raising the bar considerably for small revue but as an inspiration to a whole generation of university comedians. It was also the catalyst for a host of satirical television programmes, despite all four members denying that there was ever a conscious satirical undercurrent to the show.

Miller said, 'We didn't consciously indulge in satire. We just indulged in being funny. Because we were educated, university people, we addressed topics that had never been seen on stage before. We also had this retrospective irreverence about the heroic mythology of the war. That is why we called that sketch, "The Aftermyth of the War". I look back on it with some guilt. Peter and I did that scene with the line, 'We need a futile gesture at this time'. It was funny at the time but looking back I can understand why people who had fought in the war, or who had relatives who had laid down their lives, were upset.'

Cook however, defended the sketch and described it not as a parody of war, but a parody of war films:

War's a psychological thing Perkins, rather like a game of football, you know how in a game of football ten men often play better than eleven? Well, Perkins we want you to be that one man. I want you to lay down your life Perkins, we need a futile gesture at this stage, it'll raise the whole tone of the war. Get up in a crate Perkins, pop over to Bremen, take a little shufty and then come back. Goodbye Perkins, God I wish I was going too...
Perkins: Goodbye sir, or is it au revoir?
No, Perkins...

Whilst performing in *Beyond the Fringe* Cook became involved with the satirical magazine *Private Eye*, first published in April 1961 and following in a long English tradition of satirical magazines going back to 1670 and the wonderfully titled, *Jesuita Vapulans, or a Whip for the Fool's Back, and a Gad for his Foul Mouth* which was written and published by the gifted satirist Richard Steele.

Private Eye was the creation of Peter Usborne, Christopher Booker, Andrew Osmond and Willie Rushton. Additional articles and jokes came from John Wells, Richard Ingrams, and Cook. It was Cook who came up with the idea of having photographs of public figures with satirical speech bubbles on the cover which became the *Private Eye* hallmark.

Cook also opened his own nightclub in 1961, *The Establishment*, an intimate, membership only club offering late night drinks and food, jazz and comedy.

'Some of the things we did are as outrageous as anything that has been done subsequently,' Cook reflected years later, 'extremely bad taste flourished at *The Establishment*... I remember a crucifixion scene, with John Fortune as Christ, and Jeremy Geidt and John Bird as robbers objecting that Jesus was a, higher up than they were, and b, getting all the attention...'

One comedian who appeared at *The Establishment* was the part time Lay Preacher, and ex-Cambridge Footlights performer David Frost, who at the time was a regular performer on the intimate cabaret circuit in and around London's, West End.

The Stage said of his *Royal Court Club* performance: 'David Frost is the latest of the University types to bring a refreshing wind of change to the cabaret business.' His routines were a mixture of satire, observation, and old Variety jokes:

I'm so busy. I've got this part time job you see, as a hangman. It's all grist to the mill, isn't it? I mean, you're all over by five-past-nine, a bit like a paper round, less variety, but it's more concentrated... Although, sometimes it's later than five-past, but then you have difficult customers in any trade... Mind you, I'm not saying there's a great future in it, if anything, the bottoms dropping right out of it, what with all these people agitating, and things... Well, I say, people, but in fact they're socialists... No, I mean, if the thing fails three times, the prisoner's released, and shot!

218

He impressed television producer Ned Sherrin, who in 1961 was looking for team members to take part in a new satirical television show, *That Was The Week That Was*.

Sherrin devised, produced and directed what became known as *TW3*, and imagined that in Frost he had found a valuable member of the support cast. Frost however, had other ideas and persuaded Sherrin that he should not only perform, but also present the show, and by the time the programme aired Frost was in effect link man and co-producer.

Frost explained the programme's plan, or rather lack of it: 'We did not come with a specific agenda or political programme. We were not further examples of what the newspapers called, "Angry young men". We were the exasperated young men – exasperated by Britain's recurring failures, by the hypocrisy and complacency and by the shabbiness of its politics. When asked I said in one interview that we were against everything that makes life less than it can for people. That category alone meant that there was no danger of running short of material.'

TW3 writers and its cast, David Kernan, Roy Kinnear, Willie Rushton, Kenneth Cope, Lance Percival, Millicent Martin, and Frost, assumed their viewers had a certain level of intelligence and were up on current affairs.

They actively sought to discredit the tenet and pomposity of the powerful elite and succeeded enough for Tory MP and future Prime Minister, Edward Heath to blame *TW3* for what he called, 'the death of deference' and was especially offended at Frost going down a line of life-size cardboard cut-outs of leading politicians and in turn pushing them over.

The infamous West Midlands primary school teacher, Mrs. Mary Whitehouse in a speech to her, "Clean up TV Campaign" supporters at Birmingham Town Hall described the show as: 'Anti-authority, anti-religion, anti-patriotism, pro-dirt and poorly produced, and yet having the support of the corporation, and apparently impervious to discipline from within or discipline from without.'

Whitehouse also complained about the inspired, *Consumer's Guide to Religion* written by Charles Lewson and Robert Gillespie, and performed by Frost.

The piece, analysed in the manner of *Which Magazine*, sought to advise which religion gave British consumers best value for money. The Church of England came out on top:

It's a jolly faith, if you are one there's no onus on you to make anyone else join; in fact, no one need ever know. And it's pretty fair on the whole, too, with some of these products we've mentioned you are guilty right from the off. But the Church of England is English. On the whole you start pretty well innocent, and they've got to prove you guilty...

TW3 lasted for thirteen months, thirty-seven programmes during which time it created a new language of thought and wit, breaching the divide between current affairs and comedy, and more importantly, it changed forever television's relationship with politics, religion, and royalty.

Following *TW3* was the promising *Not So Much A Programme, More A Way of Life* with Frost and Willie Rushton as co-hosts, but after only five months it was cancelled, largely because of two sketches, one featuring a Catholic Priest and an Irish mother, and the other presenting the abdication of King Edward as a musical comedy.

The 1965 series *BBC-3* turned out to be not so much of a programme at all and lasted only two months, though it did cause one almighty stir when, during a discussion on stage censorship, the theatre critic Kenneth Tynan was asked whether he would allow a play to be presented at the *National Theatre* in which sexual intercourse was represented on stage and Tynan replied: 'Well, I think so, certainly... I doubt if there are any rational people to whom the word fuck would be particularly diabolical, revolting, or totally forbidden. I think that anything that can be printed or said can be seen.'

If it was his intention to strike a blow for freedom of speech, Tynan failed. When he said, 'fuck' there was no real conviction behind it, he was nervous saying it, he stumbled over it, more a whimper than a revelation.

The incident probably set the cause for liberated speech on television back a decade.

The Frost Report; *Quiz of the Week*; *Up Sunday*; *The Late Show* were other failed attempts to recreate *TW3* and by the middle of the decade the satire boom had all but fizzled out.

Playwright Michael Frayn wrote in his 1963 introduction to the newly published text of *Beyond the Fringe*: 'To go on mocking the so-called establishment has more and more meant making the audience not laugh at themselves at all, but at a standard target which is rapidly becoming as well established as the mother-in-law.'

Comedian Bill Oddie, a member of the *TW3* live show that toured Canada and America agreed but added that *TW3's* main contribution was the extending of the acceptable range of humour. 'Instead of doing, I say, I say, my mother in law,' said Oddie, 'you could do, I say, I say, Harold MacMillan, and it could be the same joke, and very often was the same joke.'

The Guardian newspaper said, 'Satire came in as a craze, like boots for women, it was now probably about to go out much as boots will go out next year... Whatever its defects *TW3* has done more than anything else to foster a healthy irreverence towards persons in authority. Some of this irreverence will surely outlive the craze – and may be healthier for no longer being modish.'

Peter Cook meanwhile transformed his Grole character into E. L. Wisty, a man caught in his working-class roots, uneducated and unfulfilled but with a wistful yearning for a better life:

Yes, I could have been a judge, but I never had the Latin, never had the Latin for the judging. I just never had sufficient of it to get through the rigorous judging exams, they're very rigorous judging exams, they're noted for their rigour, people come staggering out saying, 'My God what a rigorous exam', and so I had to become a coal miner instead. I managed to get through the mining exam, they're not so rigorous, they only ask you one question, 'Who are you?' and I got seventy five percent for that...

Bernard Braden invited Wisty to appear on his show *On the Braden Beat* for ATV, initially for four episodes but the character proved so popular that four turned into twenty, after which Cook teamed up with Dudley Moore for a BBC television special.

Cook created "Pete and Dud" for the special, two working class men in cloth caps and rain coats whose relationship was, in Cook's own words: 'Pete is the informed idiot, and Dud is the uninformed idiot. They're both idiots, but Pete is always slightly superior. In fact, he knows nothing either.'

The pair followed up with *Not Only... But Also*, which began its first of three highly acclaimed series beginning in 1965.

Cook and Moore tours were always hugely successful, but it was while playing New York in 1973 that a side project gained them cult status.

Plied with alcohol, Pete and Dud, a k a Clive and Derek, recorded three late night improvised head to head sessions which resulted in a ridiculously adolescent, incredibly vulgar, and rather brilliant comedy album.

Cook revealed to the *Sheffield and North Derbyshire Spectator* in 1976 how the project came about: 'Dudley Moore and I booked a recording studio for a late-night ad lib session after performing what seemed like the millionth performance of *Good Evening* in New York.'

Armed with several bottles of wine Cook said that the idea was, 'to just see what happened if we talked with no prior ideas into a microphone. We had no preconceived attitudes or intentions, and what emerged on the whole was a shower of filth with no social redeeming or artistic value.'

The 'shower of filth' was the result of three New York recordings, the first at the *Bell Sound Studios*, the second at the Greenwich Village club, *The Bottom Line*, and lastly the *Electric Lady Studios*. The recording at the *Bell Studios* arguably produced the best material, including, 'The Worst Job I Ever Had':

Clive: What's the worst job you had?
Derek: The worst job I ever had?
Clive: Yeah.

(Derek coughs)

Clive: What? Was it just that? Coughing?

Derek: Well, I had to collect up, this was a very difficult job, I had to collect up, every year, every financial year, you know, April...

Clive: Every ear? Whose ears did you collect up?

Derek: No, wait. No, year... April to April

Clive: Yeah.

(Derek belches)

Derek: Pardon. All the phlegm that Winston Churchill had gobbed out into his bucket by the bed.

Clive: Oh, God, yes, I was offered that job, but I said no. I said, I'm not going through all that phlegm, because he has so many cigars, so much brandy. I am not, as a human being, going to go around with buckets collecting that fucking phlegm. I said, I'm not going to touch it, I said, I won't touch it...

Neither thought that the recordings would amount to anything, no reputable record company would, or so they imagined, be prepared to distribute such material. However, as is often the case, recording engineers run off their own copies of studio sessions, and when copies of those private copies began circulating Cook and Moore suddenly discovered they were a cult phenomenon.

When ads started appearing in *Private Eye* offering bootleg copies for sale the pair decided it was time to cash in on the action and quickly did a deal with *Island Records*.

Derek and Clive (Live) was released in August 1976, almost three years after the original sessions in New York, and despite the prior underground trade sold over a hundred thousand copies in Britain and became their most successful LP in America.

The project proved to be a one-off, when Cook and Moore attempted to repeat the process the results were mixed, *Come Again* and, *Ad Nauseam* both failing to match the spontaneity of the *Bell Studios* original. Nonetheless, the Derek and Clive albums anticipated punk rock, *Viz* comic, and influenced and inspired "Alternative Comedy", not to mention a whole generation of smutty teenagers.

223

In 1969 the first television show dedicated entirely to jokes was aired, Granada Television's *Jokers Wild*, followed two years later by another Granada production, the ground-breaking joke extravaganza, *The Comedians*.

The Comedians was the brainchild of producer Johnny Hamp and the concept was simple, yet quite brilliant. Each comedian performed a short set of jokes before a live studio audience which was then edited to appear as if one comedian told a joke and was immediately followed by another. The result was a blizzard of jokes, as many as sixty in each half hour episode, of which there were fifty between 1971 and 1974. The first episode was broadcast on Saturday June 12, 1971 and opened with Ken Goodwin:

This feller come to our house and he said, 'do you believe in free speech?' I said I do, he said, 'well, can I use your telephone?'

After a brief musical interlude from *Shep's Banjo Boys* a voiceover announced, 'Ladies and Gentlemen, it's… The Comedians.'

Frank Carson was followed by Bernard Manning and George Roper before Charlie Williams, a black man with a broad Yorkshire accent told a joke about a "Jew boy", after which Mike Coyne told of an explorer who, 'spent thirty years in deepest darkest Africa looking for the lost Mazasuki tribe and eventually found them over a chip shop in Bradford', which he followed with, 'the new Corporation toilets in Birmingham are losing a fortune, Jamaicans are doing the limbo under the door.'

The Comedians DVD of the inaugural show has edited the race jokes, and instead begins with same Ken Goodwin joke, the banjo tune, voiceover, and George Roper:

A feller stood at the bus stop eating a meat pie and a woman's next to him with a poodle… and the dog keeps jumping up trying to get at the pie, so the feller says to the woman, 'Missus can I throw your dog a bit?' and she said, 'Yes,' so he threw the dog a hundred yards up the road…

Cut to Frank Carson:

Feller got on the plane in Australia and he went straight to the cockpit and he stuck a bloody great shotgun in the pilot's ear and said, 'Take me to London!' and the pilot said, 'I'm going to London', and the feller said, 'I know but I've been hijacked twice and I'm taking no chances.'

Bernard Manning:

Feller backs a horse called, Yellow-Yellow and wins a quarter of a million pounds. He has all his house painted yellow, yellow carpet, yellow curtains, yellow furnishings, everything yellow, and he got yellow jaundice and died, and they can't find him...

Ken Goodwin:

I was putting some toilet water on me hair and the seat fell down...

Ray Fell:

I went away on holiday and we're standing at Manchester Piccadilly station and the mother-in-law's there, not very bright... electrified system... and she said to the guard, 'Will I get a shock if I put my foot on that rail down there?' he said, 'No madam, only if you cock your other leg on that cable up there.' So she did, and we all got one...

The show received five-star reviews from all and sundry, including *The Times* and *Daily Mail*, while *The Morning Star* told its readers: 'It's very, very funny, please watch it.'
The series was subsequently voted comedy programme of the year by both the *TV Critics Circle* and *The Stage* magazine.

The comedians on the show were censored only for expletives and blue jokes. Not until the 1979 revamped series did Hamp, aware

225

of changing public sensibilities, ban race jokes and insist that Irish jokes were told only by Irish comedians.

In defence of club comedians and their racist jokes, they were comedians of their time. They grew up in an era when 'Nigger' was a common name for black or brown pets, it was the name given to the black cat on Captain Scott's Antarctic Expedition, and to the black Labrador mascot of the World War Two Royal Air Force's 617 (Damn Busters) Squadron, though for the film recounting their heroic exploits the dog's name was unimaginatively renamed, 'Digger'. There was a well-known children's rhyme that began 'eenie meenie miney moe, catch a Nigger by the toe', while popular sixties sitcoms such as *Love Thy Neighbour* and *'Till Death Us Do Part* made regular references to, Paki's, Coons, and Darkies.

They were derogatory terms, degrading synonyms that implied inferiority, and those who used the terms were aware of it, but they got big laughs, cheap ones some might say, but laughs nevertheless.

Jokes reflect a society's sense of humour at a given time and had racist jokes been frowned upon then comedians would not have told them.

Race jokes were a part of most club comic's repertoire. Perhaps if West Indian and Asian people had been encouraged to join their local club then audiences would not have been so keen to hear fellow members abused. But black and Asian people were not encouraged, in fact the very opposite.

During the early years of the CIU movement racism was not an issue and indigenous minorities throughout Britain were actively involved with their local social club. However, after the Second World War the migrants who came from the Caribbean and India were made less welcome and most clubs either set a limit on "coloured" members or discouraged them altogether.

In 1972 the CIU became embroiled in a racial discrimination issue after both the East Ham South Conservative Club and the Preston Dockers Club had refused entry to black men. The CIU won a hollow victory, the House of Lords agreeing that the *1968 Race Relations Act* did not apply to Working Men's Clubs because there was, 'a genuine system of personal selection of members', and as private clubs were exempt.

The CIU issued a statement promising to call for integration but, it added, 'Over time'.

In 1977 a new law was introduced that did not exclude social clubs from discriminatory practises which meant *officially* a social club could not refuse entrance or membership because of a man's ethnicity. Unofficially little changed.

Given such an environment it is remarkable that there were any black comics on the social club circuit, but there were, and the likes of Astor Garricks, Sammy Thomas, Josh White, and Charlie Williams were the first British, black, stand-up comedians.

Williams was the first black comedian to achieve star status. The son of Caribbean immigrants who arrived in Yorkshire shortly after World War One he, like his father, became a coal miner until he was offered professional terms with Doncaster Rovers Football Club.

After retiring from football in the early sixties he decided on a career as a comic in the Yorkshire clubs where he soon discovered that the way to win over a club audience was to poke fun at himself and his colour before moving into his regular set:

Me mother's Yorkshire tha knows, she is, Yorkshire, me dad's anybody's guess but dun't matter… I'm part Scotch really, I am, I'm part Scotch, me dad were a colour sergeant in the Black Watch!

Speaking with a broad Yorkshire accent, Williams was ever the amiable and upbeat comic, who dealt with animosity in the most non-confrontational way: 'If you don't keep quiet, I'll bring me tribe in and we'll eat the lot of yeh! We've had missionary for tea before tha knows.' Although sometimes he could be quite subversive:

Enoch Powell says, 'Go home black man', and I thought, aye, ah will, but it's a helluva long wait for a bus to Barnsley.

In a 1999 interview with *Guardian* journalist Alistair Harry, Williams said: 'I told jokes that I thought would suit the audience, I was telling jokes for the human race. So people could have a laugh. There are Jewish jokes, Irish jokes, Scottish ones, so why not coloureds? If you stop telling jokes about nationalities, you've got nothing left. But if you were offended I apologise. I didn't set out to offend. I went out so that people could laugh.'

Prior to the eighties sexist jokes were acceptable to club audiences while conversely sex jokes were not, and any comic using four letter expletives was almost guaranteed to be, "paid off" (given half the fee and shown the door).

That all changed in the eighties. Ken Dodd said in a Jonathan Brown article for *The Independent*: 'The effing and blinding – that is shock comedy that is not here to stay, after you have shocked the audience where do you go?'

Dodd was wrong, the effing and blinding was here to stay and comedians like Bernard Manning, Jim Davidson, Roy 'Chubby' Brown, Jethro, Mike Reid, and Jimmy Jones had long since recognised the fact.

It was not, as most people think, an "Alternative" comedian who first employed expletive language in front of mixed crowds. Legendry cockney comic, Jimmy Jones holds that distinction.

Jones performed on a circuit of pubs and clubs in and around London and through numerous recordings of his shows became something of a sixties cult figure amongst touring rock bands like, The Rolling Stones, Iron Maiden, and Status Quo.

Initially Jones relied on a technique whereby he never actually swore but instead used the term, 'kinnell' which he explained in his 2011 autobiography, *Now This Is A Very True Story* was short for, 'blinking hell,' he said, 'and you can please yer kin selves if you kin believe me or you kin don't.'

According to Jones the idea came to him while watching a football match in the late sixties and one team had a player called George Kinnell. When Kinnell missed a penalty the fans collectively shouted, 'Oh, Kinnell!' and Jones thought, 'I kin like that', and put it into his act.

In 1980 Jones signed a deal with *PolyGram* for Betamax and VHS recordings of his live shows, making him the pioneer of stand-up video.

'It was the video company that advised me to drop kinnell and go with fucking hell,' Jones said, 'I thought, well they must know the market, so I went bluer.'

The company was right, and sales rocketed, though bluer meant that television producers shied away from him, especially in the wake of Liverpool comedian Stan Boardman, who in the early eighties caused a major furore on the live *Des O'Connor Show* when he told a joke about the German Focke-Wulf fighter plane, and a World War Two Polish pilot who flew in the Royal Air Force and was appearing on *This is Your Life*:

So Aemon Andrews jumps out and sez, 'Charlie Polanski this is your life' and they get him into the studio and Aemon sez, 'You are the famous fighter pilot who during the war shot down twenty five German fighter planes', and Charlie was telling the story and he said, 'I vos flying over the channel and suddenly I see two Fokkers and I think to myself I must shoot one of the Fokkers down, so I shoot one of the Fokkers down and another Fokker went into the clouds so I follow him, but I lose the Fokker… and then I came out of the clouds but he is gone and in the mirror I look and I see behind me, the Fokker is behind me…' at this point Aemon Andrews interrupted and he said, 'hang on Charlie Polanski we've got to explain to the viewers that during the war the German fighter plane was a called a Focke-Wulf,' and Charlie sez, 'That is correct Aemon, but these Fokkers were Messerschmitt's!'

Like many cockney comedians at the time Jimmy Jones incorporated a West Indian accent for some jokes, he argued it was just an accent and that no one ever complained about a Welsh or Scottish accent. A valid point but for the context in which the accent was used. From his 1989 *PolyGram* recording, *An Audience with the Guv'nor*:

So, I came out of this pub well drunk and I'm heading towards south London, Peckham and this coloured feller was muckin' about on the Zebra crossing, 'First you see me, now you don't', and he had his teeth out an all. Well, I caught him on the black and he went up in

229

the air at such an angle that he came through the sun roof of the Reliant Robin, well, actually it wasn't a sun roof until he came through it… I have to say I was a bit bevied so I thought, I'm in trouble 'ere, but I found this copper, and he done him for breaking and entering…

The routine could be construed as a subtle piece of social commentary on the discriminatory behaviour of a policeman toward a black man. But Jones considered it neither social commentary nor racist, he was just trying to make people laugh, and defending the joke said: 'Take the accent away and you kill the gag. Black people in the audience always loved it. I've only ever had complaints from white people, the kind of people that are always looking to be offended on someone else's behalf.'

It is however, difficult to argue Jones' case when listening to his *Live at Kings* DVD and he begins a joke, 'So there was this coloured feller,' suddenly stopping to glance at the audience before asking, 'Is there any of them in? Cos the bastards hide in the shadows, and just my luck he'll have taken his teeth out,' before explaining his concern, 'cos they can chuck a spear two- hundred-yards!'

The comics' reign as the star attraction in social clubs began to wane in the eighties which coincided with, for the first time in the history of Working Men's Clubs, shrinking membership numbers.

Inner city pubs and bars changed dramatically over the decade, becoming more vibrant and playing loud music, which was much more alluring to young people than social clubs.

In their heyday of the sixties and seventies there were over four thousand affiliated social clubs in Britain, since then more than half have called, 'last orders'.

Yet, despite having their lowest membership numbers since the early fifties, the Working Men's Club and Institute Union is the largest non-profit making social entertainment and leisure organisation in Britain and still represents the interests of over five million members.

Chapter Twenty-Seven

The alternative before Alternative

The idea that the 1980s British "Alternative" comedians (for want of a better phrase) were the first to disregard conventional joke telling is a fallacy. Every era has produced alternative comedians and while the new alternatives were finding their feet in the early eighties there were many established comedians who fashioned jokes from observations and exaggerations of real life.

Liverpool comic Tom O'Connor created jokes from the eccentricities and foibles of working class Liverpudlians. 'I suppose the change in my cabaret act from gags to routines began with the wedding,' he explained in his autobiography, 'weddings in the old days being a heady mixture of romance, family strife, and outrageous fun.'

What are you doing on the corned beef table? You're on the ham with our family, their crowds on the potted meat! Move them down!
Oh, right, sorry, are you a friend of the groom?
Certainly not, I'm the bride's mother...

Dave Allen transformed himself into a comedic observer of the highest order in the 1970's after taking advice from Opera star, Helen Traubel: 'I was working with her in Sydney and we used to go out,' Allen said, 'and I used to talk about Ireland and just being a kid, and she said to me one night, why don't you talk about this on stage? Why go out and try and tell funny one-liners? Why don't you introduce some of this? Because it's not only funny, it's good to listen too, and it's factual. It's very real.'
Allen did just that:

School was quite terrifying. The first time you go to school. My father said to me, there'll be a boy at the school that will want to hit you. The first day in school someone will want to hit you. Now *that* is the school bully. All bullies are cowards, and he'll only hit you if he thinks you're frightened of him. So, if you hit him first he'll run away. I was expelled after two weeks for being the school bully.

For decades Glaswegian Chick Murray had indulged in surreal flights of comic chimera:

I got up this morning, I like to get up in the morning it gives me the rest of the day to myself... so I dressed, I always dress, I like to be different, but I think undressed you're a bit too different... so, I crossed the landing and went down stairs, mind you if there had been no stairs there I wouldn't even have attempted it... and I went down the street, went down the front, you can go down the front, there's no law against it, and I was walking in my usual way, nothing fancy, one foot in front of the other, that's the best way I find...

In his autobiography Bob Monkhouse wrote: 'John Paul Joans might have become the British Lenny Bruce until tragedy struck and a hit and run accident left him with severe cerebral damage.' The 1971 Granada TV documentary, *There's This Feller* filmed Joans performing in a Working Men's Club:

Would you believe that many people, in fact only three nights ago, someone complained because I had dared to use such an obscene three letter word as tit! They said, you will be banished forever! I said, come now, there are far worse pornographic words in the world than tit, would you agree with me sir? Yes, there are far worse words than tit, most people think the worst four letter word is the one to do with copulation but it's not sir, copulation is a beautiful thing, ain't it? The worst four letter word in the world for me is the word, bomb, a dirty, nasty, obscene thing would you agree? Which would you rather hold in your hand, a live bomb or a live tit?

John Dowie is a comedian often associated with the Alternative scene but one who had been plying his talents at universities, colleges, and arts centres since the early seventies. His one man shows consisted of wry thoughts, opinions, observations, and even the occasional joke:

I once bought her a book, *How to Improve your Man in Bed*. And she got somebody else.

In 1978 Dowie toured with the incredibly gifted, Victoria Wood:

She was terribly depressed about the veins in her legs. She had shorts on the other day and her husband used her left thigh to direct someone to the motorway.

The British folk scene produced a surprising number of comedians who were more observational then out-and-out joke tellers.

Despite the advent of rock 'n' roll and Beatlemania folk clubs were extremely popular in Britain during the sixties and seventies. "Folkies" set up folk evenings in pubs, clubs, and hotels, nights that had a reputation for non-commercialised, unsophisticated, laid back entertainment.

Most comedians on the folk circuit started out as musicians, playing and singing, adding the odd joke between numbers until eventually the jokes took over the act. Bob Davies from Birmingham chose Carrot as a surname to add to his nickname Jasper when he decided upon a career as a folk singer in the late sixties. He took regular jokes and personalised them:

I had an auntie once, who suffered terribly from asthma, and one night she got an obscene phone call, and after five minutes the bloke said, 'Did I phone you or did you phone me?'

As he gained more experience Carrot reversed the process and turned real life into jokes. Londoner, Richard Digance developed in much the same way:

The difference between *Cosmopolitan* and *Woman's Realm* is that *Cosmopolitan* tells you how to have an orgasm and *Woman's Realm* tells you how to knit one.

'Rochdale Cowboy', Mike Harding, a favourite on the university and college folk circuit was a humorous raconteur of the highest order:

The priest told us it was wrong to masturbate, and he said that whenever we were tempted we should take a cold shower. When I was coming through puberty I had that many cold showers now when it rains I get an 'ard on...

The formative years of Billy Connolly's comedy was a strange concoction of observational patter and traditional jokes.

He started out in Glasgow folk clubs where he was influenced by performers who added comic asides to their sets, like singer-songwriter and poet Matt McGinn; singer/comedian Hamish Imlach; and Anglo-Canadian guitarist Diz Disley who once quipped: 'I learned this song at university, with a record I bought when I was there, with some money I stole when I was there. Some people call it a grant...'

In the mid-sixties Connolly became a member of the folk group *The Humblebums* and began adding jokes to the introduction of their songs. The group split in 1971 with fellow band member Gerry Rafferty citing: 'The jokes were getting longer and the musical content shorter and I was frustrated towards the end.' Connolly agreed, 'It couldn't work anymore,' he said, 'I just had to get funny.'

His first solo album, *Billy Connolly Live* was a moderate success in Scotland, but it was the 1973 follow up, *Solo Concert* that made critics really sit up and take notice. It also earned him a certain amount of notoriety by being banned from radio stations for his depiction of the crucifixion, a monologue that came out of a joke told by a friend, Tam Quinn:

Jesus came into the bar where all the apostles were hanging out and he saw them all eating Chinese take-away.

234

Jesus said to them, 'Where did you get that?'
'Well,' said Peter, 'Judas bought it, he seems to have come into a bit of money.'

Connolly turned the joke into his infamous *Last Supper and Crucifixion* which he set, not in Galilee, but in Gallowgate, 'up by the cross', where the apostles were drinking in the pub and eagerly awaiting the arrival of Jesus, or as Connolly called him, 'The Big Yin':

Suddenly the door opens and in he comes, the Big Yin, 'Well, hello there, boys', with the long dress and the casual sandals and the aura... 'So, hello there, lads, how yers getting on and that y'know?' And the wee apostle comes up to him and says, "Hey I thought you were ney comin' and that, you know Big Yin, I thought you wasnae turning up", and the Big Yin says, 'I nearly wasnae turning up, sonny boy, I bin oot all morning doing them miracles and I'm knackered, gis a glass a that wine... ney kiddin' son I'm knackered, see them miracles I've done this mornin', take a look out that door, there's nothin' but deed punters walking up and doon that street.'

When booked to appear on the prestigious BBC chat show *Parkinson*, Connolly introduced himself to the British public with an old joke:

This feller was walking with his pal, and his pal sez, 'How's the wife?' and the feller said, 'Oh, she's dead.' 'Dead?' said his pal, 'Aye, I murdered her, you wanna see where she's buried?'
So, they go into his back yard and they get to a spot where there's a mound of freshly dug earth and a bare bum sticking out from it, and his pal sez, 'Why have yer left her bum sticking out like that?' and the feller sez, 'Well, I need somewhere to park my bike!'

Parkinson, the studio audience and millions of viewers exploded with laughter, and Britain hailed the arrival of a new comedy star.

The alternatives were admittedly in the minority, most British comedians told jokes, and many told the same jokes, and by the mid-seventies they held little appeal for most young people.

By the end of the decade British stand-up comedy needed an overhaul, change was long overdue and the catalysts for that change were the comedians who established the London *Comedy Store*, a small and inauspicious comedy club that launched an Alternative movement that redefined stand-up comedy in Britain. A movement that for a while, left the joke out in the cold.

Chapter Twenty-Eight

The Comedy Store, L. A.

Stand-up comedy in America underwent a transformation in the early seventies after a whole raft of observational comedians broke onto the scene, many of whom learned their trade at *The Improv Club* in New York, opened by comedian Budd Freidman in 1963.

The club was designed as a laid back, loosely formatted cabaret room where established acts tested material for America's most prestigious television show, Johnny Carson's *The Tonight Show* which was recorded in New York.

When the known comedians were done, unknown acts were allowed stage time and star comedians like Jay Leno, Freddie Prinze Andy Kaufman, Steve Lubetkin, Richard Lewis, Elayne Boosler, and David Brenner all started out at *The Improv*.

David Brenner's set-up, 'Did you ever notice…' defined the seventies generation of American comedians:

Did you ever notice that the evangelist guy on TV that cures people wears a toupee! I don't get it, he can fix a guy's legs, but he can't put hair on his own head.

In 1972 *The Tonight Show* announced that it was relocating to Los Angeles, while as fate would have it, only a few weeks prior to Carson's West Coast debut a new ninety-nine seat comedy club opened on Sunset Strip.

The club belonged to Las Vegas comic Sammy Shore and his business partner Rudy DeLuca who with only days to its opening, were still wrestling with names for their new venture. Shore's wife Mitzi suggested, 'The Comedy Store.'

Shore opened *The Comedy Store* not as money making venture but a place he and his showbiz friends could hang out, drink, and try out new material. The evenings were fun, free-and-easy affairs and no one knew who might drop in and perform on any given night, although as back up Shore did hire the *Comedy Store Players*, a comedy improvisation team.

Star names like Buddy Hackett, Jackie Vernon, Flip Wilson, and Red Foxx all appeared regularly, but never by appointment and audiences knew that they took a chance on the bill when they paid their entrance fee. The arrival of *The Tonight Show* changed everything.

One morning Shore got a call from the talent agent James Komack asking him to give rookie comedian Freddie Prinze some stage time because he wanted to bring some people in to watch him. Shore obliged, and the people turned out to be Jim McCawley, the talent co-ordinator for *The Tonight Show* and some *NBC* television executives.

Prinze was duly booked for Carson's show the following week where he performed a blistering set. A few days later *NBC* announced that it had signed the comedian to star in his own sitcom.

The announcement sent a clear message to every unknown comedian in America, because when Johnny Carson introduced Prinze for his *Tonight Show* debut and said, 'Here is a young comic who's appearing in town at the Comedy Store', it effectively told every comedian in the country that the path to stardom began at *The Comedy Store*. Overnight the little club became the gig they all wanted.

Sammy Shore meanwhile, had other ideas and despite the flood of unknown comedians wanting stage time he saw no reason to change how his place worked. He accommodated *Tonight Show* people when asked, but basically the club remained a place for him and his friends to socialise.

His wife Mitzi however, had a very different vision of how the place should be run. So, when Shore returned to Vegas for a brief stint she turned the club into a business and *the* place to go if you wanted to see fresh, quality stand-up comedy in Los Angeles.

She started with the décor of the performance room, removing any glitz and glitter, and painting the walls and ceiling black to match the tables. The stage was lit by a single white spotlight which focussed the audience's attention on the comedians. But the most ingenious part was the show itself.

When her husband ran the evenings, it was a "most famous goes first" policy and young hopefuls who turned up night after night rarely got a chance to perform. Mitzi decided to make the hopefuls the stars of the show.

She established a system of nightly line-ups featuring as many as twelve comedians, each one vetted by her personally, each performing one after the other for an evening of continuous comedy.

All that remained of Sammy's original idea was that of not paying the comedians, Mitzi being of mind that *The Comedy Store* was a place of opportunity, not a place of employment.

When Sammy returned he was shocked to find that in just a month his little club was a slick, money-making operation.

The Comedy Store went from strength to strength, the performance room was extended to a capacity of four hundred and fifty, while two shows nightly became standard.

The policy of non-payment remained until 1979 when comedians refused to work the club and after weeks of wrangling Mitzi reluctantly agreed to pay the performers a fee, which effectively wiped out "showcase" rooms across the country.

By the mid-eighties the demand for live comedy in America was such that there were more than three hundred comedy clubs on a circuit that supported an estimated fifteen hundred comedians.

While a new generation of comedians were giving American stand-up comedy a makeover an old-fashioned joke book marked a new scholarly approach to the study of Anglo-American folklore.

Pissing in the Snow by Vance Randolph is a volume of Ozark folktales collected by the author between 1919 and 1954, one hundred and one jokes, anecdotes, and lies, a unique and vivid picture of the type of humour enjoyed in the context of life by the Arkansas-Missouri hill folk, the Ozarks.

Prior to Randolph's book, studies of American folklore included only a selective representation of certain cultural groups while large segments of the population were ignored, specifically women and children, and rural white lower-classes.

Coarse folklore was usually censored, something Randolph refused to do, which earned him nigh on a lifetime of struggle against poverty, red tape, and indifference to his work, and is the reason why *Pissing in the Snow*, completed in 1954, was not on general release until 1976.

In the preface Randolph said: 'An anthropologist is free to publish a detailed description of any indecent situation, by using Latin derivatives instead of the vulgar English equivalents. But many folktales cannot be presented in this academic jargon, because they depend upon linguistic as well as situational elements for effect. Translate a vernacular legend into the language of the schools, and it is no longer a folktale. An honest folklorist cannot substitute *faeces* for *shit*, or write *copulate* when his informant says *fuck*, *diddle*, *roger*, or *tread*. Why should one employ such a noun as *penis*, if the narrator prefers *pecker*, *horn*, *jemson*, or *tallywhacker*?'

One time there was this silly little girl that heard about fucking, but she hadn't never done any. She took her old pappy a jug of cider while he was working the timber. 'Pappy,' she says, 'I want you to fuck me.' The old man says, 'All right,' and cut him a saw-toothed briar. He whipped her ass until she yelled like a steam whistle. So that's what she thought fucking was.

Pretty soon her and one of the neighbour boys got married. 'The very first night she says, 'I never been fucked but once, and I sure don't want any more of it.' He asked her who done it and she told him, 'My pappy.' Next day the boy went to see her pappy and the old man told him just what happened. 'Don't never call it fucking,' says pappy, 'just tell her you want to make something for the house and get her broke in that way.' So, the boy went to town and got some plates, cups, and saucers. He hid them under the bed and every time they knocked off a chunk he would fetch out a piece of china.

Next time the old man sees the girl he asks how they are getting along. She says everything is going fine. 'I told John the first night there'd be no fucking,' she says, 'me and him spends all our time making dishes, and it sure is fun. We've got enough plates, cups, and saucers for two families already, and if John don't run out of paste, we're going to make you a fine big piss-pot for Christmas.'

One time there was a young woman fetched a baby into Doc Henderson's office and she says it is losing weight. Doc examined the baby a while, and asked the woman about her victuals, but she says, 'What I eat ain't got nothing to do with the baby being skinny.' Doc figured she must be kind of stupid, so he didn't ask no more questions.

Doc examined her mighty careful anyhow, and he pulled her dress open, to see if there is something the matter with her breasts. The woman wiggled a good deal, but he sucked her tits, first one, and then the other. There wasn't no milk at all. Finally, she says, 'That's my sister's baby, you know.'

Old Doc Henderson was considerable set back when he heard that, because he never thought but that it was her baby. 'Hell's fire,' he says, 'you shouldn't have come!' And the young woman just giggled. 'I didn't,' she says, 'until you started a-sucking the second one.'

On Oct 16, 1978, Cardinal Karol Wojtyla, the archbishop of Krakow became the first Polish Pope in history, and the first non-Italian to hold the office in more than four hundred and fifty years. Polish-Americans hoped that such a prestigious appointment would finally put an end to "Polack" jokes. It only served to provide fresh impetus to a new burst of creativity:

Did you hear what the Polish Pope's first big decision was?
Wallpaper the Sistine Chapel.

They asked the Polish Pope if he thought priests should marry, and the pope said, 'Only if they love each other.'

Chapter Twenty-Nine

"Alternative Comedy"

The seventies in Britain was a decade of industrial strikes, three day working weeks, and winters of discontent, juxtaposed with the rise of environmentalism, the Gay Liberation Front, Anti-Racism movements, Punk Rock, and Alternative Comedy.

Punk Rock was regarded as the alternative to the polished, stylised rock bands, in much the same way Alternative Comedy was meant to be the antithesis of mainstream, joke telling comedians.

Since the emergence of the first British stand-up comedians in the 1930's the stand-up format had changed little, stand-up comedians told jokes, style and persona were important, but not as important as punch lines. Unfortunately, too many comedians told the same ones.

Stand-up comedy needed new blood, young blood, an alternative to club comics, and that alternative took its first tentative steps in 1979 at *The Comedy Store*, a tiny comedy club housed in a seedy strip club in London's Soho district.

Whilst holidaying in America in 1978, life insurance salesman Peter Rosengard spent an evening at the Los Angeles, *Comedy Store* which gave him the idea to open a similar club back in London.

In his search for a suitable place he met Don Ward, the owner of two strip clubs in Soho; the *Sunset Strip* and the *Nell Gwynne Strip Club* the latter of which accessed *The Gargoyle*, a small bar, come nightclub. The bar was agreed upon as the venue and the pair came to an arrangement whereby Ward supplied the staff whilst Rosengard supplied the comedians.

As the hundred or so invited guests began arriving on the opening night in May 1979 someone pointed out to Rosengard that comedians were notorious for hogging the limelight and a spotlight was needed to flash on and off to let the performers know their time was up.

Ashley, 'Billy the Kid' Roy was despatched to rent a spotlight, but unable to procure one Billy the Kid returned instead with a huge gong, reasoning that a gentle tap would inform the comics that it was time to wind down their act.

'The comics never stood a chance,' Rosengard said, 'the first one had hardly been on when someone shouted, "Get him off." Then the rest of the audience joined in and the poor man on stage, a look of terror in his eyes, was totally thrown and seemed about to cry. I gestured for Billy to tap the gong. A deafening "Gong!" rang out. It was almost as if Big Ben were in the room... the first comedian slunk from the stage. Alexei [Sayle, compere] brought on the next one. He didn't fare any better. This time somebody shouted, "Gong, gong," and Billy hit the gong again. It seemed impossible to strike it so it sounded softly, and now everybody seemed to join in, yelling, "Gong him, gong him!"'

After the first few acts were "gonged" the audience turned into a mob and screamed for every hapless comic to be the gonged off in what Rosengard described as a 'comedy massacre'.

The following morning *The Guardian* journalist Tom Tickell, who himself had been gonged, wrote in his column: 'All Rosengard has to do to make *The Comedy Store* a success is to find some comedians.'

Rosengard found it increasingly difficult to fill the bill until he decided on token payments to secure better comedians, soon after which Tony Allen, Keith Allen (no relation), Jim Barclay, Andy de la Tour, and two brilliant and inventive double acts, Rik Mayall and Ade Edmondson as *Twentieth Century Cayote*, and Peter Richardson and Nigel Planer as *The Outer Limits* were added to the regular roster of Alexei Sayle, Arnold Brown and Lee Cornes.

That small nucleus of comedians made *The Comedy Store* the place to go for new comedy in London on a Saturday night.

The comedians however, found it difficult to develop an act on one performance a week so began presenting comedy nights at the *Lord Elgin* pub on the corner of Ladbroke Grove, and it was there that the term, "Alternative Comedy" was first coined.

Tony Allen came up with the title: 'I was really against Arts Council funding,' he explained in his book *Attitude*, 'because I thought the economics should determine the style, and I couldn't understand how you could get these large amounts of money from the Arts Council and then put on something with thirty people in the audience; if you were good and it worked you should fill the place and be able to make a living out of it. So, we formed *Alternative Cabaret* – which is what I called the thing – and we all became Alternative comedians.'

Alternative comedians were an alternative to mainstream comedians, different in most every way, they dressed down to appear much like their audience, they were anti-jokes, at least in the traditional set-up/punch-line style, and were non-sexist, non-racist, and politically correct.

In 1980 television producer Paul Jackson persuaded the BBC to make a pilot variety show using *Comedy Store* comedians which was recorded in May and edited to a half hour that went out six months later. According to Jackson the show received, 'the worst audience response in the history of the department.'

Two years later the BBC2 comedy sit com, *The Young Ones* introduced Alternative Comedy to the masses.

Written by Ben Elton, Rik Mayall, Lise Mayer, with additional material from Alexei Sayle, and starring Adrianne Edmondson, Rik Mayall, Nigel Planer, and Christopher Ryan it was broadcast from 1982 to 1984 in two six-part series.

The show did relatively well in its first outing, but it was the second series and subsequent repeats that gave *The Young Ones* cult status and announced the arrival of Alternative Comedy on British television with a fanfare of surreal silliness, violent slapstick, and anarchic offbeat humour.

In the meantime, the Soho *Comedy Store* closed in December 1982 after the lease expired on *The Gargoyle* and with the new terms not to Don Ward's liking he decided to look for new premises. He and Rosengard also went their separate ways.

Ward re-opened the following year at Leicester Square, by which time Alternative style comedy clubs were springing up throughout Britain.

Alternative comedians were generally left wing and more sympathetic to the underdog, but in the eighties, many became so obsessed with being "right on" and politically correct that it unhinged the comedy.

Political correctness is an avoidance of expressions that excludes, marginalises, or insults groups of people who are socially disadvantaged or discriminated against. Political correctness does not give credence to the expression, 'It's just a joke.'

Making jokes with the sole intent to hurt is the mark of a bully and cannot ever be defended, but neither can a society that actively encourages people to take offence, and in the eighties the British turned into that society.

Fuelled by politicians, the media, and Alternative comedians, political correctness became an accusation bandied about for often the most trivial faux pas and those in the public eye had to think very carefully about what they said, or risk being branded racist or sexist.

It seriously curbed what could be joked about on radio and television, which cut adrift most club comics and their non-PC jokes.

At the same time however, many Alternative comedians became cartoon versions of liberal extremists, a corrupted, arrogant version of the non-racist, non-sexist comedians they were supposed to be. Comedian Mark Steel described some of the early Alternative venues as, 'forums for the most wretched, smug self-congratulatory stuck up twaddle ever witnessed outside an art gallery.'

In its modern sense political correctness began with the Left's enthusiasm for Chairman Mao's *Little Red Book*, which was translated into English in 1966. However, they did not take political correctness too seriously and even came up with kind of in-jokes, self-mocking with ironic meanings:

He is not a bad dancer, he is overly Caucasian.

She is not a bird, she's a breasted Briton.

245

The early history of political correctness in Britain is elegantly covered in a 1994 essay by social commentator Stuart Hall, who argued that the intellectual triumphs of the right-wing free market economies had extinguished the left-wing's causes of class struggle and social injustice which meant that the Left needed a substitute.

Hall wrote: 'In the old days, class and economic deprivation were what the Left considered the 'principal contradiction' of social life. All the major social conflicts seemed to flow from and lead back to them. The era of PC is marked by the proliferation of the sites of social conflict and to include the conflicts around questions of race, gender, sexuality, the family, ethnicity and cultural difference, as well as issues around class and inequality... '

The trouble for jokes and zealous politically correct jokers is that the words run the show. They surrender to the approved language of political correctness, and it takes over their own experiences, what they did, or observed, much to the detriment of the humour.

Whenever that happens jokers tend to blend into one another and sound much of a muchness, effected with emotion more generic than honest.

The individual humour of the experience is reduced by the collective mode of expression, or as George Orwell plaintively wrote: 'Orthodoxy of whatever colour seems to demand a lifeless imitative style.'

Fortunately, the second wave of Alternative comedians were not only less political but less concerned with being politically correct. They also brought the joke back into the spotlight. Comedians like Jeff Green, Lee Hurst, and Frank Skinner. 'I liked gags about shagging and football,' said Skinner 'and, at the end of the day so did most of my audience. Some people saw me as a backlash, but if I was it was an accident.'

I've got a mate who's a Mormon. He wrote the first ever Mormon musical, it's called Forty-Seven Brides for Seven Brothers.

Frank Skinner.

Despite political correctness, the ebb and flow of joke cycles continued as usual during the eighties, the most controversial of which was AIDS.

Acquired Immune Deficiency Syndrome is a disease in which there is a severe loss of the body's cellular immunity, greatly lowering the resistance to infection and malignancy. The cause is the human immunodeficiency virus, HIV, transmitted in blood and sexual fluids. It was first identified in the early 1980's and in the developed world the disease initially spread amongst homosexuals, intravenous drug users, and recipients of infected blood transfusions.

It mattered little that most of the AIDS jokes were ill-informed:

A feller is told he has AIDS and after the initial shock asked the doctor, 'Is there anything you can do?' 'Well,' said the doctor, 'I would advise taking a trip to India and once there, drink only tap water and eat unwashed vegetables.'

And the feller said, 'Will that cure me?'

'No,' said the doctor, 'but it'll teach you what your arsehole is really for.'

Joke cycles are primarily invented by men and their content often contains a marked anti-female bias. There are jokes about women's logic, but not men's, women drivers, not men, mother-in-law jokes but not father-in-law jokes, and even henpecked husband jokes can be construed as a veiled attack on domineering women. Numerous fat girl, thin girl, dumb girl, and "easy" girl jokes are rarely reversed to make men the butt. "Cucumber" jokes were the rare exception, a joke cycle created by women that put men on the receiving end.

The jokes first appeared in America as office photocopier jokes in the mid-eighties and resulted in a few published collections including, *Cucumbers*; *The Cucumber Book*; and *Cucumbers are Better than Men*:

CUCUMBERS ARE BETTER THAN MEN BECAUSE:

The average cucumber is at least six inches long.

247

Cucumbers stay hard for weeks.

A cucumber won't tell other cucumbers you're not a virgin anymore.

A cucumber never has to "call the wife".

No matter how old you are you can always get a fresh cucumber.

A cucumber won't be upset if he sees you out with a banana from your office.

The Cucumber cycle never really caught on in Britain, but American "Blonde" jokes did, which probably says more about the British male than it does the British female:

What do you get when you give a blonde a penny for her thoughts?
Change.

Why did the blonde look so happy when she finished a jigsaw puzzle after six months?
Because on the box it said: 2-4 years.

In the south of England, they transmuted into "Essex Girls" jokes, and added promiscuity to their stupidity:

An Essex girl was talking to her friend and she said, 'Ere you know that bruvver of yours, we was in bed the uvver night and he called me a slag.' Her friend said, 'Cheeky bastard, what did you say?'
And she said, 'Slag? Slag? I said, who you calling a slag? Then I told him to fack off out of my bed and take his facking friends wiv 'im.'

The American "Redneck" cycle also crossed the Atlantic:

248

You might be a redneck if you're hoping that one day you'll meet, "Cousin Right".

In England they became "Norfolk" jokes:

A young girl from Norfolk wrote to the local newspaper's Agony Aunt: Dear Deidre, I'm thirteen and still a virgin, do you think my brothers are gay?

It is an ancient tradition to make fun of fellow countrymen, even close neighbours, those without any distinct differences but who are for some reason or other considered inferior. The Irish joke about the people of Kerry, Italians about the Milanese, the Spanish about Catalans, Chinese about the citizens of Shansi, Indians about Gujarati people, Nigerians about the people of Ibos. In South Africa it's the people of Brakpan, a gold and uranium mining town in Gauteng province inhabited, according to the jokes, by white hillbillies:

Why is it hard to solve a murder in Brakpan? Because the DNA is all the same and there are no dental records.

In the nineties a closely related joke cycle was aimed at English, "Chavs":

You might be a Chav if you allow your fifteen-year-old daughter to smoke at the dinner table in front of her children.

What's the most confusing day of the year for a Chav?
Father's Day.

The term "Chav" was initially said to be an abbreviation for "council house and violent" but has since been proven to be a backronym (a constructed acronym created to fit an existing word). *The Oxford English Dictionary* defines Chav as: 'An informal

249

derogatory, meaning young lower-class person who displays brash and loutish behaviour and wears real or imitation designer clothes.'

Chav was a term popularised by the British media in the nineties when referring to what they regarded as an anti-social youth subculture. However, *The Times* columnist Julie Birchall argued that the word is a form of social racism and that the sneering reveals more about the Chav detractors than those of their supposed victims, while the *Fabian Society* consider it to be middle-class hatred of the working-class, describing it as, 'class abuse by people asserting authority.'

In the late eighties the pop star's obsession with cosmetic surgery created a Michael Jackson joke cycle:

How does Michael Jackson pick his nose?
From a catalogue.

But in the nineties the cycle became much darker when in 1994 the pop star paid out over twenty million dollars to thirteen-year-old Jordan Chandler in an out of court settlement over alleged paedophilia:

What do Sears and Michael Jackson have in common?
Little boy's pants, half-off.

When the Catholic Church began making similar out-of-court settlements it became the main target for the paedophile cycle:

A little Irish boy is sitting on the front step crying and Seamus asks him what's wrong and the boy said, 'Me Ma's died.'
'Oh, Bejaysus now, should I call Father Conley for you?'
And the little boy said, 'No tanks mister, sex is the last thing on my mind just now.'

A Scottish Priest made a complaint against eBay because the Wii Game Boy he ordered wasn't quite what he expected.

New technology usually creates new jokes:

Take my Wi-Fi... please!

Since the eighties programmers have designed computer software to write jokes, including JAPE (Joke Analysis and Production Engine); WAISCRAIC (Witty Idiomatic Sentence Creation Revealing Ambiguity In Context); DEviaNT, (Double Entendre via Noun Transfer); and STANDUP (System To Augment Non-speakers Dialogue Using Puns).

STANDUP has a more serious and worthy intent in that it was designed to help non-speaking children use language more effectively. The programme developed the "Joking Computer" which has a three-part system. It begins by choosing the punch line, for example finding a two-word phrase in the dictionary and then replaces the second word with something that sounds similar, for example, 'computer screen' becomes 'computer scream'. It then looks for associated words such as, 'pixel' for computer screen, and 'shout' for scream, which it puts together:

What do you call a shout that has a pixel?
A computer scream.

STANDUP has come up with classics like:

What kind of pre-school has wine?
A Play-grape.

What do you call a washing machine with a September?
An Autumn-atic washer.

I think that we can safely assume that a computer is not going to put joke writers out of work anytime soon.

Joke websites meanwhile have made the traditional joke book a harder sell, although much more disconcerting for stand-up comedians is that their jokes can be uploaded to such sites and relayed around the world in an instance.

British comedian Gary Delaney became embroiled in a row with *Sickepedia* after finding several of his one-liners on its joke website. He told the comedy website *Chortle*: 'It used to be the case that a comic's set would last decades. But now I've got jokes I wrote in May, June and July that aren't working by October because they've been absolutely trashed around the internet.'

Chapter Thirty

The Joke Professor

Alan Dundes (1934-2005) inherited the mantle as *the* authority on jokes as folklore from Gershon Legman when in 1987 he released, *Cracking Jokes.*

Affectionately known as the "Joke Professor" (although he said that he would much rather be called "professor of jokes"), Dundes was professor of anthropology and folklore at the University of Berkeley, California where his body of work played a pivotal part in establishing the study of folklore as an academic discipline in America.

In *Cracking Jokes* Dundes advocates that the study of a culture's folklore and specifically its jokes, is vital to assessing the true values and beliefs of that society.

Like Legman before him, Dundes belonged to the Freud school of thought in that he considered most jokes to be coded expressions of thoughts that we are unwilling or unable to express openly and believed that no joke endures unless it means something, even if neither the joke teller or the audience know what that meaning is.

'In fact,' he wrote, 'it is essential that the joke's meaning not be crystal clear. If people knew what they were communicating when they told the jokes, the jokes would cease to be effective as socially sanctioned outlets for expressing taboo ideas and subjects.'

He also proposed that to combat prejudice and oppression the meaning of jokes should be analysed and understood rather than glossed over, because to a degree jokes are a factor in the formation and perpetuation of prejudice and as such should be held up to the light of reason.

A lover of the joke but not so enamoured that he considered all jokes a positive force, Dundes told the *Los Angeles Times* in 1995:

253

'Women as a group have been blamed for the Garden of Eden, Pandora's Box, and the cause of death and disease. Besides women as a group, gay groups and African Americans know all about bad folklore.'

Part one of *Cracking Jokes* looks at "sick" joke cycles, specifically dead baby, disabled, and Holocaust jokes:

What's red and sits in a corner?
A baby chewing razor blades.

What's green and sits in a corner?
Same baby two weeks later.

We are ever reminded by Dundes that popular joke cycles are always a reflection of the age in which they flourish.
'Any society that can produce such jokes is sick,' he wrote, and pointedly asked why they were so severely criticised at a time when mankind was modifying technology with which human beings, babies included, could be instantly turned to dust.
'The concern,' he concluded, 'should not be with dead baby jokes, but with dead babies.'

What do you call a man with no arms and no legs in a swimming pool?
Bob.

... in a hot tub?
Stew.

... nailed to a wall?
Art.

According to Dundes, disabled jokes replace our unwillingness to express true feelings of guilt, revulsion, pity, or annoyance, and are an attempt to recognise and articulate the public's discomfort in the presence of disabled people.

Anti-Semitism is also put under the microscope by the joke professor who had already caused a major stir with an article published in *Harper's Magazine* in 1984 in which he claimed that anti-Semitism was not dead in Germany and featured as proof, "Auschwitz" jokes he had collected from German citizens on a recent visit to the country, including:

Do you know what songs are top of the Jewish hit parade?
Number 1 - Hey Jude.
Number 2 - In the Ghetto.
Number 3 – I'm on Fire.

In response to his many critics over the article Dundes said: 'Whether Auschwitz jokes are considered funny or not is not an issue, this material exists and should be recorded. Jokes are always an important barometer of the group. The jokes must fill some psychic need for those who tell them and those who listen to them. As long as the jokes are told, the evil of Auschwitz will remain in the consciousness of Germans. They may seem a sorry and inadequate memorial for all the poor wretched souls that perished at Auschwitz, but when one realises that comedy and tragedy are two sides of the same coin, we can perhaps understand why some contemporary Germans need to resort to the mechanism of humour, albeit sick humour, to try and come to terms with the unimaginable and unthinkable horrors that did occur at Auschwitz.'

Part two of *Cracking Jokes* deals with stereotypes, Elephant jokes, and using humour as covert language and jokes as ethnic slurs. A scholarly approach to understanding our susceptibility to the irrational, which Dundes hoped that armed with such knowledge we might move beyond prejudice to behaving rationally and humanely.

Other notable works by Dundes include, *Here I Sit: A Study of American Latrinalia* (toilet jokes); *Arse Longa, Vita Brevis* (AIDS); *First Prize: Fifteen Years* [dissident jokes from Eastern Europe - the title is the punch-line to the set-up, 'Did you hear about the joke contest in Bucharest?']; and with Carl Pagter, a trio of books covering jokes transmitted by photocopier machines from offices around the world.

The books, *Urban Folklore from the Paperwork Empire*, 1975; *When You're Up to Your Ass in Alligators*, 1987; and *Never Try to Teach a Pig to Sing*, 1991, contain jokes from office pools in the U. S. A., Germany, Sweden, Denmark, and Britain.

The office jokes appear in cartoon form, narrative and one-line jokes, graffiti, parodies of regulatory questionnaires and insurance claim forms. The following is a mock insurance claim from Buffalo, U. S. A., and dated 1980, but is much older and was a part of the famed cartoonist, musician, mimic, and comedian Gerald Hofnung's live act during the fifties. It first appeared in print in the form of a letter to the *Manchester Guardian* in the 1960s:

Dear Sir:
I am writing in response to your request for more information concerning block #11 on the insurance form which asks for "cause of injuries" wherein I put 'trying to do the job alone.' You said you needed more information, so I trust the following will be sufficient.

I am a bricklayer by trade and on the date of the injuries I was working alone laying brick around the top of a four-storey building when I realised that I had about 500 pounds of brick left over. Rather than carry the bricks down by hand, I decided to put them into a barrel and lower them by a pulley that was fastened to the top of the building. I secured the end of the rope at ground level and went up to the top of the building and loaded the bricks into the barrel and swung the barrel out with the bricks in it. I then went down and untied the rope, holding it securely to insure the slow descent of the barrel.

As you will note on block #6 of the insurance form, I weigh 195 pounds. Due to my shock at being jerked off the ground so swiftly, I lost my presence of mind and forgot to let go of the rope. Between the second and third floor I met the barrel coming down. This accounts for the bruises and lacerations on my upper body. Regaining my presence of mind, I held tightly to the rope and proceeded rapidly up the side of the building, not stopping until my right hand was jammed in the pulley. This accounts for the broken thumb.

Despite the pain, I retained my presence of mind and held tightly to the rope. At approximately the same time, however, the barrel of bricks hit the ground and the bottom fell out of the barrel. Devoid of the weight of the bricks, the barrel now weighed about 50 pounds. I again refer you to block #6 and my weight.

As you would guess, I began a rapid descent. In the vicinity of the second floor I met the barrel coming up. This explains the injuries to my legs and lower body. Slowed only slightly, I continued my descent, landing on the pile of bricks. Fortunately, my back was only sprained, and the internal injuries were minimal.

I am sorry to report, however, that at this point, I finally lost my presence of mind and let go of the rope, and as you can imagine, the empty barrel crashed down on me.

I trust this answers your concern. Please know that I am finished, 'Trying to do the job alone'.

The office copier facilitated the spreading of short jokes easier than narrative ones, below is an extract from an American list dated around the late seventies:

HAVE YOU HEARD THE ONE ABOUT?

The farmer that couldn't keep his hands of his wife, so he fired them?

The cow that got a divorce because she got a bum steer?

The absent-minded nurse who made the patient without disturbing the bed?

The chickens that ate racing forms and now they are laying odds?

The fellow who lost his girlfriend, he forgot where he laid her?

The two Angels that got kicked out of Heaven for trying to make a profit?

Other short joke lists are of specific genres, such as definitions, puns, and double-entendres.

The following is a selection from one such that originated in Pennsylvania in 1976:

If the girl next door forgets to pull down her shade, pull yours.

She used peroxide in her bath water because she knew that on the whole gentlemen prefer blondes.

The difference between dark and hard is that it gets dark every night.

Witches don't have babies because their husbands have halloweenies.

They were married, and the first morning after he was awakened by her inspecting him and crying. He asked her why she was crying, and she sobbed, 'Look, we almost used it all up the first night.'

Said the two old maids to the magician, 'Forget the hocus and pocus.'

Publishing issues meant that the collections were printed only after removing "obscene" items. *Urban Folklore from the Paperwork Empire* was first compiled in 1970 but remained unpublished for five years, while *Up to Your Ass in Alligators*, written in 1978 had to wait nine years for its release.

Censorship did not extend to racist jokes and a number are featured in the books, including in *Up to Your Ass in Alligators*, TAMPAGRAM, a New York photocopier joke which clearly originated in Tampa, Florida.

It is a cartoon depicting a distressed black child crying as an angry goose pulls his penis through a knothole in a fence. The caption below reads: 'It usually pays to stay on your own side of the fence.'

For a great part of the twentieth century the vogue term for referring to black people was, 'coloured'. An American copier joke from the mid-eighties:

ME

WHEN I WAS BORN - I WAS BLACK

WHEN I GREW UP - I WAS BLACK

WHEN I AM SICK - I AM BLACK

WHEN I GO OUT IN THE SUN - I AM BLACK

WHEN I GO OUT IN THE COLD - I AM BLACK

WHEN I DIE - I AM BLACK

BUT YOU!

WHEN YOU ARE BORN - YOU ARE PINK

WHEN YOU GREW UP - YOU ARE WHITE

WHEN YOU ARE SICK - YOU ARE GREEN

WHEN YOU GO OUT IN THE SUN - YOU ARE RED

WHEN YOU GO OUT IN THE COLD - YOU ARE BLUE

WHEN YOU DIE - YOU ARE PURPLE

AND YOU HAVE THE FUCKING NERVE TO CALL ME COLOURED!

Concerning race copier jokes the authors wrote: 'No one concerned with American humour or American national character should ignore the unique self-portrait of a people drawn from the urban folklore of the paperwork empire.'

Chapter Thirty-One

Black and British

In Britain up until the early eighties making jokes at the expense of ethnic minorities was acceptable, even on radio and television.

Author and essayist Hanif Kursishi, whose father is Pakistani and mother English, wrote about British humour on television during the sixties and seventies: 'Television comics used Pakistanis as the butt of their humour. Their jokes were highly political: they contributed to a way of seeing the world. The enjoyed reduction of racial hatred to a joke did two things: it expressed a collective view (which was sanctioned by it being on the BBC), and it was a celebration of contempt in millions of living rooms in England. I was afraid to watch TV because of it; it was too embarrassing, too degrading.'

The emergence of the Alternative comedians in the eighties together with a more politically correct culture heightened awareness, and racist jokes all but disappeared from radio and television.

Alternative comedy was inclusive to all and for the first-time people from ethnic backgrounds could attend a live comedy show without fear of being the butt of race jokes, while ethnic comedians on the comedy club circuit did not feel the need to ridicule themselves for laughs.

Lenny Henry, a black comedian and star name who learned his trade in social clubs, suddenly found his act unfashionable in the politically correct climate of the eighties.

A decade earlier at the age of sixteen Henry shot to fame when he won the television talent show *New Faces*, after which he played social clubs, cabaret clubs, summer season theatres, and bizarrely was the only black person in the touring cast of the *Black and White Minstrel Show*.

Henry explained to Alan Franks in a *Times* article about race jokes and why he told them: 'There were Paki jokes and Darkie jokes and jokes about being sent home, and moving in next door... Charlie Williams, who was born in Yorkshire, doing jokes about how all the blacks were talking about going back to Africa, and he'd say, send the boogers home, that's what I say. I did them because Charlie was doing them. He was the only successful black comedian in this country I could look to.'

Eventually Henry concluded that audiences were laughing *at* him, not with him, and that revelation, together with what he described as a, 'kick up the arse' from ITV producer Chris Tarrant, set in motion the change from cuddly social club comic to black stand-up comedian. In the mid-eighties on C4's *Saturday Night Live* he finally, ":came out":

I've been in the business for ten years and while I've been in the business I've been living a lie, I've been living a hidden existence, wearing certain clothes, going to special clubs, hanging out with people who are not like me... I've got to come out of the closet; I've got to tell you... I am... a black man! Oh my God I've said it, free at last, free at last, I'm so glad I told you, no more will I have to wear brown corduroy trousers, no more will I have to talk like Richard Bryers, Oh, dooo have another sausage role, no more will I have to go to discotheques and clap on the wrong beat.

At the latter part of the eighties special black comedy nights were organised in London, notably at the *Hackney Empire*; *Lewisham Theatre*; and *The Kings Head* pub at Crouch End, forming the basis of a small circuit, but if black comedians aspired to a career in comedy they had to tour the regular club circuit. Marcus Simmons was one of the first:

There's certain things that white people don't say to black people, like, 'Can you hold my purse for me?'

Felix Dexter, Junior Simpson, Curtis Walker also became major players on the national circuit, and the raunchy and charismatic, Richard Blackwood:

JAMAICANS MAKE SOME NOISE... yeah ... JAMAICANS THAT ARE BORN HERE... Jamaica, Kingston, via Surrey, my parents are from there... JAMAICANS THAT ARE HERE LEGALLY, and don't act like you don't know who the fuck you are, getting married as soon as you get off the fucking plane. I do, I do, come on, she does, she does, quickly they're coming, hurry up, she does...

British Asian comedians meanwhile made their mark with the 1996 ground-breaking television sketch show, *Goodness Gracious Me*.
The success and popularity of the series owed as much to lampooning recognizable British traits as it did to Asian culture. One of the creators of the show, Anil Gupta said that it was a deliberate ploy: 'It's enough for people to deal with that we've got brown faces,' she said, 'so let's not do anything else that's going to alarm them. Our approach was that we wanted to make some serious points, but not necessarily have them noticed, because the fundamental issue we were trying to address was, can Asians be funny to a broad UK television audience?'
Gupta went on to describe to Yasmeen Khan of *The Guardian* the show's impact on the comedy club circuit: 'When I started out, you were viewed as the freak act, the weird act because you were Asian. Black comics were different because there was an established black circuit, but there wasn't any Asian circuit at all. After *Goodness Gracious Me*, Asian comics suddenly became very popular.'

Asian comics were as daring as any on the mainstream circuit. Birmingham born Shazia Mirza was the first British female Muslim comedian, and noted for her sharp one-liners:

I can't wait for my marriage, I'm really looking forward to meeting my husband.

Isma Almas performed part of her act dressed in full Burka:

Asian women only wear the burka on special occasions, like when our kids have pissed us off we'll dress like this. Then, at home time, just watch them trying to work out which one of us is their mum...

'I grew up in Bradford and come from a Pakistani background and I'm a Muslim, and I discovered that's what I wanted to talk about...' Almas told Yasmeen Khan, 'My experience of living on a council estate, the only Asian family on a whole white estate.'

Terror attacks are a sensitive topic, especially for Muslim comedians but they tackled the issue head-on. American/Egyptian comedian Ahmed Ahmed asked:

There are so many terrorist organisations out there, how do you know which one to join? How do you know, I think they must have recruiters outside of Mosques going up to little boys: 'Habibi, come here... don't go to Al Qaeda, they are shit, come to us, they only promise you seventy virgins, we'll give you seventy-two, and a whore... and a goat!'

Chapter Thirty-Two

Religion

In 1989 Ayatollah Khomeni of Iran called for the death of Salman Rushdie for what he considered a blasphemous joke in the author's, *The Satanic Verses*.

The following year the book's Italian translator Ettore Capriolo was seriously wounded after being stabbed while William Nygaard, its Norwegian publisher was shot three times, both survived. Hitoshi Igarashi, the novel's Japanese translator was not so fortunate and was stabbed to death in 1991.

Two years later when Aziz Nesin stated his intention to translate *The Satanic Verses* into Turkish, a mob of radical Islamists turned up at the *Hotel Sivas* where Nesin and other Turkish intellectuals were meeting for the Pir Sultan Abdal Literary Festival. The mob demanded Nesin be handed over for execution, when their demands were not met they set fire to the building, killing thirty-seven people.

At the turn of the millennium the reward for Rushdie's death stood at three million dollars and in 2016 a group of forty state run media organisations in Iran added another six hundred thousand dollars to the bounty.

Rushdie lives in hiding and under heavy guard, and when he travels he does so in disguise, though his sense of humour remains undiminished:

Vanity Fair Magazine: What do you most dislike about your appearance?
Salmon Rushdie: Its infrequency.

In 2012 American *Tonight Show* host Jay Leno made a joke at the expense of American Senator Mitt Romney, depicting India's Golden Temple as his summer home.

The joke allegedly offended many American Sikhs, an online petition was set up, and there were demands for Leno to apologise. When he refused India's Minister for Overseas Affairs spoke out against the joke, while a Californian doctor, Randeep Dhillon filed a lawsuit for libel.

The online petition gained a few thousand signatures which petitioners claimed demonstrated the hurt and anger felt by American Sikhs.

Really?

There is estimated between four and five hundred thousand Sikhs living in America which speaks volumes about how the majority of Sikhs felt about the joke.

Generally, Sikhs have a very healthy sense of humour. The best ethnic humour is inwardly directed and self-deprecating and few people laugh at themselves as much as Sikhs.

Typical Sikh jokes are an acknowledgement of their strange traits, foibles, and weaknesses:

An old Sikh is on the train from Rameswaram crossing the Pamban Bridge and asked the conductor, 'How much to Dhanushkodi?'

'Two rupees,' the conductor said.

The old man pointed to his suitcase on the seat next him and said, 'How much for my case?'

And the conductor said, 'the case goes for free.'

'Okay,' said the Sikh, 'you take my case, slow the train down, I will get off and I will go come walking.'

With that the conductor got mad, opened the window and threw the case into the water.

'Oh, my gaard,' shouted the old gentleman, 'now you try to drown my little boy.'

A Sikh wife accosted her husband and accused him of favouring one of their two children, and the husband said, 'No way, which one, my Amrik or the girl one?'

Sardarji jokes on the other hand, are a contentious issue amongst Sikhs. They are the most widely circulated ethnic jokes in India, and they come in two forms, the Sikh as a trickster, like those published by Khushwant Singh, compiler of several Sardarji joke books:

Santa went to the doctors because of a skin rash on his neck and the doctor asked him, 'What soap do you use?'
And Santa said, 'Bajrang soap.'
The doctor said, 'Bajrang soap, is it an international company.'
And Santa said, 'no, Bajrang is my room-mate.'

And those that portrays the Sikh as a fool:

At the scene of a car accident a man is screaming: 'Oh God, I have lost my leg, I have lost my leg, aahh!' And a Sardar said to him: 'Control yourself, stop shouting, look at your passenger, he has lost his head, is he crying?'

When the 2005 film *Shabd* featured a Sardarji joke a group of Sikhs stormed the filmmakers *Pitish Nandy Communications* head offices. Despite *PNC* tendering written apologies stating that it intended no offence, further protests led to the Film Censor Board issuing a directive for the scene to be cut.

Two years later the *Sikh Media and Culture Watch* demanded the arrest of the Mutanga book seller, Ranjit Parande for stocking *The Santa and Banta Joke Book* (Santa and Banta are stock comic characters in Sardarji jokes):

Banta enters a shop selling curtains and announces to the salesman, Gurdaya that he wants to buy a pair of green curtains.
'Certainly,' says Gurdaya 'what size?'
'Fifteen inches,' says Banta.
'Fifteen inches,' Gurdaya laughs, 'what room are they for?'
Banta explains that they are not for a room they are for his computer monitor.
'But sir,' Gurdaya says, 'computers do not have curtains.'
And Banta laughing says, 'Helloooo… I've got Windows!'

266

Parande was arrested and charged under section 295 of the Indian Penal Code, which is, Hurting Religious Sentiment.

Of course, we could easily dismiss the idea of being arrested for a joke that "hurts religious sentiment" as something that would only happen in the volatile and highly religious Middle Eastern countries, but in 2006 the British government proposed a similar law.

In January of that year Rowan Atkinson, in a speech that was eloquent and informed, urged the government to re-think a proposed religious hatred bill and passionately defended the right to tell religious jokes.

'It's their irrational nature that leaves religious beliefs wide open to interpretation,' said the comedian, 'allowing occasional practices to be established that are wholly contrary to the morals of a civilised, liberal society. Those practices, must remain open to the widest critique, including what would be perceived as insult or abuse.'

He went on to question what constitutes insult or abuse in an irrational realm, 'Race is a rational concept,' he said, 'he is of that race, she is of this; and it is not difficult to judge with reasonable objectivity what constitutes insult and abuse. Such judgements are almost impossible with the irrational quality of religion where for some, any critique of their irrational quality of religious practice constitutes an insult, to question anything is an abuse.'

A key element of the bill was the government's attempt to distinguish between attacks on beliefs and attacks on believers, the former allowed, the latter not, but as Atkinson rightly pointed out, beliefs are only invested with life and significance by believers, and if you attack one, you attack the other, because the believers are the only people who invest the beliefs with significance or can take responsibility for them. You wouldn't need to ridicule beliefs if no-one believed them.

'From a comedian's point of view,' Atkinson said, 'you cannot make a joke about a belief or a practice without characterising it in human form. Every joke has a victim and with a religious joke, it is bound to be the practitioner, even if the target is the practice.'

Atkinson went even further and said that outmoded and hateful religious practices *needed* to be criticised: 'If the exposure of hateful

267

or ridiculous religious practices generates dislike of that religion's followers, they should accept that also and not seek legal immunity. They cannot renounce responsibility for their practices. They should defend them, justify them, or correct them.'

When the bill was finally passed it was a much-diluted version of the original and a victory for freedom of speech.

Judas: Still on for Thursday?
Jesus: Thursday?
Judas: The last supper.
Jesus: The what?
Judas: The supper, the normal supper, with the lads, yes, the, er, normal supper...

Throughout history most religious leaders have opposed anything other than mild humour aimed at their religion and a great number have punished, imprisoned, tortured, and murdered jokers who were judged to have insulted their God.

The mechanics of a joke and how it works if taken literally mean that religion and jokes do not mix easily. The overly pious oppose personality traits associated with jokes; incongruity, ambiguity, nonsense, playfulness, low dogmatism, low authoritarianism, lack of truthfulness, moral disengagement, loss of control, and transgression, specifically transgression of prohibitions related to aggression, dominance, and sex.

Jokes are often cruel, and religion preaches against cruelty. Jokes can be aggressive, and though the relationship between religion and violence is complex to say the least, in its explicit discourse, religion prohibits aggression.

Then there is the emotional aspect of a joke which is surprise, followed by laughter, a momentary loss of control. Religion is strongly associated with control. Faith itself implies a need for control, of events, and of self.

A joke is usually an invented story or a play on the truth, strictly speaking a lie, which to an ardent believer is a sin.

The zealous take a dim view of jokes about their religion, especially when their God or Prophet is the butt and in recent times there have been some chilling repercussions for what was meant to be, just a joke.

In September 2005 Denmark's biggest selling newspaper *Jyllands-Posten* published twelve cartoons under the headline, The Face of Mohammed.

In the immediate aftermath of the publishing of the cartoons Arab countries and various Middle-Eastern organisations began printing and speaking anti-Denmark rhetoric, while supermarkets across the Middle East boycotted Danish goods.

Some six months later in a show of solidarity dozens of European newspapers reprinted the cartoons which resulted in a prominent Egyptian preacher calling for a, 'Day of Rage', a day that stretched into weeks and saw hundreds of thousands taking to the streets in protest while Danish Embassies were burned down in Jakarta, Beirut, and Damascus.

In defiance European newspapers again printed the cartoons which led to more violent demonstrations and two hundred and fifty deaths across Afghanistan, Pakistan, and Nigeria.

Meanwhile radical Islamist leaders offered rewards for the heads of the cartoonists and their editors, and in 2010 a Somali Muslim armed with an axe and a knife was shot dead by police after breaking into Kurt Westergaard's home.

Westergaard is the most reviled of all the cartoonists, the one who depicted the Prophet Mohammed with a bomb in his turban. He claimed it was meant to evoke how Muslim terrorists had essentially taken Islam hostage, hence the bomb in the turban, and added that he could not imagine anyone interpreting it in any other way. Interpret it another way they did.

The French satirical magazine *Charlie Hebdo* responded to the attack at Westgaard's home by not only printing the original cartoons but also adding one of its own which depicted Mohammed saying, 'It's hard to be loved by imbeciles.'

Following an arson attack on the *Hebdo* offices the magazine featured Mohammed as editor-in-chief saying, '100 lashes if you don't die of laughter', and in 2011 its front-page headline read,

'Untouchables 2' with Mohammed pictured in a wheelchair saying, 'You mustn't mock.' A cartoon inside depicted the Prophet naked. Two years later it released a sixty-five-page illustrated special edition of a spoof biography of Mohammed.

On January 7, 2015 masked gunmen attacked the *Charlie Hebdo* offices and murdered twelve employees.

Humour is not always a positive force, some jokes have a dark side, and we should be aware of that. Sometimes jokes can lead to negative and harmful outcomes, and we should be conscious of when and how it can happen.

Religious jokes are a form of mockery and usually point to a certain degree of tension or at least disrespect between different worshippers, and yes, the tensions are relative and can be laughed off, but it is impossible to know where the line of tolerance lies (or we might argue, should lie at all). Much depends on who tells the joke and their intent. If the teller is perceived as an enemy, or a non-believer it is easy to see maliciousness where there may be none.

Francois Boespflug's excellent, *Laughing at God* from the 2011 collection, *Humour and Religion* is in favour of freedom of expression and to some extent derision, but calls for self-restraint: 'There are no right relations between couples, family, friends, community, in business, with respect to the homeland, religion or religions, without a daily dose freely administered of self-censure, in dignity and humour – this is an elementary form of charity, without which the latter is not. Not all truths are good, or to be told, and it is sometimes proof of intelligence and charity to abstain from laughter.'

Chapter Thirty-Three

The Greatest Joke Ever

Comedy is subjective, what one person finds funny someone else may find only mildly amusing, while another may not find it funny at all, and that is why we cannot claim any joke to be the greatest ever.

In the late nineties the American *Esquire Magazine* published a list of what it considered the seventy-five funniest jokes of all time, with the following Gary Shandling joke topping the list:

I went to my doctor and told him my penis was burning, and he said, 'that means someone is talking about it.

My favourite joke from the *Esquire* seventy-five is an old Jewish gem:

An elderly Jew, Sol, went to his Rabbi with a problem; 'Rabbi,' he said, 'I've got a new girlfriend, she's very young and everything is wonderful except in the bedroom, I can't satisfy her'.

The Rabbi pondered and then said; 'Next time you are making love to your girlfriend, hire a young athletic type man to swing a towel above your heads.'

So, the next time Sol was making love to his young girlfriend he had a muscular young man swing a towel above their heads, but to no avail and his girlfriend remained unfulfilled.

He returned to his Rabbi who advised him that next time if the same problem occurs he should swap places with the young man. The following night Sol and his girlfriend were making love with the young man furiously swinging the towel above their heads, but again the girlfriend was unmoved. So, as the Rabbi advised they swapped places and in minutes the girlfriend was going wild, screaming and panting, and having multi-orgasms.

271

Afterwards Sol turned to the young man and said proudly, 'See, that's how you swing a towel.'

The largest study of its kind was done by Professor Richard Wiseman of the University of Hertfordshire who attempted to identify the world's funniest joke for his 2002 experiment, *LaughLab*.

The winning joke was submitted by Manchester psychiatrist, Gurpal Gosal:

Two hunters are out in the woods when one of them collapses. He doesn't seem to be breathing and his eyes are glazed so the other hunter whips out his mobile phone and calls the emergency services.

'My friend is dead,' he gasps, 'what can I do?'

And the operator says, 'Calm down sir, I can help. First, let's make sure he's dead.'

There is a silence, and then the sound of a gun-shot.

The hunter then comes back on the phone and says, 'Ok, now what?'

The joke is a take on a 1951 *Goon Show* sketch written by Spike Milligan:

Bentine: I just came in and found him lying on the carpet there.
Sellers: Is he dead?
Bentine: I think so.
Sellers: Well, hadn't you better make sure?
Bentine: Alright, just a minute... (sound of a gun-shot). He's dead.

A good joke, but the funniest joke ever? It is impossible to say. When it comes to jokes, our upbringing, culture, personal identity, and other subjective aspects of our character that help form our sense of humour, together with a myriad of other factors, such as age, socioeconomic background, and gender, determine the type of jokes we like best.

Take just one aspect; gender.

272

The following joke got a favourable rating from over fifty percent of men, while only fifteen percent of women liked it:

A man driving on the motorway is pulled over by a police officer, and the officer asks: 'Did you know that your wife and kids fell out of the car a mile back?'
And the man says, 'Oh, thank God for that, I thought I'd gone deaf.'

Added to the impossible task of finding the funniest joke ever is what people consider unsavoury subject matter for jokes. The following will receive a different reaction from different people:

Did you hear about the back-street abortionist whose business folded? His ferret died.

It is the type of joke that some will say goes, "too far". But how far is too far, and how far is not far enough? Too far and some will not laugh. Not far enough and no one laughs.

Professor Wiseman discovered that the most non-contentious jokes received the most votes, while the most provocative jokes were ranked highest in value by some and lowest in value by others.
The winning *LaughLab* joke he rightly concluded was, he said, 'The cleanest, blandest, most internationally accepted joke... the colour beige in joke form.'

Chapter Thirty-Four

The Joke is Dead, Long Live the Joke...

In 2005 Warren St John wrote an obituary for the joke in the *New York Times* entitled, *Seriously, the Joke is Dead.* The article began:

> In case you missed its obituary, the joke died recently after a long illness of 30 years. Its passing was barely noticed, drowned out, perhaps, by the din of ironic one-liners, snark and detached bon mots that pass for humour these days.
>
> The joke died a lonely death...
>
> But when people reminisce about it, they always say the same thing: the joke knew how to make an entrance. 'Two guys waked into a bar'; 'So this lady goes to the doctor'; 'Did you hear the one about the talking parrot?' The new humour sneaks by on cat's feet, all punch line and no set up, and if it bombs, you barely notice. The joke insisted on everyone's attention, and when it bombed – wow!

St John was I believe, cheerleading for the joke while casually lambasting the comic observers and reminding us just how much more joke tellers put on the line.

Telling a joke is much braver than observational humour. If an observation dies, the observer can hide behind the fact that it was just that, an observation, but once someone announces, 'Did you hear the one about?', expectations are heightened, and they must deliver or suffer the humiliation of poker-faced silence.

The joke is far from dead, enter 'joke' into an internet search engine and see just how alive and well it is. Go into any pub and hear raucous laughter and you can be almost certain that the joke is involved. It will never die.

The joke is a psychological, social, and cultural phenomenon, and is constantly re-inventing itself in response to each new generation's social, cultural, and psychological needs. It will live forever because it will always adapt. Two Vaudevillians talking:

Who was that lady I saw you with last night?
That was no lady, that was my wife.

Two social club comics:

Who was that lady I saw you with last night?
That was no lady, that was my brother, he only walks that way…

Two American Rappers:

Who was that ho I saw you with last night?
That was no ho, that was my bitch.

Jokes have a special place in human life, they are funny stories, and people love stories, we learn to understand the world through stories, be it orally from our elders, or through literature, folklore, films, and jokes.

An elephant and a mouse are talking philosophy and the elephant says, 'Why is it that we are both God's creatures, with souls of equal worth, and yet I am so huge and strong and magnificent, while you are so tiny, puny and grey?'
'Well,' says the mouse, 'I've been ill, haven't I?'

Picasso said, 'The purpose of art is washing the dust of daily life off our souls.' I believe jokes serve the same purpose.

Jokes are a product of human ingenuity that, at their subtlest and most refined fall within the domain of art and can cleanse us of that, 'dust of daily life'.

A Joke is one of those rare magical elements in our lives, yes, it can be common, coarse, crude, unsophisticated, unintelligent, but it can also be clever, subtle, incredibly creative, self-corrective, and not least therapeutic.

Joke lover and father of psychoanalysis Sigmund Freud believed that when a joke is told it opens a window in our minds and all our dark thoughts, all the bats and bogeymen, fly out, which leaves us with a marvellous feeling of relief and elation.

Then again, comedian Ken Dodd said, 'That's alright for Freud to say, he never had to play Glasgow Empire, second house on a Saturday night!'

About the Author

J K Dowd is the stand-up comedian, Dave Kristian. This is his first book. (If you liked it please rate it on Amazon, thanks.)

Contact: Amazon Authors Page.

Printed by Amazon Italia Logistica S.r.l.
Torrazza Piemonte (TO), Italy

54622921R00167